Informal Manufacturing
Conditions and Prospects

Informal Manufacturing

Conditions and Prospects

Dr. Vasudha Joshi
Reader
Ness Wadia College of Commerce, Pune

NEW
NC
CENTURY

New Century Publications
Delhi India

NEW CENTURY PUBLICATIONS
34, Gujranwala Town, Part-2,
Delhi - 110 009 INDIA
Tel.: 7247805, 7138192
Fax: +91-11-7464774
E-mail: indiatax@del2.vsnl.net.in

ICSSR Consultant: Professor Amitabh Kundu

First Published 2003

ISBN: 81-7708-046-6

This publication was partially financially supported by the ICSSR. The responsibility for the facts stated, opinions expressed, or conclusions reached, is entirely that of the author and that ICSSR accepts no responsibility for them.

Published by New Century Publications and printed at Singhal Print Media, Delhi -110 007

PRINTED IN INDIA

Preface

This book examines the essential but non-dynamic and unrecognized part that informal sector plays in the Indian economy. As our planners' initial faith in state-led growth under a large public sector is now buried, the subject of informal sector has become particularly relevant. The prospects for working class and informal sector appear to be invariably tied together.

Coexistence of several modes of production such as own account work, family business and factory production is the focus of this study which provides an important insight into the working of the Indian economy. To understand the mutual relations among these different modes, a bottom-top, subaltern approach is attempted in this book.

The study of informal sector is important because the crucial task of making productive use of abundant, surplus labour in the Indian economy remains neglected. A two-pronged employment strategy has been followed in the country, viz. special employment generation programmes and measures to transfer more resources to workers with low productivity. Programmes for transferring resources (e.g. Integrated Rural Development Programme) have sought to upgrade the resource-base of informal sector.

While it is true that economic growth is the final creator of employment, there are severe limits to labour absorption in the organized sector. Furthermore, the public sector as a whole is not likely to play an important role in the economy in the years to come.

Though the employment generation and resource transfer programmes continue, the organized sector is not performing to expectations as envisaged by the planners. Capital has and continues to generate more surplus to take the economy forward but it has failed to provide productive employment to workers.

Therefore, large enterprises have every incentive to make use of cheap, unprotected labour in small firms and informal sector. This is reflected in the widespread use of contract labour in the organized sector. It is used in large enterprises for housekeeping, material handling, transport and maintenance activities. It is also used for managing temporary peaks in regular production work. Subcontracting of some parts of the production process has been increasingly resorted to since the mid-1970s. It offers two substantial benefits, viz. lower cost and flexibility.

Informal sector has been neglected by the government as well as by the trade unions. Trade unions have not been active in this field because they require at least a few permanent workers at a fixed location to become operational. However, non-government organizations (NGOs) have been active in it. Their experience shows that government measures to improve the conditions of informal sector workers have been marked by rigidity and a strait-jacket approach.

What the informal sector workers basically need is income and social security. For this purpose, an employment guarantee programme for urban areas can be added to the existing battery of special employment programmes.

The issue of informal sector always raises uncomfortable questions like the supremacy of capital over labour. It is the responsibility of the state to ensure that the accumulation process takes place within a framework which guarantees some basic minimum rights of labour. In order to maximize profit, capital looks for every opportunity to externalize its costs. It wants free access to infrastructure created out of public money. The State must be strong enough to resist this pressure and to force some internalization of costs on the part of capital. Cost of maintenance and reproduction of labour force must be borne by capital. Hence the suggestion for tax on ancillarization and subcontracting.

I am indebted to Dr. Sulabha Brahme who made specific comments and constructive suggestions at various stages of the completion of this project. My next debt is to my father, Shri P.M. Joshi who induced me to take up this project. Mr. A.R. Contractor, Mr. Hiralal Kirad, Mrs. Kelshikar, and Mr. S.S. Ambike provided valuable help and co-operation.

Utpala Joshi, my sister, took time off her very busy schedule and helped me in finalising this work. Mr. V.N. Inamdar painstakingly prepared a typed copy of the text. I am grateful to all of them.

Vasudha Joshi

Pune
November 2002

Contents

Chapter 1

Informal Sector: Genesis and Development

The term informal sector (IS) has been attributed to Keith Hart (1971) but the origin of the concept of IS can be traced to earlier contributions in sociology. For example, Geertz's study of two Indonesian towns (1963) was concerned with the transformation of a 'bazaar economy' (traditional economy) into a 'firm (modern) economy'. The informal system originally referred to the parallel system of labour organization and wage bargaining that existed side by side the formal employer-labour relationship in industrialized countries. In less developed countries (LDCs) it was not just the presence of a parallel system but the juxtaposition between two distinct modes or ways of living and the imposition of Western ideas on the Orient which received wide attention in sociology and social anthropology.

In economics also, prior developments (i.e. those before the publication of Hart's paper or ILO-Kenya Mission Report, 1972) were already leading towards IS as a substantive category. Thus Harris-Todaro model of rural-urban migration (1970), looked upon the urban labour market as consisting of two sectors viz. Protected (modern) and unprotected (informal) sectors. The model viewed migration as an equilibrating force that cleared the labour market given the difference between rural wage based upon cost of living differential and the facility of job search in urban areas. Simultaneous existence of open unemployment and migration in the labour market indicated the possibility of market failure. Harris-Todaro model sought to explain this anomaly by introducing a new variable in the picture, viz. the probability of obtaining a modern sector job in the urban economy.

In this model, migration depends upon the difference in expected real income between urban and rural areas.

Expected real income in urban areas = real wage x probability of getting a protected sector job

and

Probability of getting a protected sector job = $\frac{\text{New job openings in protected sector}}{\text{Number of job-seekers in the unprotected sector}}$

With an urban real wage premium and a rate of job creation that exceeded the rate of natural population growth, migration was induced and urban labour supply exceeded the number of available jobs. The excess job-seekers were temporarily accommodated in IS where they formed a queue for of getting a protected sector job was reduced and migration flow was checked. Operating through the probability variable IS thus helped to regulate migration.

Harberger (1971) argued that unprotected sector wages were the best approximation to the supply price of labour in urban areas. Otherwise opportunity cost of urban labour was equated with agricultural wage. At one time (Nurkse, 1953) the marginal product of labour in agriculture was thought to be zero and so urban labour's opportunity cost was also zero. Harberger did not accept this view. He argued that had urban labour's opportunity cost indeed been zero, rural-urban migration would have been far greater than what was observed. He drew attention to the contribution of IS in providing subsistence to those who would otherwise have been openly unemployed.

Around this time, it was also being gradually accepted that the Western concept of open employment was not directly applicable to LDCs. Only those persons who are willing to work at the prevailing wage rate and who are actively seeking work are counted as openly unemployed. Past savings or institutional support in the form of income-sharing within family or state unemployment benefits enable a person to fulfil the above two conditions. Their absence leads to a suppression of open unemployment and vice versa. (The concerned literature has also explored the role of generous unemployment benefits in reducing the motivation to seek work.) IS can play a dual role in this connection in the sense that it might enable its participants to engage in both income-earning activities and job search simultaneously. Therefore, IS can compete with other institutional arrangements in regulating the quantum of open unemployment benefit and IS are inversely related to each other as rivals.

	(1) State unemployment benefit		(2) Is		(3) Open Unemployment	
	High	Low	High	Low	High	Low
1	✓			✓	✓	
2		✓	✓			✓

In situation 1, high unemployment benefit leads to low IS presence and high incidence of open unemployment. In situation 2, low unemployment benefit leads to high IS activity and low level of open unemployment. (1) and (2) are inversely related but (1) and (3) are positively linked. It is of course probable that (1) and (2), pulling each other in opposite directions, nullify each other and then fail to influence the impact of open unemployment. The policy implication is that if unemployment benefits are considered very costly, the state ought to promote IS. Conversely, if it wants to limit the size of IS, it has to offer unemployment benefits. Then the quantum of open unemployment will be within acceptable limits.

In LDCs, observed rates of open unemployment have generally been low and the role of IS is not insignificant in this connection.

Thus as a regulator of both rural-urban migration and open unemployment, the contribution of IS was gradually being recognized in economics. The above developments treated IS as a labour market category. The ILO-Kenya Mission Report treated IS as a product market category. It reviewed IS as a cluster of economic activities which escaped recognition, enumeration, regulation and protection by the government. According to the report, these activities were none the less productive and hence it made a strong case for promoting IS.

Stewart (1978) made a distinction between traditional and modern activities in urban areas in LDCs. She conceptualized the urban economy as below:

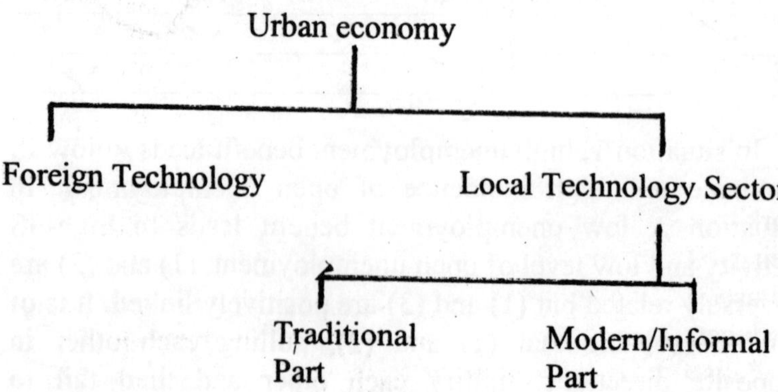

IS, in this approach, comprised a group of new activities that had appeared in the wake of industrialization.

Berger and Piore (1980) start with the observation that duality is not peculiar to only LDCs but can be seen in developed countries also. Thus the traditional sector in Italy, France, Japan and even U.S.A. performs an important economic role. In their conceptualization, the basic reasons why this dualism exists are two-fold. Firstly, it is a reflection of the dualism in modern economics between capital and labour. Capital – particularly plant and equipment – is a fixed factor which cannot be forced to bear the cost of its own unemployment whereas labour, the residual factor, can be. So employers are very careful in planning the utilization of their capital.

The concept of IS attracted a lot of attention since it provided a vital missing link in particularly development economics. The nature and role of small-scale development in classical political economy. Petty commodity production was extensively studied in Marxist literature. In neo-classical economic thought, however, small production units had been ignored. IS hence appeared to fill an important gap.

In Marxian economics, LDCs, petty producers and peasantry constituted weak links of the capitalist system. (Petty producers or petty production constitutes the bulk of IS.) Petty producers or petty production constitutes the bulk of IS.) Petty producers stand in between capitalist and the working class. They consider themselves to be capitalists but their interests are close to that of the working class for both are used by capitalists to externalize their costs. A few petty producers might be able to transform themselves into capitalists but most of them are forced to eventually join the working class; some may even join the industrial reserve army. The periodic crises to which capitalism is subject are opportunities to challenge and overthrow it. In LDCs, the underdeveloped working class has to win the support of both peasantry and petty producers in this task.

Petty commodity producers have been defined as those who are capable of reproducing themselves as private producers of commodities without employing wage-labour and without selling their labour-power. Another definition emphasizes the following features:

(a) Production for the market.
(b) small, scale of operations in terms of volume of output, size of workforce, size of capital and level of technology,
(c) ownership of means of production by the direct producers.

Petty commodity production (PCP) constitutes a distinct mode of production as compared to the main capitalist mode in LDCs. It can also be viewed as a transitional mode between the pre-capitalist and capitalist modes. The former represent a cyclical movement of productive forces which permits sustenance but not growth. In contrast, the capitalist mode represents continuous generation, reinvestment of surplus and a revolutionary movement of productive forces.

Tension exists between these modes and a gradual transformation of PCP into the capitalist mode is ruled out. The relationship between them is a complex mechanism of conservation and dissolution. Because of the following factors, conservation becomes the dominant tendency in LDCs:

1. PCP cheapens worker's consumption and helps to increase surplus.
2. It also subsidizes the rural subsistence economy.

3. It adopts a number of coping mechanism and does its utmost to survive. The coping strategies include use of family labour, reduction in consumption, circulatory migration, engaging simultaneously in a number of income-earning activities, if possible, etc.
4. PCP prevents open unemployment from becoming very high and it enables the state to switch resources form providing social security.
5. To the extent PCP producer cheap, low quality goods with low income-elasticity of demand, it occupies a non-competing domain from the capitalist mode and can co-exist with it.

Petty commodity producers continue to exist but are unable to transform themselves into capitalist entrepreneurs because:

1. Entry into their fields is easy and so they are subject to market-specific involution.
2. They are forced to go for mixed portfolios in order to minimize risk. So growth prospects become limited.
3. Technology is generally not neutral to scale; it has a bias against small producers.

Once petty production becomes non-viable, it is attached to the capitalist mode in an explicitly subordinate manner. Putting out work, subcontracting, piece-rate contracts are manifestations of this subordination. They help the capitalist mode to reduce risk, gain flexibility and reduce its costs.

Petty producers form only one part of IS. The rest comes from the industrial reserve army which comprises the unemployed, under-employed and the marginalized elements. The reserve army exerts a downward pressure on wages and 'curbs the pretensions' of labour (Marx).

In Marxian analysis, both PCP and reserve army are integral parts of the capitalist system. Both help in the accumulation process. PCP allows large capitalists to lower their costs and to lower the cost of workers' consumption. The reserve army acts as a check on wage-workers in large enterprises and their wage-fund. Because of this contribution to the accumulation process, IS does not disappear. Later, it expands in LDCs. Demographic response of the poor-high fertility to have more helping hands in the family-ensure continual growth of surplus labour pool and so of IS. IS is, therefore, a functional part of capitalism.

Similar arguments have been made about the relation of women's economic role to capitalism. Women are a part of reserve army; they move in and out of labour force depending upon; the needs of capital. Secondly, since family survival is the compulsion behind them, women are forced to carry out a number of economic activities, whether home-based or otherwise, under conditions of absolute surplus extraction. Many of these activities are unremunerated or under-reported. Thirdly, through their unremunerated services and ability to stretch wages, housewives enable capital to pay lower wages than would otherwise be needed for the reproduction of labour power. The housewife's unpaid labour is transferred to capital as surplus. Because of this functional similarity, the association between IS and women is close and a majority of working women may be found in IS.

Dependency theory, one strand within Marxian theory, views the problems of petty producers in IS as being those of LDCs in microcosm. It maintains that IS cannot develop its own logic of capital accumulation and growth as long as it coexists unequally with large scale capitalist enterprises. The same applies to LDCs as a whole which are a part of subordinate, peripheral capitalism, controlled by core capitalism. The core capitalist system retains the productivity gains accruing within it and also appropriates those that arise in the periphery. Profit maximization in the periphery requires wage minimization stating cheaper consumption of workers. In core capitalism, wage minimization turns out to be counter-productive. To check the tendency of over-production, it is necessary to place more purchasing power in workers' hands and hence increase their wages. The marginality school in Marxian tradition attaches importance to the backwash effects of the capitalist development process – manifest in IS – which simultaneously gives rise to under-development.

This comprehensive treatment remained outside the purview of mainstream economics and therefore the concept of IS, advocated by ILO, was hailed as an important addition to the development literature. Since many heterogeneous activities were bracketed together in IS, the concept meant many things to many people. Mazumdar (1975) saw it as an easy-entry, residual sector crowded with secondary workers having low productivity. It was thought that self-employment would be the dominant form of organization in IS. As a relic of pre-capitalist production relations, the underlying motive of IS activities was thought to be maximization of total income rather than profits.

ILO saw IS in a more positive light. It looked at IS as a seedbed of native entrepreneurship. Self-sufficiency of this sector, following the low income-elasticity for its products, was noted. It was accordingly seen as a viable sector producing cheap wage-goods. IS was also described as the employer of last resort and its contribution as safety net for the urban poor was emphasized.

The variety of views about IS and its heterogeneous content created plenty of confusion. In the words of Moser (1984), "The IS is still too broad to be meaningful; at one end is a pool of surplus labour, at the other a skilled high-income earning entrepreneur; at one end a proliferation of residual enterprises involutionary in nature, at the other a skilled high-income earning entrepreneur; at one end a proliferation of residual enterprises involutionary in nature, at the other end of the spectrum dynamic evolutionary enterprises." The lines of demarcation between IS and other sectors in the economy were not clear. Thus Holmstrom (1984) constantly emphasizes that the organized sector consists of firms which have many casual, temporary and contract workers whose employment is unprotected and who there fore belong to IS. In other words, firms may belong to the organized sector but their workforce may partially be in IS.

This would indicate that the formal sector (FS) and IS are not two independent categories. Rather, "they are in a continuously fluctuating state of interaction and parts of one sector may be dominated and created by parts of the other". (Bromley, 1970.) therefore, it is necessary to distinguish between the product market approach to IS (making it a cluster of micro-enterprises) and the labour market approach (IS a aggregate of unprotected labour). In other words, both enterprises (including family-enterprises or households as producing units) and individuals are included in IS. The former may belong unambiguously to IS while individuals may combine formal and informal activities. Alternately, the distinction between producing units and labour units in IS needs constantly to be kept in mind. This is a very important point. In the product market approach, FS firms enjoy privileged access to credit, foreign exchange and tax concessions while the competitive advantage of IS firms lies in escaping taxation, social security levies and also such regulation as might exist about working conditions, wages and job security.

Critics of the concept of IS have pointed out that FS, IS classification is crude, over-simplistic and that reality in LDCs is too complicated to be explained by this new version of economic dualism. Till, date, ambiguity remains about whether IS is an urban phenomenon or it also covers agriculture and the rural economy. One is therefore not clear as to what remains in the economy. One is therefore not clear as to what remains in the economy after counting FS and IS. Heather Joshi (1980) has mentioned the importance of dynamic relationships among three sectors, viz. FS, IS and the domestic sector. Unpaid labour, family labour and households as economic units would presumably be included in the domestic sector.

Martine Guerguil (1988) has, one the other hand, stressed the residual nature of IS but stated that domestic and criminal activities are not a part of it. Latin American scholars have explored the association between informality and underground economy. Domestic work and home-based production are very much a part of IS according to many others. M. Abdel – Fadil (1992) has used a colour-code to distinguish among the following sectors:

1. White (formal) sector – private formal and state sector activities,
2. Mauve sector – small business and personal services operating on the fringe of the white sector,
3. Grey sector – 'self-provision household activities, moonlighting and the gift economy'. These activities, conducted on the fringe of legality. (The term 'grey segment' is being increasingly used today in industrial analysis. For example, one talks of the grey end of the computer hardware and electronics industries. The grey

end is inhabited by small firms which smuggle raw materials, which have very low overheads and which excel in reverse engineering.)

4. Black sector – all illegal activities.

IS would be the total of mauve and grey sectors in this classification.

Because of the heterogeneity of activities included in IS, characteristics which are used to define informality do not apply to all the activities. For instance, ease of entry is a foremost feature of informality and yet many informal activities (e.g. shoe-shining and even rag-picking at the lowest level of informal activities) may defy this feature.

When diverse elements get clubbed together in one category, it becomes difficult to identify those parts which have some growth potential vis-à-vis those which face involutionary prospects. Then there arises the danger of making wrong policy recommendations. Thus policies which are designed to help small enterprises will not necessarily help their wage workers. Policies which benefit wage workers in FS may harm the interests of casual/temporary workers, home-based workers, etc. independent manufacturing units in IS may not welcome the promotion of subcontracting links between formal and informal enterprises; policies which help informal firms carrying on legal business may not help those carrying out illegal activities, etc. therefore a single policy prescription for IS is ruled out. IS is so large and diverse that a range of measures from direct assistance, incentives-rehabilitation and even persecution is called for.

Castells and Portes (1989) have talked of an informal economy, giving up any attempt to define and distinguish IS within an economy. Their focus is on unprotected labour or labour that is denied protection of either the State of unions.

1.1 Definition of Informal Sector

The above ambiguity is reflected in the various definitions of IS. Most of the definitions simultaneously emphasize a number of attributes of informality. Firm size, type of employment, technological competence, income level, capital employed and legal status are the oft-used criteria to delineate informal activities. Among the many definitions that are around , the following stand out:

The ILO-Kenya Mission stated the following features, making it clear that the degree of their application differed from activity to activity:

(a) no access or limited access to resources such as institutional credit, foreign technology,
(b) small-scale operations,
(c) ease of entry,
(d) family ownership of enterprises,
(e) competitive markets,
(f) reliance of indigenous resources,
(g) labour-intensive, adapted technology,
(h) unremunerated, invisible nature of activities.

The features of FS were the obverse of IS activities. The definitions suggested at the 14th International Conference of Labour Statisticians, ILO (1987) distinguishes between registered and unregistered units and the difference between the two boils down to scale of wage-employment, provision of social-security for wage-labourers and source of energy for the manufacturing process. Joshi and Joshi (1976) have emphasized three variables, viz. Relationship with government, market structure (whether competitive or not) and nature of technology for distinguishing IS activities. These definitions approach IS as a product market category.

Squire (1981) has given the most clear-cut definition of IS as a labour market phenomenon – IS is a sector in which return to labour is determined by the forces of demand and supply. Wages in FS are higher due to institutional factors such as

(a) labour legislation stipulating minimum wage and working conditions,
(b) trade unionism,
(c) hire and wage policies of multinationals and public sector enterprises.

It has been shown that the market also has a tendency to create clusters with more than the market-clearing wage. Efficiency wage concept, internal labour markets in large organizations, human capital attributes, different supply prices of temporary and permanent migrants and the different proportions in which they can possibly be used in small and large enterprises are the factors which give rise to this effect (Mazumdar, 1983).

An interesting attempt to integrate the various strands of Marxian thinking on IS is made by Nattrass (1987). Here IS becomes a set of petty production activities manned by persons in the industrial reserve army, the marginal pole and also those holding formal jobs. In other words, IS gets defined at the interface of FS, reserve army and marginal pole. Diagrammatically.

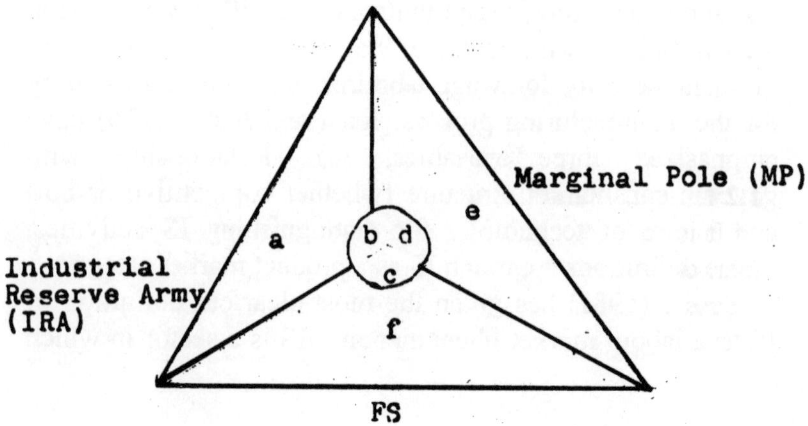

IS = b + c + d

IRA = a + b

A = full-time job seekers; not productively engaged, hence not a part of IS,

B = persons who have stopped their job-search and have entered IS temporarily.

They are capable of obtaining work in FS.

FS = f + c

F = persons working full-time in FS,

C = persons working in FS who supplement their income with that from informal activities.

MP is characterized by the lack of access to basic resources (e.g. land, capital, including human capital) and therefore it operates around residual resources.

MP = e + d

E = the truly marginalized elements within MP which are not active in informal production, e.g. beggars.

D = persons who are marginalized but are still working in IS e.g. rag-pickers.

This approach leaves out enterprises employing wage-labour in IS and is hence inadequate. Nattrass then clarifies that informality should be associated with any two of the following characteristics :

- labour-intensive operations,
- small-scale operations and
- existence outside official rules and regulations.

1.2 Implications

It is clear from the foregoing analysis that in the labour market approach IS comprises unprotected labour. This means that the following groups are included in it:

(a) wage-workers in enterprises (even formal enterprises) whose employment is not protected by institutional and /or market factors mentioned above.

(b) Own-account workers whose employment is not protected by the requirement of capital, skill and barriers to entry arising from organization, and

(c) Service-providers, e.g. domestic servants, cleaners, etc.

The emergence of IS, in this approach, is fundamentally due to labour surplus in the economy. The important question, in this approach, is : what impact does unprotected labour have on market theories (or labour segmentation theories) take the position that barriers between FS and IS are strong and hence unprotected labour cannot affect protected labour. Skill-formation and productivity in FS insulate it from IS. The reserve army formulations is that protected and unprotected labour are linked together and the latter drives down the wage level of the former. It appears that the labour segmentation theories explain the short-run position but bail to take into account the wage-employment trade-off that is seen in FS.

At the same time, mainstream economic theories do not accept the reserve army formulation. Their position is that IS does not enable capitalists to pay lower wages; there is no empirical support to such a relationship. Their argument is in fact, reverse, viz. IS enables labour to resist the very low wage levels that would otherwise result, given the large labour surplus in LDCs. In other words, IS can be looked upon as an alternative to the direct exploitation of labour by capital.

In the product market approach, IS becomes a sector of unregistered (or perhaps illegal) micro-enterprises which employ in inferior technique of production that earn less than the average rate of return (Gibson, Kelly, 1994). IS is forced to adopt and inferior technique because of scarcity of capital. Unregistered or illegal activities exist either because of the pressure to reduce labour costs and gain flexibility or because of the inability of LDC governments to enforce existing regulations. Lack of registration and invisibility in official records work in two directions. Non-compliance with statutory provisions regarding resource-use leads to lower costs but also lack of access to resources, particularly technology. The net impact of these two and its implication for the growth dynamics of IS become important issues in this formulation. The crucial question is whether IS will be able to formalize itself and earn the average rate of return in the process of growth and whether it has the potential for autonomous growth. Marxian approach has raised the following policy issues in connection with IS:

1. Should working class struggle for industrialism and the collective benefits it provides to workers or should it support the individualism of tiny enterprises?
2. Should petty capitalism of the poor be seen as a form of creative energy or as exploitative individualism?
3. Can IS grow only in an involutionary manner or is evolutionary growth possible?
4. Can IS expand its sphere or scale of operations?

1.3 Dynamics

Dynamics and growth prospects of a product market phenomenon need to be considered. As regards IS, this enquiry can proceed along two separate paths (Tokman, 1978). The first emphasizes special features of IS and grants it functional independence, at least in the short run. The following features are mentioned:

1. IS units carry out activities that are considered unprofitable by FS. Very small volumes of activity, low-

income elasticity of demand and perhaps fluctuations in demand, labour-intensity of operations, etc., fluctuations in demand, labour-intensity of operations, etc., induce in where there are no growth prospects (since survival is its motive).
2. Factor-use and factor proportions are likely proportions are likely to be different in IS. Recycling of waste material, use of second-hand or self-fabricated machine tools, local technology, greater use of family labour, use of residential accommodation for industrial work, use of informal finance, etc., are special features of IS. Uniformity in resource-use, following from compliance with statutory provisions is also absent.
3. The objective of carrying out these activities, given the application of a number of own resources of space, family labour, savings, etc. is probably sustenance or maximum total income rather than maximum profit.

These features, particularly the combination of low technology, non-specialized resources and low income-elasticity of demand appear to make IS self-sufficient. As a lower-order category, it can then co-exist with IS.

A number of attempts have been made to organize informal activities along this path (Navavaty, 1994). These attempts have made use of the following measures for ensuring sustainability.

- organizing sections of informal workforce,
- eliminating middlemen,
- forging closer links with consumers,
- making use of various government schemes from administration to marketing.

Their experience suggests that organizing and continuing these activities in the short-run is difficult but not impossible.

- getting access to technology,
- withstanding competition in the market,
- being at the receiving and of external changes, e.g. change in tastes and technological change.

This leads to the conclusion that IS and FS do not constitute exclusive categories. The option of pre-empting profitable opportunities in IS appears to be always open to FS. Independence in the short run and co-option in the long run seems to be the common pattern.

The other path begins by recognizing that FS and IS are related and linkages related to production, technology, personnel, finance and marketing exist between them. The following are common examples of these links :

- sub-contracting and putting out arrangements,
- procurement and recycling in IS of used materials in FS,
- use of cheap and quick repair facilities in IS by FS,
- use of their formal working place by FS workers for informal activities,
- use of formal channels for procuring materials and other services for informal housing and construction.

These are two-way linkages, i.e. both the sectors are earn some income. The links enable IS to exist and to earn some income. They enable FS to lower its cost of operations, to externalize the burden of adjustments with changing environment and to gain flexibility. These linkages are expected to exist as long as cost differences exist between the two sectors. Complementrarity, perhaps induced complementraity, rather than isolation or competition mark the inter-relationship between the two sectors in this perspective. In the course of time, some IS firms might fully specialize in producing some intermediates for FS sand elevate themselves to the position of formal job-shops.

Given technological possibilities and the existence of surplus labour willing to work at less than the subsistence wage also, capitalists have plenty of opportunities to switch activities between FS and IS. So they make use of IS. IS contributes to the accumulation process. Mainstream economic thinking takes the position that IS will be used by capitalists since it exists but accumulation process will continue without also. Instead of complementarily between FS and IS, it is more appropriate to talk of the dependence of IS on FS, given the difference in technology and resource endowments.

To conclude, available literature on IS veers round the view that IS will be a permanent feature of LDCs; it will act as reserve army of labour, its formalization will not be automatic; rather, substantial barriers will prevent it and it will get stuck in a zero-profit, long-term equilibrium. At the same time, it will counter accentuation of inequality by giving a breathing space to the poor.

Some analysts have pointed out that traditional firms and dual labour markets have also expanded in developed countries. They view these as rational ways in which a society makes use of its resources to resolve current conflicts. IS enables us to realize the inadequacy of the dominant paradigm and takes us to a more nuanced understanding of institutions which determine individual responses as well as social structures in societies.

Chapter 2

Past Studies on Informal Sector

In spite of its nebulous nature, the concept of IS has proved to be popular in literature. The chief appeal of the concept lies in that it facilitates the study of different forms of labour-use in the urban economy. Much of the research on IS has been directed to the quantitative estimation of the number of workers in IS and their earnings. Theoretical contributions have been comparatively few. A summary of the research so far is presented in this chapter. The summary is organized as follows:

Section 2.1 summarizes the major theoretical contributions on IS. Section 2.2 provides the historical backdrop of the work on IS as a theoretical tool in the LDC setting. Section 2.3 makes a detailed review of the major Indian surveys of IS. Section 2.4 takes a look at small industries sector in India. Only the disadvantaged, traditional, very small industries sector in India. Only the disadvantaged, traditional, very small units in this sector can be said to belong to IS; the modern units are linked with large, formal units in different ways and they are themselves formal in the sense of being recognized, having access to government, to modern, capital intensive technology, etc. These units dominate the SSI sector. Further a definition based on size of investment rather than number of persons employed is used here to delineate small unites from large ones. Therefore, it is not possible to relate the literature and database on SSI sector easily to IS literature. Very few studies of SSI sector deal with its relationship with large units. An overview of a few of those that do is presented in this section.

2.1 Theoretical Contributions

Right from the Kenya Mission Report (1972), ILO has continued to draw attention to the productive potential of IS but the theoretical work has been rather skeptical about the contribution of IS. Initial work, outside the framework of ILO (Mazumdar, 1975), looked upon IS as a residual sector that mainly provided services and that trailed behind FS in terms of growth of labour productivity, wages and income. The sector, in short, lacked any autonomous growth potential. Informal workers were mostly secondary earners and IS was not even the major point of entry for migrants from rural areas. This pessimistic view was replaced by cautious optimism when an intermediate sector was located within IS (Steel and Yasuoki, 1978). The intermediate sector was taken to mean small establishments which engaged labour at a positive marginal product and used intermediate technology plus moderate amount of capital per worker. IS proper then became a casual work segment with near-zero marginal productivity. It was argued that the intermediate sector made it possible to reduce unemployment without sacrificing output and without aggravating the problem of rural-urban migration. The intermediate sector had to be nurtured and the policies recommended for the purpose were:

- reduction of import-based and capital subsidies to large establishments in the short run,
- provision of credit, materials, managerial assistance to intermediate units plus the creation of a climate facilitating effective competition between large and intermediate units in the medium run, and
- redistribution of income in the long run to endure self-sustaining growth of intermediate units.

The idea that rural migrants get absorbed in the urban economy through the IS has been there right from the beginning. It was expanded in other contributions. It was argued that IS facilitated on-the-job search for formal jobs. This led to a formulation in which IS occupants had a better chance of finding an FS job as compared to those in the rural economy urban but a worse chance than the openly unemployed persons in/areas who could engage in job-search full time (Fields, 1990).

Fields built his labour market model around the decision-rule – take an IS job if it pays you to take one. The options in his model are:

1. To remain in rural areas and earn the agricultural wage without entertaining any hope of getting an FS job.
2. To search for a FS while being unemployed in the city. The decision rule will be: take an FS job if it is offered, otherwise be unemployed.
3. To search for an FS job while being employed in IS. This entails a lower probability of success than under (ii). The decision rule is: take FS job, if offered, otherwise earn an IS wage.

Because IS was assigned a better job-search probability as compared to the rural economy, this model arrived at the result that average IS earnings in equilibrium would be lower than agricultural earnings. Mazumdar had earlier arrived at the same result. This result has been contested in other studies (Bombay, Ahmedabad). So Banerjee (1986) suggests a modification in the above model. He considers three variables, viz. Gross income, search costs and waiting period before the desired job is attained. Banerjee argues that low gross income in rural areas is associated with low search costs while the high gross income in urban IS is accompanied by high search costs from transient informal jobs but according to Banerjee, the distance between the desired job and jobs with free entry is quite high in urban areas and it imposes considerable psychic costs on the concerned persons. Once this feature of search costs is taken into account one can allow for the possibility of net urban informal income (i.e. gross income from urban informal employment – search costs) being lower than net rural income even when gross urban informal income exceeds gross rural income. All that Banerjee's modification requires is that the cost of search from the transitory job exceeds the costs of the rural-based search by a greater margin than the difference between the transitory urban income and rural income.

However, the more fundamental objection of Banerjee is that he questions the very basis of the probabilistic migration models which make IS a transitory phenomenon or a non-target for employment in the rural migrants' journey towards FS. In his study of migrants to Delhi, Banerjee found that more than half of the IS entrants were attracted by the job prospects (particularly non-wage jobs) in IS itself. (More details of this study are given later.)

To take the above important point into account, Fields suggests that IS be bifurcated into an upper tier and a lower tier segment. The latter would be the easy-entry segment approaching the conception of the probabilistic migration models. In other words, people in this lower tier IS or FS. The upper tier IS segment does not have free entry. Its occupants probably have past linkages with FS, but they do not aspire to go back to it. They are content with their income and prospects in the upper tier segment. The lower tier would be a staging post.

Stark (1982) has tried to extend Todaro's migration model by incorporating a linkage coefficient (to denote the connection between FS and IS) which seeks to determine the intersectoral allocation of labour and the intra-urban allocation of rural migrants between IS and FS. He too, like Mazumdar, arrives at the result that the determinants of IS growth originate in the external environment – FS. He recognizes that the linkage coefficient can be both positive and negative i.e. expansion of FS can be both positive and negative, i.e. expansion of FS can lead to both expansion and contraction of IS. He takes one more possibility into account, viz. If rural migrants accept IS jobs, they send a signal about their inferior human capital acquisitions and this exerts a downward pressure on their future employment and earning prospect the results he arrives at are that again in migration decision the dominance of one sector Fs cannot be presumed and that the role of is urban growth cannot be predetermined analytically.

Thus, in the labour market approach to IS, its role in the rural-urban migration process appears to be more complex than was thought initially. IS, too, (like FS) is found to pull rural people out on its own; nor does it do this as a stop-gap arrangement.

Datta Chaudhury (1989) concentrates on the producing units in IS. Capital costs and wages differ between FS and IS and therefore they are linked together. As long as these cost differences exist, IS will exist. If cheap credit is provided to it, it will, in the course of time, specialize in producing intermediate products. It may even take over completely the production of intermediates form FS. Therefore IS might temporarily expand while FS in contracting.

In Gibson and Kelly's formulation (1994), IS is defined as a sector that uses inferior technology. FS wage equals IS earnings, i.e. wage plus profit. Multiple (inferior) production processes exist in IS initially. Because of competition among IS units, only the most profitable process remains finally. The formalization of this process is, however, blocked and the informal process remains in a no-profit, long-term equilibrium. IS functions also as reserve army of labour – it shrinks while FS expands and vice versa. However, IS producers tend to reduce the exploitation of workers in FS (by providing opportunities for self-employment) and bring about redistribution of income.

The concept of informality has been extended also by tracing its links with illegality (Tokman, 1991). The idea that informal activities were clandestine activities was present in ILO-Kenya Mission Report but it was not expanded. Two lines of enquiry can be distinguished in the available literature on this issue. According to the first, informal activities arise due to the pressure to reduce labour costs and to gain flexibility. Decentralization to avoid or diminish trade union power is another motive. While the desire to do away with rigidity caused by legal provisions is found in both developed countries and LDCs, its effects are dissimilar in the two. In developed countries, in the absence of a chronic labour surplus, decentralization could well mean increased labour remuneration accompanied, however, by loss of job security. Surplus labour exists in LDCs and so the desire for decentralization leads to a whole lot of informal activities which are not dynamically related to FS. in the second line of enquiry, attention is drawn to the inadequate legislation and inefficient bureaucracy in LDCs. The difficulty in enforcing the existing regulations leads to a large number of activities existing beyond the pale of law. Paradoxically, therefore, laws and governments are responsible for the existence of informal, i.e. non-regulated, activities.

2.2 Historical Backdrop

ILO launched the World Employment Programme (WEP) in 1969 to focus attention on employment as an independent policy objective in its own right. Otherwise the emphasis used to be on gross national product (GNP) with the understanding that industrialization would lead to an increase in GNP which would automatically lead to growth in employment and productivity. Three country missions – Colombia, Sri Lanka and Kenya – were carried out as a part of WEP for the purpose of recommending employment policies applicable to these countries. The mission reports highlighted several structural imbalances, e.g. between rural and urban sectors or between sector as factors that brought about lack of sufficient employment. Colombia Mission Report identified poverty as the most important aspect of the employment problem. Sri Lanka Mission found that types of work people were willing and able to do were not matched by the available opportunities. A package of structural reforms comprising land reforms, reorganization of educational system, national wage policy, etc. was recommended to solve this problem.

The Kenya Mission Report concentrated on the working poor and stated that the main problem was one of employment (earning low incomes in spite of long hours of work) rather than unemployment. This report identified IS as the abode of rural migrants who were thrown out of the rural economy due to lack of access to land and who could not be absorbed in the urban, modern industrial sector. A series of city-studies was also carried out to complement the country-studies. Calcutta, Jakarta, Sao Paulo, Bogota and Abidjan were the cities surveyed for this purpose. The framework for these city-studies was provided by a paper by Bairoch (1973) which focussed on excessive urbanization and rural-urban migration in LDCs and the consequent swelling of the urban tertiary sector which was seen as an obstacle to development. According to Bairoch, the choice was between urban over-unemployment and rural under-employment and he advocated the creation of job opportunities in rural areas to check the urban drift. The city- studies, however, contradicted this position to varying extent and drew attention to the productive capacity of IS. They generally made a case for measures to increase urban employment.

More city-surveys were carried out by ILO under WEP till the end of 1970. Colombo, Manila in Asia, Cordoba, Campinas in Latin America and Lagos, Freetown, Kano and Kumasi in Africa were the cities studied. The size and composition of informal activities, linkages of informal enterprises, age composition, earnings and migration status of IS workers were the aspects regarding which these studies collected information. They also sought to estimate the proportion of informal workers/population in the total urban population by treating workers in enterprises below a certain employment size as informal workers. The comparative picture that emerges form these studies is shown in Table 2.1.

Many more surveys of IS have been carried out till date. Table 2.2 sets out the estimated share of informal employment in certain LDCs.

The above figures are not strictly comparable due to the different time frames. Still it may roughly be surmised that the proportion of IS employment is low (around 30 per cent) in Latin America. Africa exhibits a wide range of variation form 25.4 per cent to 65.6 per cent and Asia (only two countries) takes a middle position, clustering around 40 per cent.

Table 2.1 : Comparative Features of the Urban Informal Sector

(Range of Variation)

Particulars	Asia	Africa	Latin America
1. The Sector in urban labour force (%)	19-17	50-65	25-38
2. Recent migration (%)	55-60 (Colombo-14)	80-95 (Kano-35)	55-73
3. Age of unit (< 5 years, %)	38-51 (Manila-Low)	50-67	11-45
4. Entrepreneur's median age (years)	35-37	28-35	40-41
5. Own-account workers in IS (%)	50-90 (Ahmedabad-34)	50-75	40-50
6. Manufacturing workers in informal sector (%)	5-28	20-42	15-33
7. Entrepreneur's income	> LM	> LM/FS	> PCY
8. Wages	> LM	> LM	- - - -
9. Sale to households (% of product – value)	80	72-87	82-83

LM = legal minimum wage. FS = formal sector average.
PCY = per capita income.

Notes : for the purpose of the above tabulation the cities that are included are Colombo, Manila, Jakarta, Ahmedabad in Asia, Cordoba, Campinas in Latin America, Lagos, Freetown, Knao and Kumasi in Africa. Ahmedabad study (Papola, 1981) was not an ILO study. Particulars in brackets are about places with outlying values which are excluded from the range figures above them.

Source : Roy, Basant, 1990.

Table 2.2 : Estimated Proportion of IS in the Non-agricultural Labour in Selected Developing Countries

Country	Year	Share of Informal Employment
<u>Africa</u>		
Algeria	1985	25.4
Burundi	1979	65.6
Cote d'Ivoire	1975	48.1
Egypt	1976	58.7
Morocco	1982	56.9
Senegal	1979-80	40.3
Tunisia	1980	36.1
<u>Asia</u>		
Iran	1986	43.5
Pakistan	1973	39.0
<u>Latin America</u>		
Argentina	1985	28.9
Brazil	1985	30.1
Colombia	1985	35.4

Costa Rica	1985	28.3
Chile	1985	37.2
Guatemala	1985	33.5
Mexico	1985	29.5
Peru	1985	34.9
Venezuela	1985	26.2

Source: Jacques Charmes in "The Informal Sector Revisited", 1990

Table 2.3 depicts the sectoral distribution of informal employment in select countries of the world. From the data, with the same constraints as noted above, it would appear that in Latin America and Asia, fewer workers are engaged in production as compared to commerce and services. In Africa, at least half of the workers are engaged in production. Some additional information about the professional status of informal workers (i.e. wage-workers, own-account workers, apprentices and family workers) that is available through the same source shows that the extent of wage-employment is substantially lower and that of apprentice-ship higher in Africa.

2.3 Indian City Studies

The Indian studies – city-studies with varying scope and rigour are classified in Table 2.4.

An overview of these studies is presented below:

Ahmedabad (Papola, 1981)

The study sets out to identify IS and its various segments in the urban economy and to estimate its contribution in terms of income and employment generation. The study is based on a sample survey of establishments (employing less than 10 workers) as well as workers in IS. The former comprised establishments engaged in manufacturing, trade, commerce and services while workers covered three categories, viz. Regular workers in small establishments, own-account or independent workers and casual workers. For an overall estimate of informal workforce, irregular workers in large establishments are included but they are not surveyed in the study. The total number of workers in IS and their segments were estimated on the basis of 1971 census data. It was found that 47 per cent of the workforce in Ahmedabad city was in IS, with 26 per cent being in small

Table 2.3 : Sectoral Distribution of Informal Employment

Country	Year	Production (1)	Commerce (2)	Services (3)
Mexico	1987	23.5	27.7	48.7
Colombia	1984	26.7	30.1	42.4
Egypt	1976	39.4	34.0	26.6
Pakistan	1972-73	21.6	37.4	37.9
Mali	1976	52.7	22.8	24.5
Morocco	1982	51.7	23.3	23.7
Tunisia	1980-81	54.7	23.8	21.5

Note : Columns 1+ 2 + 3 = 100.0.
Source : As in Table 2.2.

Table 2.4 : Classification of Indian City-Studies

A Rigorous City-studies	B Rigorous Studies of Parts of IS in the urban economy	C Other City-studies
1. Ahmedabad – Papola, 1981		
2. Calcutta – Bose, 1978	3. Calcutta – Banerjee, 1985	
	4. Calcutta – Romatet, 1983	
5. Bombay – Joshi And Joshi, 1976		
6. Bombay – Deshpande, 1979		
7. Delhi – Majumdar, 1980	8. Delhi – TCPO, 1983	
	9. Delhi – Banerjee, 1986	
10. Bangalore – Aziz, 1984		12. Madurai – Hariharan, Benjamin, 1991

11. Coimbatore – Harriss, 1982		13. Patiala – Vishwa Mitter, 1988
		14. Visakhapatnam – Ramana, 1988

establishments, 14 per cent is independent workers and 7 per cent as casual workers in households. The study estimates that IS contributed around 28 percent of the GDP generated in Ahmedabad city. Of this, 23 per cent was contributed by establishments and 5 per cent buy independent and casual workers together. Only manufacturing establishments were expected to sustain themselves and perhaps grow in future although their employment generation capacity per unit of capital would decline over time. The study cautions that the following points need to be considered before making a case for the growth of these establishments.

(a) exploitation of labour far exceeds that in FS,
(b) in spite of (a) above they tend to prefer the use of capital and
(c) the better-off establishments are more dependent on their FS counterparts.

Other findings of the study were that migration to Ahmedabad was a smooth process with an average waiting period of 45 days. Three-fourths of the workers earned at least 50 percent more in the first job in the city in spite of migration being mostly due to a push out of rural economy rather than the pull of the urban economy. Rejects from FS joined IS and half of the informal workers did not aspire for a change and so it was concluded that the labour market was tending towards segmentation from the formal sector labour market. Opportunities for graduating form IS to FS appeared to be limited.

Calcutta (Bose, 1978)

Bose's study of informal units in Calcutta was in the nature of follow-up of Lubell's study for ILO, 1974 (see page 33). The study makes use of both primary and secondary data. The former was collected through a survey of slum industries in Calcutta.

By using details from the census of the 1961, 1971 and Annual Survey of Industries, the size of IS in Calcutta was estimated. Employment in IS was estimated to be 28 per cent in 1971. Employment in informal manufacturing was 38 percent and in informal non-manufacturing activities was 23 per cent of the total. In 1961, employment in informal manufacturing was as much as 54 per cent. Past surveys of informal industries in Calcutta (7 in all) were reviewed. For the survey of slum industries which was carried out in 1974, clusters of these industries were identified. Eleven such clusters were surveyed and 646 industrial units in them were classified into 12 industry has not been defined in the survey. 112 units (17 per cent) with 1,806 persons (41 per cent) employed had more than 10 employees each. These industries made use of productive capital (fixed plus working capital) worth only Rs. 4,400 per employee as against only fixed capital of Rs. 15,000 per employee in the registered factory sector in 1968. Some case studies from the survey are also presented. They give information about the conditions in which production of footwear, garments, light engineering and electrical components, etc. is carried out in these slum industries.

The picture that emerges from these studies reveals two parts of IS; the modern part depends heavily on large, modern unites which compel it to operate in different market which has higher factor prices and lower product prices and which reap the main benefit of this price differential. The traditional part of IS produces cheap goods for poor people and adequacy of effective demand is a major constraint for it.

A survey of 34,316 pavement dwellers (about one-third of them being income-earners), the most informal section in industries. This survey found that 35 per cent and 28 per cent of the income earners were in regular and casual employment respectively. It was also estimated that the proportion of people above poverty line was considerably higher among pavement dwellers as compared to the general population.

The study finally presents an outline of a development programme starts with the premise for IS as a whole. This programme starts with the remise that the structure of the rest of the economy needs to be changed for facilitating the development of IS. It then recommends a changed industrial mix to favour agricultural modernization, area-based integrated development of agriculture and greater diversion of organized credit towards IS. Preparation of informal ancillary unit development plans by big industrial units and effective organization of these units are recommended. Finally the need for networking among informal ancillary units and other informal units in both industry and agriculture is stressed.

Nirmala Banerjee's study of Calcutta (1985) is restricted to women workers in IS. IS or rather, unorganized sector was defined as a residue after registered factories, public and semi-public agencies, education, health, other professions, shops and commercial institutions, motor transport units, construction and hawking units were excluded from establishments. The study is based on a sample survey of 400 women workers, 56 per cent of whom were engaged in domestic service, 26 percent were skilled workers and the balance 18 per cent were unskilled workers. The conclusions were that : employers (demanding labour) were not interested in a stable, long-term relationship with the workers. Flexible employment contracts existed and they enabled the employers to drive a hard bargain. There was no system of granting annual increments or promoting the workers. In fact, no arrangement for imparting training to workers existed. Similarly there was no channel for providing information about jobs to aspiring candidates and so, even without barriers to entry, getting a job was considered difficult. Rejecting piece-workers to unionise were the methods used for enforcing discipline.

E. Romatet's small Study (1983) of Calcutta made use of both secondary and primary – from a survey of 53 slum industries – data. Slum industries were identified on the basis of their informal appearance. In about half of the surveyed units the owner's income was nearly equal to the wage earned by hired workers in FS. The units had no control over the selling price of their products. They managed to survive by paying very low wages to their workers.

Bombay (Joshi and Joshi, 1976)

This study is; based on secondary data from the censuses of 1961 and 1971 and a survey done by Lakdawala at al in the 1950s. Joshi and Joshi have estimated the size of the unorganized sector in Bombay by using the 1961 census figures. Unorganized sector is taken to consist of all establishments employing less than 25 workers. This is a much higher cut- off point as compared to what has become the norm (mostly 10 workers) and the study itself notes that unorganized units hire no more than four workers per unit.

Unorganized sector workforce is classified into two categories, viz. employees in non-household industry and other i.e. single workers, family workers, workers in household industry and also cultivators and agricultural labourers. As per 1961 census details,

Unorganized sector thus accounts for half of the total labour force in the city. Services account for 30 per cent and manufacturing 26 per cent. Wage-workers were more common in manufacturing as compared to trade or services and within the former also modern industries like engineering had greater wage-workers while the traditional textile industry employed more family labour.

(Figures in thousands)

Total Workforce In Mumbai = 1687.7				
	Organised employees	837.6+2.5* (49.6%)	=	840.1* (49.8%)
	Unorganized employees	752.3+93.5* (44.6%)	=	845.8 (50.2%)
	Employers	96.0 (5.7%)		

(* This breakup is suggested by the authors)

Deshpande (1985) divided the Bombay labour market into two categories – regular and casual. The former was subdivided into factories and small establishments, mostly shops and commercial establishments. The small establishments segment (roughly) and the casual segment might be taken to represent IS. The study is a sample survey of 6,000 workers. Deshpande has separately estimated that the unorganized workers in Bombay declined from 42 per cent to 39 per cent between 1961 and 1971.

The study shows that skill differentials give rise to narrower wage differentials in the IS as compared to FS, due to the absence of a fine division of labour. A list of 17 occupations common to all three segments is given and it is shown that casual wages < small establishment wages < factory wages. It is suggested that these three segments constitute non-competing groups. It was also found that real wage over time had increased substantially in the factory segment. Nothing definite could be said about IS since wage had increased in the small establishments segment and declined in the casual segment. Lack of any institutional protection exposed the casual workers to the competition from fresh migrants and depressed their wages.

Migrant casual workers were found to be older, less educated and more likely to be married at the time of migration. They were morel commonly landless rural workers and had few personal contacts. Migrant small establishment workers were usually young (36 per cent were students at the time of migration), unmarried males looking for a career in the city. Factory workers were more commonly cultivators previously. Data on intersectoral mobility showed the if the badli system in textile industry was excluded, very few factory workers mobility from small establishments to factories was greater. The study concluded that the Bombay labour market was segmented and the segmentation process has rural roots.

Delhi (Majumdar, 1980)

Majumdar has estimated the magnitude of IS in Delhi on the basis of census figures for 1961 to 54 per cent in 1971. The proportion of migrants in the informal labour force was found to be 77 per cent. Primary data was also collected through an occupational survey in which certain occupations were identified as informal occupations. These were mostly service occupations. It was found that the changing pattern of urban life gave rise to a large number of new occupations in IS.

The Town and Country Planning Organization – TCPO, Ministry of works and Housing (1983) carried out a sample survey of informal establishments concentrated in one particular industrial estate – the area was actually meant for public recreational use – in Delhi. Two hundred and fifty establishments were covered in the survey. Seventy two per cent of them were manufacturing units, 20 per cent were engaged in trade and commerce and 8 per cent in repairs and services. Workers in 70 of the sample establishments were young (less than 10 years old) and had monthly turnover of less than Rs. 20,000. 70 per cent of the workers were found to be skilled, their acquisition of skill being on-the-job.

Banerjee (1986) has carried out a study of IS in Delhi for the purpose of studying the relation between migration and the phenomenon of dual labour market in the urban economy. Specifically, he wanted to test the validity of what he calls the probabilistic models of migration (Todaro, 1969; Fields, 1975; Mazumdar, 1977). These models start with the premise of dualism in the urban economy and formulate that rural urban migration is a two stage phenomenon. In other words, FS attracts the rural migrants who first enter IS which is a free-entry sector, carry out their job-search while simultaneously earning some income for their sustenance and are eventually able to land FS jobs. Is thus becomes the staging post and these models support the graduation (from IS to FS) hypothesis.

The study is based on a sample survey of migrant household heads in Delhi. IS was defined on the basis of employment size with a cut-off limit of 20 employees. Within IS, distinction was made between wage employment and non-wage employment. Identification of FS on IS on the basis of occupational classification was also attempted but was not pursued further retailers, wholesalers, handcart pullers, hawkers and vendors) were common to both sectors. Findings of the study were the following:

1. More than half of the IS entrants had been attracted to Delhi by the opportunities available.
2. Slightly less than one-fourth of IS informal wage sector intranets were able to move to FS. The proportion of direct entrants to FS was higher than this.

3. Only a small proportion of informal wage sector employees where seeking alternative jobs.
4. Although labour turnover was higher in IS as compared to Fs, job stability and tenure among informal non-wage workers was comparable with that of FS workers. Turnover in informal wage sector too, was dominated by voluntary job changes and reflected a systematic and cautious job-search process.
5. Non-wage workers did not see their activity as a step towards wage employment. Only a small proportion of them was engaged in searching for wage employment. Entry into non-wage occupations was restricted by the requirements of capital, skill and the presence of informal networks which exercise control over location and zone of operation.
6. Average monthly earnings of informal non-wage workers were 47 per cent higher than those of wage-workers. The order of earnings was; informal non-wage workers, formal wage workers. This supports observation (5) above.
7. Process of wage determination is different in IS as compared to FS. But returns to education and experience are similar in both sectors. IS tends to be more competitive, i.e. unlike FS, IS does not distinguish between castes, manual and non-manual workers, salaried and daily wage status, etc.

By putting the above findings together Banerjee concludes that the assumptions and implications of probabilistic migration models are not valid.

Bangalore:

The study by Aziz (1984) estimates the size of employment in IS in Bangalore on the basis of 1971 census data. Employment size and a cut-off point of 10 employees is used to segregate IS from FS. IS workforce is estimated to be 40 per cent of the total labour force. Aziz then proceeds to further classify IS into organized and unorganized segments, two reasons are forwarded for this step: some establishments having < 10 workers have to get licences and thus have a formal relationship with the state. Secondly, factories employing between 10 and 20 workers and not using p0wer in the manufacturing process do have to reckon with trade unions. Both these establishments enter IS in the usual method of estimating IS workforce but they are actually formal units. Hotels and restaurants, medical, sanitation, educational services, finance, insurance, real estate services and electricity, gas and water supply establishments fall in this category and are called organized informal establishments. The rest that is those engaged in manufacturing and repairs, trade and commerce, construction, agriculture and personal services fall in the unorganized informal segment. As per 1971 Census data, these two segments accounted for 8 per cent and 32 per cent of the total workforce (total (IS = 40 per cent). The study then goes on to present the working of the waste recycling industry which is one part of is.

Coimbatore

Harriss (1982) estimates, on the basis of the 1971 Census and Directorate of Employment and Training figures covering factories employing 25 and more workers, IS workers to be around 60 to 65 per cent of the workforce in Coimbatore. It is also estimated that about slightly less than half the manufacturing workers in the city worked in IS.

For studying the informal economy and its linkages with FS, Harriss has carried out a sample survey of manufacturing establishments and workers. The survey includes both registered and unregistered production units and organized and unorganized workers. The unregistered production units are called petty commodity production units (PCPs) and they are defined as units where producers supply their own labour, use raw materials and tools over which they have some control and sell the commodities they produce for reproducing themselves and their production processes. The PCP units are further classifies as those engages in traditional and new occupations. Unorganized workers similarly consist of both workers in unregulated workshops and vulnerable workers. The category of vulnerable workers as suggested by Bromley and Gerry (1979) basically means casual workers. The following classification of workers is thus adopted:

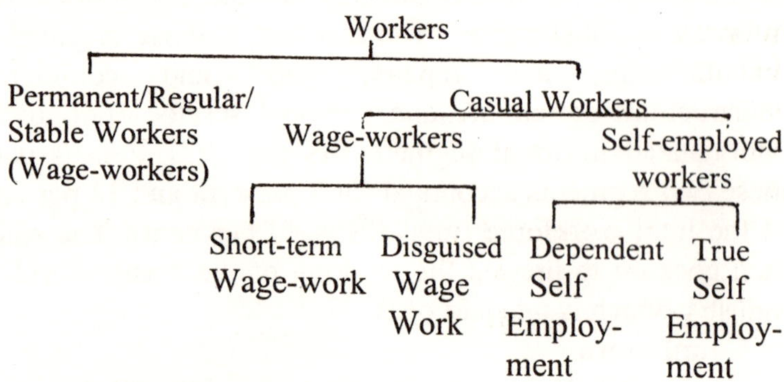

The study found that:

1. small unregistered workshops which had substantial linkages with large factories were prominent in Coimbatore. The linkages were both input and output-related. Large factories were interested in these links for controlling their own labour process and for reducing labour process and for reducing labour costs. The "free" workshops operated in very competitive markets and so

the possibility of their sustained growth was constrained. At the same time, their markets were persistent.

2. PCP units engaged in new occupations were similarly subordinated to more organized units and their market depended upon income generated in the rest of the economy.
3. PCP units in traditional occupations were linked with finance and trading capital and they too were subject to an involutionary pattern of growth.
4. Labour market in Coimbatore was strongly segmented.

Then there are three other surveys in category C of Table 2.4. The survey of Madurai (1991) found that IS was equivalent to about 32 per cent of the city labour force. Manufacturing workers came to around 23 per cent of the total workers in IS. Among the IS establishments, about half (47 per cent) were less than five high proportion (73 per cent) of the labour force to be in IS. The own-account workers in IS were found to be 67 per cent. About half (48 per cent) of the workers received wages that were less than the legal minimum wage. The Vishakhapatnam study (1988) found that there was scope for occupational and intersectoral mobility in the urban economy.

2.3.1 Summary of Major Points

Given the heterogeneity of activities lumped together in the concept of IS, the above studies have sought to identify and concentrate on one particular segment within IS. In the labour market categorization, this segment is referred to as upper tier or non-wage segment. In the product market approach, it is called the intermediate sector or modern (or even organized) segment and it is supposed to have some chance of growth unlike other segments in IS.

Among the Indian city-studies, those with the product market approach (Ahmedabad – Papola, Calcutta – Bose, Romatet, Coimbatore-Harriss. Papola and Harriss have also adopted the labour market approach) have reached the following results:

(a) The modern segment of IS, comprising manufacturing establishments, is dependent on FS.

(b) The growth prospects of this segment are limited though its market is persistent. Growth prospects and dependence on FS are positively linked.

(c) FS-IS links are used by the former for controlling its own labour process and lowering labour cost. According to Bose, these links are used by FS to compel IS to operate in a market with low product price and high factor prices. According to Romatet, factor prices – basically wages – have got to be low if IS units are to survive.

Indian city-studies with the labour market approach (Ahmedabad – Papola, Calcutta – N. Banerjee, Bombay – Deshpande, Delhi-B. Banerjee and Coimbatore – Harriss) have arrived at the following conclusions:

(a) The formal labour market is segmented from the informal labour market. Fs ejects can join it but IS occupants cannot graduate to FS.

(b) In the absence of an elaborate division of labour, skill differences lead to a narrow wage difference in IS as compared to FS.

(c) Because of its low skill content, labour is a general purpose input in IS and so employers are not interested in a stable relationship with workers. (this conclusion was reached on the basis of the study of women workers in IS.

(d) Comparison between FS wage-workers and IS wage-workers brings out only dissimilarities but FS wage-workers and IS non-wage workers are comparable in terms of tenure and stability of employment.

(e) Because of the non-wage component of IS, its role in the rural-urban migration process is more complex than that suggested by the Todaro migration model.

2.4 SSI Sector in India

The sizable literature on small-scale industries (SSI) sector in India should also be relevant as its non-factory units are a part of informal sector. SSI sector in India comprises a very large number of industrial units which fall in two categories, viz. modern and traditional. modern units have access to modern technology and state machinery which has provided a number of incentives and benefits and markets. Some of them trade untraditional textiles and handicrafts but are modern, export-oriented units. Traditional small units are tiny, disadvantaged units which exist in large numbers but which do not make a mark in economic terms, except probably in employment.

According to Holmstrom, the continuum of small units in India starts with those units at one end which gave been started by big industries for taking advantage of State promotion and assistance programme. At the other extreme, there exist small units which enjoy genuine cost advantages flowing from entrepreneurship, cheap labour, flexibility, cheap machinery, local started because the owners as technician-entrepreneurs and financier-entrepreneurs or those with a commercial orientation and opines that the latter are more successful!) most of the small units prefer to remain small in order to be eligible for State assistance. The extent of sickness in SSI units in the country is very high.

On the whole, analysts have concluded that over the years, modern SSI units which exist in a complementary capacity to large-scale units have done well as compared to traditional units. These units have no truck with the informal sector.

Brahme, Paranjape (1979) have made, on the basis of their sample study of SSI units in Pune Metropolitan Region, two important points in connection with this sector. Firstly, they argue that instead of traditional units and their owners being enabled to move upward, a new entrepreneurial class with middle-class origin, has been created in this sector. Secondly, they point out that large industrial units have made use of State promotional measures to make small units viable. In other words, large units want small units to become viable at social cost. Once these units become viable (due to state incentives and concessional finance provided buy public financial institutions), large units are ready to use them to externalize their costs. A long mechanism from delayed payment of bills to use of cheap labour in small units through subcontracting and putting out, has been fashioned to made this transfer. Therefore the state finds, paradoxically, that the more it helps small units, the more they become dependent on it. Modern SSI units have become integrated with the economy only to the extent they are a part of this mechanism to help large units to pass on their costs.

The perspective is very important because it gives an insight into the relationship between FS and IS also. Most of other studies of SSI are, however, straightforward and outside this perspective. These studies are, therefore, not directly relevant to the study of IS. The same is the case of database on SSI sector.

In official reports on SSI units, these units are defined in terms of capital investment rather than number of workers employed. Therefore, it becomes difficult to find out which of them are informal units. Given that the modern units dominate this sector, we have ignored the database on this sector. Later, we have dipped into it occasionally to understand the results from our survey of informal manufacturing units in Pune.

Chapter 3

Quantifying the Informal Sector

Decennial census reports, Five Year Plan documents and economic surveys help in building up an overall picture of IS in the Indian economy. A residual approach has to be used while using these sources. in other words, the unorganized sector employment is derived by netting out the organized sector from the economy. This approach is useful for getting an idea of the break-up of number of persons employed in the two sectors, their composition and relative change in their proportions over the years. Table 3.1 gives the latest break-up of population and workforce in the Indian economy.

Economic census reports on the other hand, give us a direct insight into FS. The government initiated the scheme of economic censuses in 1976 to cover the unorganized, non-agricultural sector. The Central Statistical Organization (CSO) has so far carried out economic censuses (Ecs) in 1977, 1980, 1990 and 1998. As a back-up to Ecs, National Sample Survey Organization (NSSO) has carried out surveys focussing on particular parts of the unorganized sector such as non-registered manufacturing, trading enterprises, transport and storage units, ect. EC and these sample survey reports give detailed information on number of enterprises, their location (rural/urban) and industry-wise break-up, number of persons employed in them and certain structural features of these enterprises in terms of their inputs and output.

On the basis of ECs, National Accounts Statistics prepared by CSO give the break-up of national income and

Table 3.1: Population and Workforce: 1981-2001

(in Lakhs)

	1981	1991	%age growth (1981-1991)	1991-2001	%age growth (1991-2001)
1. Population	6833.3	8463	2.16	10252.5	1.94
2. Workers	2507.9	3173.6	---	4019.0	---
(a) Main Workers	2289.2	2885.9	2.34	3127.0	0.81
(b) Marginal Workers	218.7	287.7	2.78	892.0	11.98

Source: Decennial Census Reports

factor incomes in the organized and unorganized sectors. Information from these different sources is presented in Table 3.2.

3.1 Overall Picture

Thus in 1991, 91 per cent of the workers in the country was in the unorganized sector. There has been only a marginal terms employment in the unorganized sector has grown at the rate of 28.4 lakhs per annum in these 40 years. Rate of growth of employment in the organized sector has not had any impact on the growth in unorganized sector over the years. At the same time the share of the organized sector in net domestic product (NDP) continues to grow steadily. Between 1980-81 and 1990-91, the organized sector's share in NDP rose from 30 per cent to 36 per cent to 64 per cent. This reiterates a well-known paradox, viz. the organized sector is the dynamic, growing part of the economy but in terms of employment , its contribution is negligible, particularly in absolute terms. Therefore the unorganized sector is the main sector from the point of view of employment. It will not be out of place to mention one interesting point here: From 1994 onwards, rate of growth of population, labour force and employment have declined in the economy. Rate of growth of employment in some parts of the organised sector such as agriculture and construction has become negative since 1994. It is the unorganized sector which continues to generate employment to take care of the growth in labour force but its rate of growth is also declining now. (Economic Survey, 2001-2002.)

The unorganized sector turns out to be so large because the entire employment in agricultural and small scale industries (SSI) sectors is included in it. Actually a part of SSI comprises modern, capital-intensive units. In agriculture

Table 3.2 : Employment in Organised and Unorganised Sectors, 1961 to 2000

(Figures in Lakhs)

Year	Organised Sector	Unorganised Sector	Total
1961	146 (7.7)	1741 (92.3)	1887 (100.0)
1971	202 (8.9)	2067 (91.1)	2269 (100.0)
1974	225	-	-
1981	229 (10.7)	2140 (91.2)	2369 (100.0)
1983	240 (8.8)	2680 (91.2)	2880 (100.0)
1987-88	257 (8.8)	2680 (91.2)	2937 (100.0)
1991	267 (9.3)	2594 (90.7)	2861 (100.0)
1993-94	272 (8.6)	2887 (91.4)	3158 (100.0)
1999-2000	281 (8.3)	3086 (91.7)	3367 (100.0)

Notes : 1) The figure of workers in unorganised sector is obtained by deducting organised sector workers from total workers as per the decennial census.

2) figures in brackets are percentages to total.

3) Organised sector worker are those reported by Five Year Plan Drafts.

Sources: 1. G. Parthsarthy

2. 1993-94 and 1999-2000 figures are taken from Report of the Special Group on Targeting ten Million Employment Opportunities, Planning Commission, May 2002

too, owners of large landholdings manage their holdings with commercial motives and this tendency has become widespread following the green revolution. This new class of farmers appropriately belongs to the organized sector within agriculture. Small and marginal farmers and landless agricultural labour on the other land, belong to the unorganized sector.

The retabulated figures, after correction along the above lines, for organized and unorganized sector workers appear in Table 3.3. Table 3.3(a) shows the broad break-up of workforce in 1991.

The unorganized labour force comprises 75 per cent of total agricultural labour and 60 per cent of total non-agricultural labour in the economy.

After splitting up agriculture and small-scale industries (from the latter powerlooms and modern small industry have gone to the organized sector and traditional industries sector have gone to the unorganized sector) the share of unorganized sector in the total workforce comes down to 70 per cent. In the modified scheme also there has been marginal change in the change in the proportion of organized and unorganized sectors in the total workforce in the decade 1980-1991. Within these two sectors, however, there have taken place some significant changes. Powerlooms and modern small scale industry in the organized sector and traditional industries in the unorganized sector have grown significantly while there is a decline in employment in private sector establishments and curiously enough, in the ranks of non-agricultural labour and own account workers in trade and services. The share of agriculture in both sectors is significant.

Table 3.3 : Employment in Organised and Unorganised Sectors – After Modification, 1981, 1991

(Figures in Lakhs)

Particulars	1979-80/ 1980-81	1990-91/ 1989-90	Per cent share in Two sectors in 1990-91/ 1989-90	Per cent change In the Decade
I. Unorganised Sector				
1. Small, marginal farmers and Agricultural labour	1180	1390	70.1	17.8
2. Workers in the traditional industries in non-agricultural sector(e.g. Khadi, Village industries, handloom, handicrafts, sericulture and coir, etc.)	130.8	219.2	11.0	67.6
3. Other non-agricultural labour	286.7	250.5	12.6	-12.6
4. Own account workers in trade and services	143.3	125.5	6.3	-12.6
Total (1+2+3+4)	1740.8 (71.1)	1984.9 (69.4)	100.00	14.0
II. Organised Sector				
1. Large and medium landholders In agriculture	400.0	460.0	52.6	15.0
2. Non-agricultural labour:				
a) Public sector employees	156.0	180.0	20.6	15.4
b) Private sector employees in establishment with more than	74.0	70.0	8.0	-5.7

10 workers				
c) Powerlooms	11.0	45.0	5.1	318.2
d) Modern small scale industry				
	67.0	119.6	13.7	78.5
Non-agricultural labour	308.0	414.6	47.4	34.6
Total (1+2)	708.0	874.6	100.0	23.5
	(28.9)	(30.6)		
Grand Total (I+II)	2448.8	2859.5		16.8
	(100.0)	(100.0)		

Notes : The methodology adopted for this bread-up is not clear. Labour in household industry plus non-factory, non-household industry has been shown under traditional industries in non-agricultural sector. Data on non-agricultural labour in traditional industries has been taken from Seventh Plan Report 1990-91. Workers estimated from household data and census data on cultivation.

Source: G. Parthasarthy, "Unorganised sector and Structural Adjustment", op. cit.

Table 3.3 (a)Broad break-up of Workforce in 1991

(Figures in lakhs)

	Organised Sector		Unorganised Sector		Total
Agricultural labour	460		1390		1850
	(24.9)		(75.1)		(100.0)
Non-Agricultural labour	415		595		1010
	(41.1)		(58.9)		(100.0)
Total	875	+	1985	=	
	(30.)		(69.4)	2860	
					(100.0)

3.2 National Accounts Statistics

National Accounts Statistics are compiled by CSO. It presents various aggregates of national income and factor incomes by institutional sectors and by industry of origin. It recognizes the following institutional sectors:

(a) Public sector,
(b) Private corporate sector,
(c) Cooperative societies, and
(d) Household and private unincorporated enterprises.

The first three sectors above make up the organized part of the economy while (d) above becomes the unorganized part. For the purpose of collecting data, the unorganized segment of any sector in the economy is defined to comprise those operating units whose activity is not regulated under any legal provision so that data about it are not available in regular fashion. Thus all factories not registered under the Factories Act constitute unorganized manufacturing segment. All non-public operating units become the unorganized segment of trade, hotels and restaurants, storage, warehousing and service activities because regular accounts of their activity are not available. In other sectors, certain activities such as air transport, communication, banking, provident fund and insurance institutions, public administration and defence, research, scientific services, recognized educational institutions, international bodies, etc., by their very nature, belong to the organized sector.

Information about the unorganized sector as defined above is collected from economic censuses and national sample surveys. The share of organized and unorganized sectors in NDP in the years 1993-94 and 1999-2000 is presented in Table 3.4.

Table 3.4 sets out the industrywise break-up of NDP contributions by organized and unorganized sectors. Mining,

Table 3.4: Share of Organised and Unorganised Sectors in Net Domestic Product by Industry

(Rs. in crores)

Industry	1993-94 (at current prices)			1999-00 (at current prices)					
	Organised sector	Unorganised sector	Total	Organised sector	Unorganised sector	Total	Organised sector	Unorganised sector	Total
1. Agriculture, forestry and fishing	8046	221783	229829	13999	422844	436843	8808	266050	274858
2. Mining and quarrying	13861	1089	14950	28944	2255	31199	19156	1492	20648
3. Manufacturing	65774	37965	103739	127387	82419	209806	90168	57953	148121
4. Electricity, gas and water Supply	8169	632	8801	21350	1307	22657	13766	843	14609

5. Construction	18929	19820	38749	43941	57580	101521	24107	31589	55696
6. Trade, hotels, and restaurants	10865	85762	96627	47110	188888	235998	32751	131313	164064
7. Transport, storage and communications	21000	16721	37721	45437	52088	97525	30801	35309	66110
8. Financing, insurance, real estate and business services	39706	40835	80541	119377	80032	199409	78739	52788	131527
9. Community, social and personal services	70499	16536	87035	198997	39257	238254	120033	23679	143712
10. Net Domestic product at factor level	256849	441143	697992	646542	926670	1573212	418920	600425	1019345

Source : National Accounts Statistics, CSO.

quarrying, electricity, gas and water, railways, communications, baking and insurance, pubic administration and defence belong mainly to organized sector. (Electricity, gas, water, railways, communications, public administration and defence belong exclusively to the organize sector.) Agriculture, forestry and fishing, trade, hotels and restaurants transport by means other than railways, real estate and business services are found mainly in the unorganized sector. Within the non-agricultural part of the unorganized sector, trade, manufacturing, construction, financing, real estate, business services and transport and storage are the more productive segments.

National accounts statistics also report factor incomes in organized and unorganized sectors. This is presented in Table 3.5. Factor income is equal to net values added and is the sum total of compensation of employees, operating surplus and mixed income (accruing to both labour and entrepreneurship) of self-employed persons. Operating surplus is the sum total of property incomes, i.e. rent and interest and residual profit or loss. Mixed income of self-employed persons includes compensation to employees of own account workers and also profit or loss generated in unincorporated enterprises.

What is striking about this data is the relative stability of employees' compensation (in percentage terms) over this period of 13 years. The share of operating surplus has increased by 4.2 per cent during this period and to that extent, the share of mixed income has gone down. This suggests that the organized sector is gaining ground. Within the organized sector, share of employees' compensation has declined by 7 per cent and the share of operating surplus has increased correspondingly.

Table 3.5 : Factor Incomes by Institutions

(Rupees in Crore)

	1980-81			1990-91			1992-93		
	Organised Sector	Unorgani -sed Sector	TOTAL	Organised Sector	Unorgani -sed Sector	TOTAL	Organised Sector	Unorgani -sed Sector	TOTAL
(a) Compensation of employee	24550 (74.2)	16047 (20.8)	40597 (36.8)	105161 (68.4)	58252 (21.4)	163413 (38.4)	136470 (67.4)	74373 (21.1)	210843 (38.0)
(b) Operating Surplus	8523 (25.8)	--	8523 (7.7)	48645 (31.6)	---	48645 (11.4)	66109 (32.6)	---	66109 (11.9)
(c) Mixed Income	---	61219 (79.2)	61219 (55.5)	--	213544 (78.6)	213544 (50.2)	--	278417 (78.9)	278417 (50.1)
Total net domestic product (or net value	33073 (100) (30)	77266 (100) (70)	110339 (100) (100)	153806 (100) (36)	271796 (100) (64)	425602 (100) (100)	202579 (100) (36)	352790 (100) (64)	555369 (100) (100)

added, i.e. a+b+c									

Notes: 1. Figures in brackets per cent to total.

2. Figures in brackets on the last line show shares of organised and unorganised sectors in total factor income.

Source: National Accounts Statistics of India: 1950-51 to 1994-95, EPW Research Foundation.

This data shows that shares of factor incomes have been fairly stable over this decade in all the industries. However, the most interesting point is the range of variation: in case of mixed income, from 100 per cent in construction and in case of compensation to employees, from 3 per cent in finance and business services to 74 per cent in construction.

This data also shows that in the unorganized sector, the share of employees' compensation has declined over the years in agriculture, transport, storage and communication. Otherwise and particularly in service sectors, it has gone up. This means that the share of mixed income has gone up in agriculture, transport, storage and communication and has declined in the rest of the industries. This could be due to nothing more than better reporting of activities or else it could mean greater formalization and greater use of wage labour. Table 3.6 highlights the factor income shares by industry of origin in the unorganised sector. Table 3.7 presents the rate of growth of employment in organised and unorganised sector.

3.3 Economic Census and NSS Rounds

This is the most important source of information on the unorganized economy. As stated at beginning, it does not view the unorganized sector as a residual sector but quantifies it directly. ECs are carried out by the Central Statistical Organization (CSO). Economic Census of 1998 is the latest. ECs of 1980 and 1990 were carried out along with the house-listing operations of the decennial population censuses. CSO is trying to conduct Ecs quinquuennially. So it wanted to undertake fourth EC in 1996 but could do so in 1998 only. Agricultural and non-agricultural enterprises are covered in ECs and the statistics are reported separately for rural and urban areas. (Agricultural enterprises exclude

Table 3.6: Factor Income Shares by Industry of Origin: Unorganised Sector

	1980-81 Compens-sation of employees	Mixed income	Total	1989-90 Compens-ation of employees	Mixed income	Total
1. Agriculture, forestry and fishing	20.9	79.1	100.0	18.5	81.5	100.0
2. Mining and quarrying	7.1	92.9	100.0	7.4	92.6	100.0
3. Manufacturing	13.6	86.4	100.0	14.9	85.1	100.0
4. Electricity, gas and water supply	-	100.0	100.0	-	100.0	100.0
5. Construction	73.0	27.0	100.0	74.3	25.7	100.0
6. Trade, hotels and restaurants	19.2	80.8	100.0	19.3	80.7	100.0
7. Transport, storage and communication	34.0	66.0	100.0	30.3	69.7	100.0
8. Financing, insurance, real estate and business services	1.3	98.7	100.0	3.4	96.6	100.0
9. Community, social and personal services	28.5	71.5	100.0	36.7	63.3	100.0
ALL SECTORS	20.8	79.3	100.0	21.7	78.3	100.0

Table 3.7: Rate of Growth of Employment in Organised and Unorganised Sectors

Activity/Sector	Employment	Growth Rate % per annum	
	Weight: 1999-00	Organised Sector (1994-2000)	Unorganised Sector (1994-2000)
1. Agriculture	56.7	-1.00	0.03
2. Mining and quarrying	0.67	-1.30	-2.40
3. Manufacturing	12.11	0.87	2.95
4. Electricity, gas and water supply	0.34	0.51	-17.00
5. Construction	4.44	-0.69	5.85
6. Trade, hotels and restaurants	11.15	1.43	5.79
7. Transport, storage and communication	4.05	0.21	7.59
8. Financing, insurance, real estate and business services	1.38	1.27	8.30
9. Community, social and personal services	9.16	0.8	-3.56
ALL SECTORS	100.00	0.56	1.12

Source: Report of Special Group on Targeting Employment Opportunities, Planning Commission, May 2002.

agricultural production and plantation and cover remaining agricultural activities such as livestock breeding and keeping, bee-keeping, fishing, hunting, forestry and agricultural services.)

The follow-up of EC 1977 was carried out by NSSO in its 33rd Round (July 1978-June 1979). It covered own account enterprises engaged in manufacturing and repairing activities. As a follow-up to EC 1980, non-directory establishments and own account enterprises (see below) in manufacturing and repairing activities were surveyed by NSSO in its 40th Round during 1984-85. A similar survey was undertaken again in the 45th Round during July 1989 to June 1990. Following EC 1990, four follow-up surveys were carried out by the NSSO from 1992 to 1997. NSS 53rd round in 1997 covered residual unorganised trade sector.

Prior to EC 1977, NSSO had independently carried out some rather sketchy surveys of the unorganized sector. These were:

7th Round : October 1953 to May 1956,
14th Round : July 1958 to June 1959,
23rd Round : July 1968 to June 1969 and
29th Round : July 1974 to June 1975.

The 14th Round exclusively and 23rd Round mainly dealt with household industries. They did not specify any upper limit on the number of workers employed in them. The 29th Round was supposed to cover the whole unregistered sector but its coverage was incomplete with respect to the non-household segment. It specified an upper limit of 5 on the number of hired workers in household industries.

ECs and NSSO use the following classification scheme for analysing the unorganized sector. The unorganized sector.

An enterprise is defined as an undertaking engaged in some gainful activity of production of some goods and/or services by the members of a household with/without hired labour.

Enterprises

- On-Account Enterprises (OAEs)
- Establishments

An OAE is an enterprise engaged in manufacturing activity or repairing service with the help of household labour only (i.e. without any hired labour).

An establishment is an enterprise which employs at least one hired worker on a fairly regular basis.

Establishments

- Non-directory Establishments (NDEs)
- Directory Establishments (DEs)

An NDE is an establishment which has less than 6 workers (both household and hired) and annual output/turnover/receipts of less than Rs. 1,00,000.

A DE is a larger establishment with more than 6 total workers and annual output/turnover/receipts exceeding Rs. 1,00,000.

ECs cover the entire unorganized sector while specific NSS reports focus on manufacturing, trading, service activities, etc. For covering unorganized manufacturing, the classification scheme uses the categories NDMEs and DMEs, i.e., non-directory manufacturing establishments and directory manufacturing establishments. These are NDEs and DEs engaged in manufacturing. Table 3.8 depicts the growth of unorganised workers as per economic census.

A comparative picture of the unorganized sector that emerges form EC 1980 and 1990 is presented in Table 3.9.

The conclusion that can be drawn from this Table is that agricultural enterprises have shown the maximum growth in this decade, both in terms of employment and number of enterprises. However, in absolute terms, agricultural enterprises are a small entity. In case of urban/non-agricultural enterprises, employment growth rate is below that of number enterprises. The reports mention that among agricultural enterprises, establishments contributed more to the growth in employment. This might mean that the reported employment growth is durable and that it is not distress self-employment created because there are no jobs available elsewhere. On the whole, the unorganized sector has created sizable employment rose marginally during this period. It is, therefore, said that the future of employment in the country lies in small industrial units, service industries and the informal sector.

Tables 3.10 and 3.11 show the overall picture of the unorganized economy in the country as per Economic Census, 1998.

Thus, in terms of employment, manufacturing, community, social and private services, and retail trade, in that order, are the most important activities in the non-agricultural unorganized economy. In terms of number too, these three activities dominate the scene but their order is reserved.

Statewise break-up of the unorganized sector shows that Maharashtra and West Bengal have a share of 10.7 per cent each of all enterprises and with a share of 10.5 per cent each

Table 3.8: Growth of Unorganised Workers as per Economic Census

(figures in lakhs)

Particulars	1980	1990	1998
1. Rural sector (excluding farm sector and plantation)	242.26	321.76 (2.88)	381.32 (2.15)
2. Urban	289.52	382.10 (2.81)	424.99 (1.34)
TOTAL	531.79	703.86 (2.84)	806.31 (1.71)

Note: Figures in brackets denote growth rates.

Source: Report of Special Group, Planning Commission, May 2002. There is some difference in EC 1998 figures of employment. EC 1998 details are given below. Planning Commission figures have been retained for the sake of overall growth rates.

Table 3.9 : Comparison of EC 1998 and EC 1990 : All India

(figures in lakhs)

Location/ Activity	EC 1998		EC 1990		% Increase	
	No. of enterprises	Usual employment	No. of enterprises	Usual employment	Enterprises	Employ ment
1. Rural	177.08(58.3)	399.01(47.9)	143.72(58.63)	321.76(45.71)	23.21	24.01
2. Urban	126.41(41.7)	433.98(52.1)	101.35(41.37)	382.10(54.29)	24.73	13.58
3. Total (1+2=3)	303.49(100.0)	832.99(100.0)	245.07(100.0)	703.86(100.0)	23.84	18.35
3a. Agricultural	34.75 (11.4)	67.49(8.10)	23.16(9.45)	47.25(6.71)	50.04	42.84
3b. Non-agricultural	268.74(88.6)	765.50(91.9)	221.91(90.55)	656.85(93.29)	21.10	16.54

Sources : 1. The Economic Census 1998, All India Report.
2. The Economic Census 1990, Report.

Table 3.10 : Number of Unorganised Enterprises and Employment Therein : All India, 1998

(Number in lakhs)

Particulars	No. of Enterprises			Persons Usually Employed		
	Own account enterprises (OAEs)	Establish ments	Total	OAEs	.	Total
a) Agricultural enterprises	31.03	3.72	34.75	53.54	13.95	67.49
b) Non-agri-cultural enterprise	182.73	86.01	268.74	268.86	496.64	765.50
Total	213.76	89.73	303.49	322.40	510.59	832.99

Source : The Economic Census Report, 1998.

Table 3.11 : Activity-wise Break-up of Number of and Employment in Non-agricultural Enterprises : All India, 1998

(Number in lakhs)

Major activity group	No. of enterprises	Employment
1. Mining and quarrying	0.36	4.91
2. Manufacturing	55.36(20.60)	225.29(29.43)
3. Electricity, gas and water	0.38	4.39
4. Construction	2.87	7.76
5. Wholesale trade	7.20	19.64
6. Retail trade	106.94(39.79)	185.37(24.21)
7. Hotels and restaurants	11.89(4.42)	30.98(4.05)
8. Transport	8.97(3.38)	19.79
9. Storage and warehousing	0.80	2.74
10. Communications	2.49	8.71
11. Financial, Insurance and Business services	6.90	29.95 (3.91)
12. Community, social and private services	64.53 (24.01)	225.89 (29.51)
13. Others – Unspecified	0.06	0.09
Total Non-agricultural activities	**268.74(100.00)**	**765.50 (100.00)**

Note : Figures in brackets are percentages to total.

Source : The Economic Census Report, 1998

of all employment. They are the main providers of employment in the country. Among establishments (i.e. enterprises which use hired labour), Tamil Nadu had the highest share at 12.1 per cent of all units. Maharashtra was second in this respect but its share in employment in establishments was the highest at 14 per cent. Dadra and Nagar Haveli provided employment to 13.59 persons per establishments while the figure varied between 2 to 6 per cent in other states.

Interestingly, among the establishments (i.e. enterprises which use hired labour with/without household labour) operating in the unorganized sector, Maharashtra, followed by Tamil Nadu, had the highest share – 12.5 per cent in respect of number of establishments and 14.4 per cent in respect of employment in them. Establishments in Maharashtra were also larger, employing 7.36 persons on an average as against 6.40 at all India level.

At all India level, 94 per cent of the unorganized enterprises were under private ownership. Out of total of 303.40 lakh enterprises, 56.9 enterprises (18.8%) operated without premises; their number being far larger in rural areas as compared to urban areas. Out of total enterprises, 93.1 per cent had perennial activities. Size class of employment distribution of these enterprises showed that 94 per cent of them had between 1 and 5 employees, 3.3 per cent had between 6 and 9 employees, and 2.8 per cent had 10 employees or more each. However, in terms of persons employed, 58.6 per cent of the employees worked in the smaller enterprises (employing 1-5 employees) while as many as 33.1 per cent worked in the larger enterprises employing 10 workers or more.

As for employment, 433 lakh hired workers constituted 52 per cent of total employment in unorganised enterprises.

In rural enterprises, proportion of hired labour to total was 41 per cent and in urban enterprises it was 62 per cent. Female employment constituted 17. 3 per cent of total employment. This proportion was 22.5 per cent in rural areas and 12.5 per cent in urban areas. Of all the workers engaged in these enterprises, 38.7 per cent were engaged in own account enterprises and the rest 61.3 per cent in establishments.

Having taken a bird's eye view of EC statistics, we turn to NSS rounds. Their reports provide a wealth of details about OSEs in rural and urban areas and in all the States. The number of enterprises, workers employed in them, economic characteristics of enterprises in terms of their inputs, particularly fixed and working capital, output, value added and also some important ratios such as value added per worker, value added to output, value added to fixed capital, input-output ratio, etc., are the details that are given in these reports. The break-up of this information is available industrywise also. Unfortunately, the format of presentation of this information varies from report to report. Successive reports build up on the experience of previous reports. New information is presented in subsequent reports. Some old details get dropped in the process and comparability, consistency of date suffer. At the aggregate level, it is difficult to relate this date with that available form other sources. However, it must be emphasized that the disaggregative details available in NSS reports are not available in any other source.

In both the 33rd and 45th Rounds, unorganized enterprises engaged in manufacturing and repair activities were surveyed by NSSO. This is presented in Table 3.12. The two Rounds reveal that a majority of unorganized enterprises were OAEs. They accounted for as much as 83 per cent of

Table 3.12 : Number of Persons Employed and Number of Enterprises as per NSSO Surveys : All India

(Number in lakhs)

NSS Round	Year	No. of persons employed	No. of enterprises
14th Round	1958-59	166.6	130.0
23rd Round	1968-69	139.2	85.7
29th Round	1974-75	161.3	88.1
33rd Round	1978-79	144.0	84.7
45th Round	1989-90	296.3	157.3

Notes: The above figures are not comparable because the first three Rounds pertain to mainly the household segment. For 33rd and 45th rounds the figures exclude Directory Manufacturing Units, i.e. those with more than 6 workers and annual output exceeding Rs. 1,00,000.

Sources: (1) For information up to 29th Round: Basant Rakesh, Kumar, B.L., "Data Base for Study of Household Manufacturing Sector, Problems of Comparability", Economic and Political Weekly, Vol. XXIV, No. 20, May 19, 1990 (2) For 33rd and 45th Rounds: respective NSSO Reports.

total employment in unorganized manufacturing as per the 45th Round. They were also predominantly rural while a majority of NDEs was urban.

As shown in Table 3.12, 157.31 lakh enterprises were engaged in unorganized manufacturing and repair activities during July 1989 to June 1990 (45th Round). Of them, 90 per cent were OAEs and only 10 per cent NDEs. These OAEs were mostly rural, while the majority of NDEs were urban. All these enterprises were engaged in a variety of activities. In urban areas, manufacture of beverages, tobacoo products, jute and other textiles, basic chemicals and chemical products, cotton textiles, textile products, etc., took place in OAEs while NDEs were engaged primarily in the manufacture of electrical equipment, basic metal and alloys, transport equipment and parts, paper and paper products, etc.

The 45th NSS Round estimated that 296.28 lakh persons were employed in these 157.31 lakh enterprises. 73 per cent of these workers were in rural areas and 27 per cent in urban. OAEs accounted for 83 per cent of total workers were female workers. The number of female workers per thousand male workers was 682 in rural areas and 323 in urban areas.

Unorganized enterprises (OAEs + NDEs) in urban areas contributed output worth Rs. 13392.36 crores and value added of Rs. 6209.04 crore. NDEs's contribution was twice that of OAEs' in output but only 4/3 that of OAEs in value added. Total capital (fixed plus working) was Rs. 11193 per worker in OAEs in urban areas and Rs. 30622 (or nearly thrice) per worker in urban NDEs.

The ratio of value added per worker to salary/wage paid to him/her was 3.16 in rural NDEs and 3.43 in urban NDEs.

Table 3.13 presents a comparative picture of per enterprise estimates of some key variables on the basis of NSS reports.

3.4 Manufacturing Segment of Informal Sector

If one concentrates on only the manufacturing activities then workers employed in establishments registered under the Indian Factories Act, 1948, fall in the registered or organized sector. This information is provided by the Annual Survey of Industries (ASI). Workers employed in smaller establishments belong to unregistered or unorganized or informal manufacturing sector. By deducting the registered manufacturing workforce (as per ASI data) from total workforce in manufacturing as per the decennial census the number of workers in informal manufacturing can be calculated.

Informal manufacturing workforce is divided into two segments, viz. non-factor, non-household segment and household segment. The household segment represents mainly family labour while the non-factory, non-household segment covers hired labour in small establishments that are not covered by the Factories Act. Calculations regarding these two segments of informal manufacturing sector from 1961 to 1991 are presented in Table 3.14.

Table 3.14 shows that the proportion of workers in informal manufacturing declined between 1961 and 1981 but rose between 1981 and 1991. In other words, the proportion of organized manufacturing workforce first rose between 1961 and 1981 and then declined till 1991. The proportion of workers engaged in the household industry has, however, been steadily declining over the years.

Table 3.13 : Some Key Variables Per Enterprise

Particulars	33rd Round (1978-79)		45th Round (1989-90)	
	OAEs	NDEs	OAEs	NDEs
1) Number of employees	1.65	3.05	1.74*	3.10*
2) Fixed assets (Rs.)	2235	7377	5310	7819
3) Output (Rs.)	4942	10173	16915	96902
4) Value added (Rs.)	2832	8413	9514	39622

Notes : 1. These figures pertain to urban areas only.

* The number of employees per enterprise in the 45th Round has, however, been worked out on an overall (urban plus rural) basis.

Source : NSS Reports for 33rd and 45th Rounds.

Table 3.14 : Estimate of Main Workers in Informal Manufacturing:1961-1991, All India

(Figures in lakhs)

Particulars	1961	1981	1991
1. All manufacturing	175.23	251.45	286.71
2. Household industry	96.51(55.1)	77.13(30.7)	68.04(23.7)
3. Non-household industry (3 = 1 - 2)	78.72	174.32	218.67
4. Registered factory/organised industry	30.50(17.4)	77.15(30.7)	77.43(27.0)
5. Non-factory, non-household industry (5 = 3 – 4)	48.22	97.17	141.24
6. Informal manufacturing = 2 + 5 (household + non-factory, non-household industry)	144.73(82.6)	174.30(69.3)	209.28(73.0)

Note : Figures in brackets are percentages to all manufacturing workforce.

Sources:

1. Row 4 i.e. registered factory workforce reported by Annual Survey of Industries. For 1991, ASI data pertains to 1998-89.
2. G. Parthasarthy, op. cit.
3. Ramaswamy, K.V., "Small-Scale Manufacturing Industries, Some Aspects of Size, Growth and Structure", Economic and Political Weekly, Review of Industry and Management, Vol. XXIX, No. 9, February 26, 1994, pp. M-13-23.

It will be interesting to cross-check the figures of workers in informal manufacturing as computed above with those reported in NSS 33rd and 45th Rounds.

Informal manufacturing workforce in 1981 is 174.30 lakhs as per Table 3.14. As per Table 3.12, the 33rd NSS Round has estimated this workforce at 144 lakhs. Of course, NSS figure pertains to 1978-79 and only the decennial census reports distinguish between main and marginal workers. The NSS figure comprises all workers : household, own account and hired workers. However, the 33rd Round figure excludes workers in DESs.

In 1991, as per Table 3.14, there were 209.28 lakh main workers in informal manufacturing. The 45th NSS Round figure for 1989-90 is 296.28 lakhs. If the number of workers in DMEs were to be included, this figure would turn out to be higher.

Thus, NSS figures turn out to be way above the figures per decennial censuses as in Table 3.14. It is not possible to relate them with each other.

As per EC 1990, the total number of persons in the unorganized sector is 720. 75 lakhs (see Table 3.7). As per NSS 45th Round, there were 296.28 lakh workers in unorganized manufacturing in 1989-90, DMEs being excluded. Thus the manufacturing workforce (OAEs + NDCs) comes to about 41 per cent of the total unorganized workforce. EC 1990 has, however, reported 218.16 lakh workers in manufacturing who make up 32.41 per cent of the total unorganized workforce. Thus even EC and NSS figures do not tie up.

3.5 Conclusion

Several sources of data exist on unorganized/informal sector. These sources have varying degrees of coverage.

Therefore, cross-checking of data or tallying one source against another is not possible. ECs and NSS reports constitute the mainstay of the database on unorganized sector. After putting together the information available in these sources, the following broad conclusions can be drawn:

1. Unorganized workers are the most important segment of the total workforce. If entire agriculture is total workforce is 90 per cent. If the organized segment of agriculture is separated, its share in total workforce declines but is still around 70 per cent. These percentages have changed only marginally over the years.
2. Share of unorganized sector in manufacturing workforce is also around 70 per cent and this share has risen since 1981.
3. Barring agriculture, trade, manufacturing, construction, business services and transport are the important segments of the unorganized sector in terms of net domestic product generated.

Chapter 4

Informal Sector in Pune: A Historical Review

4.1 Historical Account of Industrialization of Pune

Pune, an important educational centre in the country and the cultural capital of Maharashtra since the 18th century, has today also become a major manufacturing centre. It was an important urban centre of the Maratha empire but it was during the Peshwa rule that it acquired the status of a capital city. After the annexation of Peshwa Kingdom in 1818, the British rulers set up defence establishments in Pune owing to its favorable climate and proximity to Bombay. In the 19th century and early 20th century, a number of leaders such as Mahatma Phule, Agarkar, Karve, Justice Ranade, Gokhale, Tilak emerged in Pune and they led the social reforms movement in Maharashtra and the independence movement in the country.

The beginning of the industrialization process in Poona could be traced to the reign of Bajirao IT who had, around 1800, invited silk weavers from Nasik and Paithan to Poona. However, with the annexation of the Kingdom, this activity declined. The introduction of the railway line between Bombay and Poona in 1856 gave an impetus to the traditional copper and brass industry on Poona, which in 1884 was estimated to provide employment to nearly 2400 persons. The British government set up an ammunition factory at Kirkee in 1869 and it introduced Poona to he modern factory system in organized industry. The following were the other big factories established in and around Poona in the 19th century:

1885 – Deccan Paper Mills

1888 – Poona Metal Works (later called Gujarat Metal Factory)

1893 – Raja Bhadur Motilal Poona Mills

1898 – Paisa Fund Glass Factory (Talegaon).

Till the first half of the 20th century, industrial activity in Poona remained confined to the above large factories and a few household industries. Census records for this period is presented in Table 4.1.

The above census figures are full of gaps. The decline in total workers between 1921 and 1931 and the continuous decline in workers engaged in industry in these two decades in noteworthy. However, the most important point is that a very large and growing number of workers in Poona was engaged in public administration and liberal arts. These and the workers engaged in trade show that one-third of the workforce in Poona was in the service sector.

Poona: A Resurvey, 1956 has also stated that the activities that had grown during 1936 and 1954 were those connected with government and administration. These in turn gave a boost to industry to some extent and to wholesale trade. Growth in the latter was thus of a derived nature. Till 1960s therefore Poona was primarily an administrative centre.

Kirloskar oil Engines Ltd. – a private sector large factory manufacturing indigenous diesel engines – set up by Shri S. L. Kirloskar in 1946, paved the way for Poona's growth as a modern manufacturing town and also a centre of engineering industry. In the post-1950s, a number of large scale engineering units were set up on Bombay-Pune road. In the aftermath of the riots following Independence and partition of the country, a separate township to resettle the refugees was created at Pimpri near Pune. These refugees were mostly from Skindhi community which is renowned for its

Table 4.1 : Occupational Classification of workers in Greater Poona, 1911 to 1931

Occupation	1911		1921		1931	
	No.	%	No.	%	No.	%
Industry	20373	30.1	18721	19.1	17494	21.2
Transport	5534	8.2	4297	4.4	3451	4.2
Trade	9434	13.9	12264	12.5	9462	11.4
Public administration and liberal arts	13504	20.0	19419	19.8	19527	23.6
Sub- total		72.2		55.8		60.4
Total Workers	**67654**	**100.0**	**97907**	**100.0**	**82640**	**100.0**

resourcefulness and business acumen. This factor also helped in spurring the development of Pune.

Till 1960 the number of small workshops/industrial units, catering to the needs of large units in Pune, was limited. In 1956, the Poona Municipal Corporation established an industrial estate at Hadapsar, and eastern suburb of Pune. In 1962 Maharashtra Industrial Development Corporation (MIDC) set up industrial estates at Bhosari, Pimpri and Chinchwad. The large industrial units attracted others which started spreading around Pune along three major roads: one leading to Bombay, another to Ahmednagar and another to Solapur. With their growth, a new city of Pimpri-Chinchwad, with a separate municipal corporation (established in 1982) developed near Pune in due course of time.

Pune city and its surrounding areas which were subject to the pull of industrialization are known as Pune Metropolitan Region (PMR) since the passing of the Pune Metropolitan Region Development Act in 1966. PMR at present covers a total area of 1514.03 sq.kms of which 86 per cent is rural and 14 per cent is in municipal or cantonment centres. Thus PMR consists of two cities, viz. Pune city and Pimpri – Chinchwad, defence areas administered by cantonment boards/ Defence department at Pune, Kirkee, Dehuroad and Khadakwasla, smaller towns like Alandi and Dehu administered by municipal councils and around 130 villages.

Between 1961 and 1971, the pace of industrial development in PMR became very rapid. The industrial estates started attracting a number of industrial units and areas adjacent to industrial estates also started witnessing rapid growth. Starting of Hindustan Antibiotics at Pimpri and Tate Engineering and Locomotive Co. Ltd. at

Chinchwad gave a big boost to industrialization and chemical, engineering, transport equipment industries started coming up. They in turn activated smaller industries such as printing, wood packaging, etc. small industrial units continued to remain mostly within the limits of Pune city.

After 1971 the government took some policy initiatives to curb the growth of industries in PMR. Need for dispersing industrial activity to other locations such as Nasik, Aurangabad and Nagpur and the increasing pressure on civic amenities and municipal finances in PMR forced government's hand and it adopted the following measures:

(a) Reserving different areas for different purposes through the formation of Zones under the PMR Development Act.

(b) Prohibiting further establishment of industrial units except in areas earmarked for the purpose.

(c) Denial of state incentives to industrial units in PMR.

These measures have effectively curbed the establishment of new large and medium units in PMR. At the same time existing large units have continued to grow. They have expanded their production under automatic licensing provisions expanded their production under automatic licensing previsions and have also diversified into new areas. Small units which serve these large units have grown exponentially since 1977. Government policy measures which have led to the dispersal of large and medium industrial units around PMR have not affected small units which continue to crowd in residential areas in Pune city and Pimpri-Chinchwad. The smallest industrial units, employing upto five workers, have shown a distinct tendency to crowd in residential areas.

The current trend is that the process of industrialization has spread in Pune district to areas surrounding PMR. Areas such as Saswad, Jejuri, Daund, Wagholi, Koregaon-Bhima, Sanaswadi and Ranjangaon, Chakan, Chikhli, Pirangut and Bhor are getting industrialized rapidly.

4.2 Analysis of MCCI Data

An analysis of data on industrial units in PMR listed in the directories published by Mahratta Chamber of Commerce and Industries reveals that in 1995 there were 195 major industrial enterprises in PMR with capital investment of Rs. 1 crore and above. Each employed 871 persons on an average. They accounted for barely 3 per cent of the total industrial units in PMR but 51 per cent of all employees, 97 per cent of all capital employed and 88 per cent of total turnover. The large units have continued to grow over the years and a larger and larger share of capital employed and turnover is getting concentrated with them. In terms of number of employees, however, they are yielding ground to medium scale businesses. This is highlighted in Table 4.2.

Thus the number of persons employed in industry ahs grown by 300 per cent between 1978 and 1995. However, the share of large units in total employees ahs started declining since 1985. The share of small units (with capital employed upto Rs. 15 lakhs) also shows an almost secular decline. Medium scale units do not compensate for this decline but non-reporting units do: This reduces the utility of MCCI data. (the rise in the number of non-reporting units over the years is surprising registration. Only very small and truly informal units would shun this registration!)

Engineering and fabrication units account for the largest number of units in PMR, followed by Printing, Treatment on metal Products and Electrical machinery. Employment, capital employed and turnover are, however, highest in

Table 4.2 : Distribution of Industrial Units in PMR According to Capital employed and Number of Employees

Capital employed per unit (Rs.)	Number of employees			
	1978	1985	1990	1995
0-15 lakhs	43,180(38.6)	321,962(22.2)	46,753(23.6)	36,698(10.87)
15 lakhs – 1 crore	10,273(9.2)	18,560(12,5)	27,263(13.8)	49,291(14.6)
1 crore and above	58,512(52,2)	89,366(60.2)	1,13,540(57.4)	1,73,695(51.5)
Non-reporting units	-	7,582(5.1)	10,274(5.2)	77,733(23.0)
Total	1,11965(100.0)	1,48,470(100.0)	1,97,830(100.0)	3,37,417(100.0)

Notes : 1) Figures in brackets indicate percentages of total.

2) In 1995 big factories have reported consolidated figures for all their factories, i.e., those in Pune and in rest of the country. 1995 figure of 3,37,417 total employees is to be taken with a pinch of salt.

Source : MCCI Directories, 1990, 1995.

transport group, thanks to just a few very large firms such as TELCO and Bajaj Auto. Small units employing upto 10 workers were, till 1984, engaged primarily in fabrication, wood, paper, chemicals, rubber and plastic, electrical, electronics and engineering industries.

Since the late 1970s, the large industrial units have followed the practice of subcontracting an increasing part of their manufacturing activities to smaller units. Government's policy of encouraging self-employment and the emergence of a new middle class which is technically qualified and which considers self-employment to be more lucrative and rewarding as compared to wage-employment have also helped in the prominent ancillarization phenomenon seen in PMR. Engineering units have production processes with discrete parts and they find it very convenient to offload parts of manufacturing. Large industrial units in PMR have also shown a growing tendency to use contract labour to take care of temporary swings in activity and also to restrict permanent jobs to highly qualified 'knowledge workers'.

The pattern of industrial employment growth in PMR has thus taken the following form:

Large scale industrial units first created employment in their own units. Then they influenced the creation of ancillary units and through them generated indirect employment. Both these developments gave a boost to the service sector which provided more employment. These tendencies have been accentuated since the late 1970s. From 1984 onwards, the absolute number of employees in the organized sector has remained virtually constant (see below). They have been surrounded by a larger number of indirect/satellite workers. It has been estimated that for every person employment in an engineering unit, total employment of around 8 persons (i.e. 7 persons working in dependent small units) is created. A chemical unit is estimated to create total employment of around 4.7 persons. This indirect employment creation is estimated to take within 10 to 15 years from the establishment of large units.

4.3 Analysis of Census Data

The decennial census data do not report data for PMR. Pune urban afflomeration (UA) or Pune district-urban are the comparable geographical units for tracing the above developments in Pune. Pune UA is comparable to PMR. Pune district-urban, in particularly the 1991 Census, represents an entity larger than PMR since, as noted earlier, industrialization in Pune district is now spreading much beyond PMR. From 1971 to 1991, Pune UA has represented 86 to 89 per cent of Pune district-urban in terms of total workers. Preference has accordingly been given to Pune UA figures wherever they are available.

The relevant information from Census records is set out in the following tables. Table 4.3 gives absolute figures of population, total workers, main and marginal workers and their industrial classification from 1951 to 1991. The next two Tables (Table 4.4 and Table 4.5) present per cent distribution of total or main workers (concept of main and marginal workers was introduced in census statistics from 1981 onwards) as per both industrial and occupational classification. Industrials classification of workers in available form 1951 onwards whereas occupational classification is available since 1961. Further, occupational distribution for 1991 could not be obtained and this distribution from 1961 to 1981 pertains to Pune district-urban and not further down.

Table 4.3: Industrial Classification of Workers (Both sexes) in Poona/Pune

Particulars	1951		1961			1971			1981			1991		
	Poona City Corporation area	%**	Poona district - all towns, all persons	Poona Town + Dehu Town Group	%**	Poona district urban-all persons	Poona city agglomeration	%	Poona district-urban	Poona urban agglomeration	%	Pune district-urban	Pune urban agglomeration	%
1. Total population	4,80,982		9,39,906	7,78,328		13,29,774	11,35,034		19,71,082	16,86,109		27,97,402	24,85,014	
2. Total workers	1,46,087		2,90,058	2,37,603		3,90,555	3,37,078		6,10,969	5,26,985		8,87,956	7,92,392	
3. Main workers	-		-			-	-		5,93,585	5,11,901		8,71,952	7,78,801	
Classification of workers:														
a) Cultivators			10,572	4,260	1.8	8,304	3,851	1.1	10,166	5,105	1.0	14,248	7,938	1.0
b) Agricultural labourers	1,121	0.8	5,206	2,837	1.2	6,565	3,233	1.0	11,069	6,273	1.2	14,278	8,288	1.1
c) Livestock, forestry, fishing, hunting, orchards, etc.			-	-		6,010	4,163	1.2	8,967	7,041	1.4	8,049	5,715	0.7
d) Mining and quarrying	747	0.5	3,364	2,840	1.2	1,731	1,657	0.5	798	649	0.1	1,635	1,355	0.2
e) Household industry			12,085	8,765	3.7	7,924	5,387	1.6	14,523	11,959	2.3	15,574	13,227	1.7
f) Manufacturing other than household industry	27,880	19.1	63,361	55,309	23.3	1,17,573	1,05,125	31.2	1,93,619	1,75,302	34.2	2,57,591	2,38,754	30.6
g) Construction	9,985	6.8	10,331	9,223	3.9	16,629	14,172	4.2	35,740	31,371	6.1	92,041	86,283	11.1
h) Trade and commerce	25,929	17.7	41,371	35,272	14.8	61,207	51,847	15.4	99,013	85,313	16.7	1,61,920	1,42,581	18.3
i) Transport, storage and communication	10,698	7.3	30,180	23,984	10.1	34,247	29,377	8.7	55,592	45,154	8.8	70,414	61,499	7.9
j) Other services	37,845* 31,882@	25.9 21.9	1,13,588	95,113	40.0	1,30,365	1,18,266	35.1	1,64,158	1,43,734	28.2	2,36,162	2,13,164	27.4
4. Marginal workers	-		-	-		-	-		17,384	15,084		22,521	19,569	
5. Non-workers			6,49,848	5,40,725		9,39,219	7,97,956		13,60,113	11,59,124		19,12,550	16,95,614	
		100.0			100.0			100.0			100.0			100.0

* Includes Electricity, gas, water and Sanitary services.

@ Not adequately classified.

** These refer to percentages to Total/Main workers. From 1961 to . these percentages pertain to the geographical unit in the second column of each year data.

Table 4.4 : Industrial Classification of Workers in Pune Urban Agglomeration : Per cent Distribution

Particulars	1951 Poona city Corporation Area	1961 Poona Town + Dehu town group	1971 Poona city Agglomeration	1981 Poona Urban Agglomeration	1991 Poona Urban Agglomeration
a) Cultivators		1.8	1.1	1.0	1.0
b) Agricultural labourers	0.8	1.2	1.0	1.2	1.1
c) Livestock, forestry, fishing, hunting, orchards, etc.	-	-	1.2	1.4	0.7
d) Mining and quarrying	0.5	1.2	0.5	0.1	0.2
e) Household industry		3.7	1.6	2.3	1.7
f) Manufacturing other than household industry	19.1	23.3	31.2	34.2	30.6
g) Construction	6.8	3.9	4.2	6.1	11.1
h) Trade and commerce	17.7	14.8	15.4	16.7	18.3
i) Transport, storage and communication	7.3	10.1	8.7	8.8	7.9
j) Other services	25.9*	40.0	35.1	28.2	27.4
k) Activities not adequately described	21.9	-	-	-	-
Total workers/Main workers	100.0	100.0	100.0	100.0	100.0

* Includes Electricity, gas, water and sanitary services.

** Since 1981 the classification is of main workers.

Table 4.5 : Occupational Classification of Workers in Pune District – Urban : Per cent Distribution

Occupational Division	Description	1961	1971	1981
0-1	Professional, technical and related workers	7.8	9.3	10.1
2	Administrative, executive and marginal workers	4.8	7.8	6.5
3	Clerical and related workers	19.2	13.8	13.9
4	Sales workers	11.8	11.3	9.6
5	Service workers	13.8	11.5	9.8
6	Farmers, fishermen, hunters, loggers and related workers	1.8	1.7	1.4
7,8,9	Production and related workers, transport equipment operators and labourers	40.6	43.0	45.6
10	Workers not classified by occupations	0.2	1.6	3.1
Total	100.0	100.0	100.0	100.0

The absolute figures of workers engaged in various occupations between 1961 and 1981 are again presented in Table 4.6.

To understand all this data better, first of all, annual average growth rates of population and total workers have been calculated. They are presented below:

Pune UA	1961-71	1971-81	1981-91
(a) Population	4.6	4.9	4.7
(b) Total Workers	4.2	5.6	5.0

That the annual growth rate of number of workers exceeds the growth rate of population from 1971 onwards, ought to indicate the rapid growth of industrialization during this period.

Industrial classification of workers shows that the share of workers engaged in manufacturing has grown till 1981 and between 1981 and 1991, the share of workers in construction has grown. The share of workers in services, i.e. trade and commerce, transport, storage, communication and other services declined between 1971 and 1981 and then remained constant.

Occupational classification of workers reveals that percentage of workers engaged in production and related activities and also professional and technical activities – the upper and lower ends of the occupational ladder – have grown fast. During 1971-1981, production-related workers continued their growth while the professional category slid back. Clerical, sales and service workers started growing more in this decade.

Thus census data fully bear out the shift in Pune's development from an administrative to a manufacturing centre.

Table 4.6: Occupational Distribution of Workers in Pune District – Urban (Both sexes)

Occupational Division/ Group	Description	1961	1971	1981
0-1	Professional, technical and related workers	21,333	35,027 (6.4)	57,997 (6.6)
	08 Nurses, pharmacists	2,372	4,680 (9.7)	5,266 (1.2)
	15 Teachers	8,429	11,922 (4.1)	18,975 (5.9)
2	Administrative, executive and managerial workers	13,230	29,284 (12.0)	37,097 (2.7)
	24 25 26 Directors, managers, working proprietors in other than financial institutions	4,055	5,711 (4.1)	13,145 (13.0)
3	Clerical and related workers	52,620	51,996 (-0.1)	79,390 (5.3)
	32 Stenographers, typists	2,317	3,010 (3.0)	4,535 (5.1)
	35 Clerical workers - Miscellaneous	33,051	31,086 (-0.6)	48,137 (5.5)
	39 Telephone, telegraph and telecom workers	702	990 (4.1)	2,054 (10.7)
4	Sales workers	32,324	42,492 (3.1)	54,753 (2.9)
	43 Salesmen, shop-keepers and related workers	12,649	13,570 (0.7)	25,706 (8.9)
5	Service workers	37,948	43,204 (1.4)	56,225 (3.0)
	52 Cooks, waiters, bartenders	14,067	8,305	11,311 (3.6)
	53 Maids		5,893	10,220 (7.3)
6	Farmers, fishermen, hunters, loggers and related workers	4,845	6,375 (3.2)	7,839 (2.3)
	65 Farm workers	3,891	3,891	4,492 (1.5)
7,8,9	Production and related workers, transport equipment operators and labourers	1,11,376	1,61,408 (4.5)	2,61,449 (6.2)
	72 Metal processors	3,206	1,850 (-4.2)	4,650 (15.1)
	75 Spinners, weavers, knitters	3,022	4,020 (3.3)	5,205 (2.9)
	78 Tobacco preparers, tobacco product preparers	4,902	3,203 (-3.5)	2,251 (-3.0)
	79 Tailors, cutters	6,554	7,797 (1.9)	11,459 (4.7)
	81 Carpenters, joiners, cabinet makers	4,709	7,009 (4.9)	10,145 (4.5)
	83 Tool-makers	15,490*	20,409	29,503 (4.5)
	84 Machinists		27,045	40,062 (5.0)
	85 Electricians and electronics workers	2,144	8,135 (27.9)	13,709 (6.8)
	87 Plumbers, welders	-	4,750	6,623 (3.9)
	89 Potters, kilnmen, glass formors	1,497	3,720 (14.8)	6,794 (8.3)
	92 Compositors, printers	3,006	4,165 (3.9)	5,485 (3.2)
	94 Miscellaneous craftsmen and production process workers	2,989	3,310 (1.1)	2,776 (-1.6)
	95 Bricklayers, plasterers, other construction workers	4,451	11,902 (16.7)	24,212 (10.3)
	99 Labourers	35,906	10,468 (-7.1)	24,229 (13.1)
X	Workers not classified by occupations	604	5,900 (87.7)	17,659 (19.9)
	Total : All Divisions (0—X)	2,74,280	3,75,686 (3.7)	5,72,410 (5.2)

Notes : * Includes Plumbers and welders.

Figures in brackets show the annual average growth rates in the previous decade.

4.4 Organized and Unorganized Workforce

Data in Table 4.7 show that the number of unorganized workers in Pune increased continuously but for a sudden decline in 1971. The decline in the number of unorganized workers between 1954 and 1971 might be a genuine development due to the growth of administration and white collarization during this period or it might be due to the change of estimation method. The noteworthy point is that unorganized workers were 36 per cent of main workers in 1981; they became 56 per cent of main workers in 1991.

The data that have been brought together in this Table are not comparable. Still they have been put together because a broad picture spanning nearly 60 years is then available. This picture shows that workers in the organized sector in Pune increased form 25 per cent of total/main workers in 1936 to 79 per cent in 1971 and then declined to 44 per cent in 1991. Alternately, the share of unorganized workers in the workforce declined from 75 per cent in 1936 to 21 per cent in 1971 and then it started increasing to reach a peak of 56 per cent in 1991. This corresponds with the general pattern of development in Pune, viz. growth of jobs in government departments, then in organized firms in the private sector and the tapering off of this increase from the 1980s onwards.

Several adjustments have had to be made to piece this picture together. Two separate methods have been followed here to estimate the number of unorganized workers. From 1971 onwards, the residual approach has been used. Use of this approach means that size of an enterprise becomes the criterion for demarcation: workers in units of a certain size and above falling in the organized sector and the rest in the unorganized sector. For 1936 and 1954 two detailed city study reports are available for Pune. They are based on sample surveys of households carried out in these two years.

Table 4.7 : Informal Sector in Pune : 1936-1991

(1) Particulars	(2) 1936	(3) 1954	(4) 1971	(5) 1981	(6) 1991
1. Population	2,75,023[a]	6,51,000[b]	11,35,.034	16,86,109	24,85,014
2. Total workers	90,844[a] (100.0)	1,97,726[b] (100.0)	3,37,078 (100.0)	5,26,985	7,92,362
3. Main workers	-	-	-	5,11,901 (100.0)	7,78,801 (100.0)
4. Workers in organised sector	22,638 (24.9)	69,006 (34.9)	2,27,000 (79.2)	3,29,100 (64.3)	3,46,164 (44.4)
5. Unorganised workers	68,206 (75.1)	1,28,720 (65.1)	70,078 (20,8)	1,82,801 (35.7)	4,32,637 (55.6)

Notes: 1 Population figures pertain to Pune urban agglomeration of comparable units in earlier years.

1. Figures for workers in organised sector, from 1971 to 1991 pertain to Pune District. (Source: The Maharashtra State Employment Review.)
2. For 1971, 1981 to 1991, the figure of unorganised workers has been derived by deducting the number of organised workers from total/main workers. For 1936 and 1954, the approach is different.

a. Population of Greater Poona in 1931 was 2,50,187 and 2,98,001. (Poona: A Socio-Economic survey, 1937.) On the basis of the annual average growth rate of 0.019 per cent, population in 1936 has been estimated at 2,75,023. On the same basis, the total number of earners in 1936 have been estimated at 90,844 starting from 82,640 earners in 1931.

b. 'Poona: A Re-Survey, 1956' has estimated this figure. The number of earners in 1954 has been worked out from the 1951 Census figure of earners.

In 1936, the sample comprised 8 per cent of population an 6.5 per cent of earners in Pune. In 1954, the sample of 5,601 families and 8,176 earners represented 4 per cent of these respective categories.

Both the survey reports have given a detailed occupational distribution of the earners. This distribution comprised 14 grades ranging from skilled, unskilled manual work, cultivators, small, medium business, low, intermediate and higher professions, owners of factories, pensioners, ect., and each grade is made up of the number of occupation. For example, unskilled manual work comprised 12 occupations in 1936 and 22 in 1954. Skilled manual work consisted of 13 occupations in 1936 and as many as 32 in 1954. There were only three types of small businesses in 1936 but 16 in 1954.

For want of any other basis, we looked at the description of each occupation and decided whether it would fall in the organized or unorganized sector. Admittedly, this is not a very foolproof basis for demarcation but no other method was available.

This simple exercise yields the following data. Out of 5,895 sample earners, 4,426 or 75.08 per cent earners turn out to be in the unorganized sector in 1936. So out of total earners estimated at 90,844, 75.08 per cent or 68,206 earners are in the unorganized sector and the remaining 22,638 (or 24.92 per cent) in the organized sector.

In 1954, 5,322 or 65.1 per cent of 8,176 sample earners were in the unorganized sector. Therefore, out of the total 1,97,706 total earners, 1,28,720 earners (65.1 per cent) were in the unorganized sector and the balance 69,006 in the organized sector.

Table 4.8 shows that the unorganized workforce engaged in manual work (grades I, II and V) increased from 71 to 78 per cent. (Very high growth of highly skilled and

Table 4.8 : Occupational Distribution of Unorganized Workers

Grade	Description	1936		1954	
		No. of earners	% of earners	No. of earners	% of earners
I	Unskilled manual work	1,546	34.9	2,064	38.9
II	Skilled manual work	1,206	27.3	1,168	21.9
III	Lowest professions and administrative posts (priests, compounders, office peons, etc.)	338	7.6	379	7.1
IV	Small businesses	719	16.3	6643	12.5
V	Highly skilled and supervisory manual work	388	8.8	918	17.2
VI	Shop assistants	72	1.6	102	1.9
VIII	Repair shops	51	1.1	-	-
XII	Beggars and prostitutes	92	2.1	27	0.5
XIII	Unclassified	14	0.3	-	-
	Total	4,426	100.0	5.322	100.0

supervisory manual work was somewhat offset by the decline in skilled work). In Poona as a whole, the activities that grew during this period were those related to government and administration. To cater to the population growth in this period, some new, manual, manufacturing activities must have been initiated in the unorganized sector. (The decline in the per cent share of small businesses could mean that the average size of a business unit increased.)

Unorganized Workers in Pune from 1971 Onwards

The annual state employment reviews of Maharashtra give figures of organized workers. This source of information is used to derive the figures of unorganized workers from 1971 onwards.

Many adjustments are, however, necessary here too. Information about organized workers is reported only at district level and that too, in an aggregative form. From 1968 to 1981, only the break-up of organized workers between public and private sectors is available and from 1982-83 onwards, their industrial classification is given. Information in the state employment reviews is based on Employment Market Information Programme which covers all public sector organizations and all non-agricultural establishments in the private sector organizations and all non-agricultural establishments in the private sector employing 10 or more workers. (In Greater Bombay, the cut-off point is 25 workers.)

The first anomaly in the computation of unorganized workers is that figures of total workers relate to Pune Uas, while the organized workers' figures pertain to Pune district. Allowing this anomaly to remain means making an assumption that the organized workforce in the district primarily comes under Pune UA. This is not an unrealistic assumption to make particularly as the spread of industrialization in the district outside Pune UA began only after 1991.

The second adjustment is that industrial classification for 1982-83 has been adopted for 1981 and that on 31-3-1988 has been adopted for 1981 and that on 31-3-1988 has been adopted for 1991. For 1971, however, industrial classification of organized workers is not available. Therefore the 70,078 unorganized workers in 1971 are distributed among services, manufacturing, mining and quarrying and agricultural operations in the same proportion of total workers. Our analysis is confined to 1981 and 1991.

A bulk of the organized workforce in Pune belongs to manufacturing followed by community, social and personal services. Many large manufacturing enterprised surrounded by medium and small ancillaries are to be found in PMR's industrial estates. Their workers and employees form the biggest component of organized workforce. The organized workforce in services belongs to government administration (including defence establishment), education and medicine in the public sector and various professional and business enterprises in private sector. Workers in trade and commerce, i.e. those employed in big shops, wholesale firms and firms employing more than 10 workers and providing services such as advertising, broking, financial services, etc., form the third biggest segment of organized workers. Those who are in transport, storage and communication are mainly engaged in public sector undertakings connected with public transport, warehousing, postal services and telecommunication.

In the unorganized workforce, trade and services (Table 4.9 items h, I and j) predominate, followed by manufacturing and construction. In percentage terms, the share of trade and services and manufacturing was constant

Table 4.9: Poona Urban Agglomeration – Estimate of Informal Workforce – 1971 to 1991

Particulars	1971			1981			1991		
	Total workers	Organised workers	Unorganised workers	Total/Main workers	Organised workers	Unorganised workers	Main workers	Organised workers	Unorganised workers
a) Cultivators	3,851			5,105			7,938		
b) Agricultural labourers	3,233		2,338 (3.34)	6,273	5,574	12,845 (7.03)	8,288	5,205	16,736 (3.87)
c) Livestock, forestry, fishing, hunting, orchards, etc.	4,163			7,041			5,715		
d) Mining and quarrying	1,657		344 (0.49)	649	327	322 (0.18)	1,355	55	1,300 (0.30)
e) Household industry	5,387			11,959	-	11,959 (6.54)	13,227		13,227 (3.06)
f) Manufacturing other than household industry	1,05,125 (31.19)		25,922 (36.99)	1,75,302 (34.25)	1,34,923	40,379 (22.09)	2,38,754 (30.66)	1,42,335	96,419 (22.29)
g) Construction	14,172			31,371	15,537	15,834 (8.60)	86,283	14,633	71,650 (16.56)
h) Trade and commerce	51,847			85,313	33,408	51,905 (28.39)	1,42,581	31,005	1,11,576 (25.79)
i) Transport, storage and communication	29,377		41,474 (59.18)	45,154	23,319	21,835 (11.94)	61,499	23,940	37,559 (8.68)
j) Other services - Community, Social and Personal services	1,18,266			1,43,734	1,16,012	27,722 (15.17)	2,13,164	1,28,994	84,170 (19.45)
Total/Main Workers	3,37,078	2,67,000	70,078	5,11,901	3,29,100	1,82,801 (100.00)	7,78,801	3,46,164	4,32,637 (100.00)

Note : Figures of unorganized workers are residual figures.

Source : 1) Total/Main workers - Decennial census reports.

2) Organised workers - Annual Maharashtra State employment reviews.

in the decade but construction registered a big rise. The nature of activities involved here is different from the organized sector. Unorganized workers in trade and commerce are engaged in retail trade. They are small shopkeepers and hawkers working on their own or as employees of small shopkeepers. Small shopkeepers sell groceries, paan or cloth with the owner assisted by one or two helpers. Small eateries and handcarts selling food items are also covered here. Hawkers sell vegetables, fruit, fish, plastic utilities, glass and ceramic ware, goggles, ethnic items, clothes, bedsheets, etc. at street corners or by going from door to door.

There exist a number of small shopkeepers dealing in scrap (used paper, plastic, glass bottles etc.), second-hand goods and also smuggled goods confiscated by the Customs Department. These are all mostly non-licensed activities. Hawkers are engaged in a continuing war with municipal and cantonment authorities over the issue of encroachment. Unorganized workers in transport segment are truck drivers, cleaners, taxi, car and rickshaw drivers and porters who carry passengers and goods from one place to another. There is a sizable number of load bearers in the grain and vegetables market in Pune. Some of them are getting unionized, otherwise they are unprotected workers.

Unorganized workers engaged in community, social and personal services provide mostly personal services which take varied forms. There are domestic servants, a majority of them being women in Pune, who work for upper and middle class families. There are barbers and dhobis (washerwomen), shoeshine boys, private tutors, car attendants, parking lot attendants, dabbawalas or tiffin carriers, priests, astrologers, street dancers and acrobats, night watchmen and courier boys, bicycle and other repairers, tailors, etc. list is endless because poverty makes people desperate to create work in order to survive. Rag-pickers and sweepers are also included here. Sweepers who are municipal employees belong to the organized sector. They, in many cases, subcontract their work and theses subcontractees fall in the unorganized sector because they do not enjoy any protection. There are a number of casual or 'badli' sweepers registered with local authorities. They have been working for a long time in that capacity without any security or prospects of permanency. They too, belong to the unorganized sector.

Unorganized workers in manufacturing work as wage-workers in small workshops or they are own-account workers. Due to the popularity of subcontracting, downstream linkages from big manufacturing firms have developed in almost all industries in Pune. In engineering, electronics and chemical industries, parts of manufacturing activities also and not just housekeeping or maintenance work, get downloaded. These links cover bigger ancillary units that deal directly with big firms and their own sub-contractors and they end into seat shops or slum industries where unskilled workers work in primitive conditions or work I is out to women to be carried out at home by them. The bigger ancillary units belong to the unorganized sector. In tobacco processing industry, the work of rolling 'bidis' is put out to women who carry it out with the hope of their family members. This practice is going on for the last ¾ decades. The same is the case of food processing, garment making industries.

Unorganized workers in manufacturing work as wage-workers in small workshops or they are own-account workers. Due to the popularity of subcontracting, downstream linkages from big manufacturing firms have developed in almost all industries in Pune. In engineering, electronics and chemical industries, parts of manufacturing activities also and not just housekeeping or maintenance work, get down-loaded. These links cover bigger ancillary units that deal directly with big firms and their own sub-contractors and they end into sweat shops or slum industries where unskilled workers work in primitive conditions or work is put out to women to be carried out at home by them. The bigger ancillary units belong to the organized sector and the downstream units and their workers belong to the unorganized sector. In the tobacco processing industry, the work of rolling 'bidis' is put out to women who carry it out with the help of their family members. This practice has continued on for the last ¾ decades. The same is the case of the food processing and garment making industries.

Unorganized workers in construction consist of contract labour supplied by 'Mukadams'. Big construction firms practise extensive subcontracting. 'Vadars' are employed in clearing up old sites, leveling them up and taking away rubble. 'Lamani' women carry bricks, concrete blocks, mortar, tiles, etc. on new sites. Even skilled workers such as bricklayers, plasters, painters, etc. mostly belong to this sector.

Many people in the unorganized sector earn their living in what are considered as non-economic activities. Begging is receiving a transfer payment and so is non-economic. Prostitution is a personal service which is not illegal but is beyond normal moral code and very few studies of income earned and efforts made in this field exist. Then there many criminal and illegal activities suchas bootlegging, gambling, thieving, smuggling, etc., which have gone up on Pune in the process of growth and because of proximity to Mumbai. It must also be remembered that moonlighting also exists:

people will supplement their organized sources of incomes with side activities, e.g. typists in big offices doing typing on a private basis either at home or with the use of office typewriters! Poverty also induces people to engage in more than one economic activity at a time.

To 'flesh up' the unorganized workforce further, we have made another tabulation. Its purpose is to use one more classification of main workers which is available in Census reports. After excluding cultivators, agricultural labourers and workers in household industry form main workers the remaining, i.e. workers in non-household industry, trade, commerce and services are classified as employers, employees, single workers and family workers. This classification should also be made use of in analyzing the unorganized sector because apart from wage labour, family labour and many own account activities are also prevalent in it.

The tabulation is presented in Table 4.10. Since the figure of organized workers is available for Pune district, we start with the industrial classification of main workers in Pune district in 1981. This removes one anomaly in earlier calculations in the table viz. main workers in Pune UA and organized workers in Pune district.

There were 3,29,100 organized sector workers in Pune district in 1981. There were 17,386 establishments in the organized sector in 1981. Assuming that each of these establishments had one employer each, one can say that there were 17, 836 employers in the organized sector and the rest (i.e. the total 36,242 employers – 17,836 employers in the organized sector) were in the unorganized sector. Thus main workers can now be bifurcated into the organized and unorganized sectors.

Table 4.10: Organised and Unorganised Workers in Pune District, 1981

Census Code	Activity/Occupation	No. of workers	Reclassified as: Number	Reclassified as: Activity	Reclassification of workers in non-household industry, trade, etc.: Number	Reclassification: Activity
I	Cultivators	4,96,165	6,94,260	Cultivators and agricultural labourers		
II	Agricultural labourers	1,98,095				
III	Livestock, forestry and fishing	29,828			36,242	Employers
IV	Mining and quarrying	1,135				
V	Manufacturing, processing, service and repairs:				5,58,315	Employees
	a) Household industry	31,764	31,764	Workers in household industry		
	b) Other than household industry	2,43,702	7,29,435	Workers in non-household industry, trade, business, profession and services	1,24,494	Single workers
VI	Construction	48,635				
VII	Trade and commerce	1,20,676				
VIII	Transport, storage and communication	71,082				
IX	Other services	2,14,377			10,386	Family workers
	Total	14,55,460	14,55,460		7,29,435	

Source : Census 1981, Maharashtra, General Economic Tables, Part III A and B(ii), Pune District.

Thus, there were 11,08,525 earners in the unorganized sector in Pune district in 1981. Leaving out cultivators and agricultural labourers (since we want to look at urban informal sector), there were (11,08,525 – 6,94,260 =) 4,14,265 earners. They consisted of 2,29,215 employees, 1,24494 single (or own account) workers, 31,764 workers in household industry, 18,406 employers and 10,386 family workers. It is very much probable that all single workers do not fall in the unorganized sector; many professionals properly belong to the organized sector and therefore the figure of unorganized earners is somewhat overstated. The important point brought out by this analysis is that although hiring out labour was the most important mode of earning income, striking out on one's own, working along with family members, working in household industries (for a wage or for subsistence) and hiring out other workers were also important modes. Several types of activities existed side-by-side for earning a living.

For the purpose of understanding the relative shares of organized and unorganized workers in main workforce over time, the figures from Table 4.9 have been presented again in the following Table 4.11.

The annual average growth rates show that the unorganised sector has shown the highest growth rate between 1971 and 1991w in Pune. During 1981 and 1991, growth rate of total workers remained constant while the growth rate of both organised and unorganised workers declined. The decline was not so large as to bring about a decline in absolute numbers. However, the strength of organised workers increased by just 0.5 per cent annually. So the unorganised workforce absorbed a major part of growth of workforce during this period. As pointed out earlier, the increase in the unorganised sector has been

Table 4.11 : Growth Rates of Organised Sector and Informal Sector Workers in Pune Urban Agglomeration

(Figures in lakhs)

Particulars	1971	1981	1991
1. Total/Main workers	3.37	5.12(5.2%)	7.79(5.2%)
2. Workers in organised sector	2.67	3.29 (2.3%)	3.46(0.5%)
3. Workers in informal sector	0.70	1.83(16.1%)	4.33(13.7%)

Note : Figures in brackets indicate annual average growth rates for the previous decade.

mainly in services. Owing to rapid growth of manufacturing activity in Pune since the 1970s, the population of Pune has been growing constantly and sizeable migration to Pune has been taking place both in the working and non-working (mainly students and other members of families of migrant workers) components of population. A number of services must be made available to a growing population and so the informal sector could grow, absorbing all those who could not find a place in the organised sector. Unorganised workforce in manufacturing and construction has also grown during this period. However, while all this growth is sizeable in terms of numbers, the nature is of dependent, supply rather than demand-induced activity. Dynamism, qualitative growth, upward mobility, etc. are not to be found in this sector.

Chapter 5

Methodological Issues

5.1 Conceptual Framework

With the variety of activities that are carried out in IS, several classifications of these activities are possible. In the first classification, IS activities can be grouped into manufacturing, services and trade sectors and within each sector they can be sub-classified as own-account, household and wage-labour activities. This is shown in Chart 1.

Another classification distinguishes between firms/ enterprises and workers first. Among micro-enterprises it distinguishes between owner-entrepreneurs and workers and among workers, it distinguishes among wage-workers, home-based workers and own-account workers. This is shown in Chart 2. The third classification is that adopted by Self-Employed Women's Association (SEWA). This is shown in Chart 3. According to SEWA, the National commission on Labour (1969) had included the following categories among unorganized labour:

1. Contract labour unorganized workers,
2. Casual labour,
3. Labour employed small-scale industry,
4. Handloom/Powerloom workers,
5. Bidi and cigar workers,
6. Employees in shops and commercial establishments,
7. Sweepers and scavengers,
8. Workers in tanneries,
9. Tribal labour, and
10. Other unprotected labour.

A typology or hierarchy of these various activities in IS, on the basis of size of income, can be constructed as below:

Chart 1 : Classification I

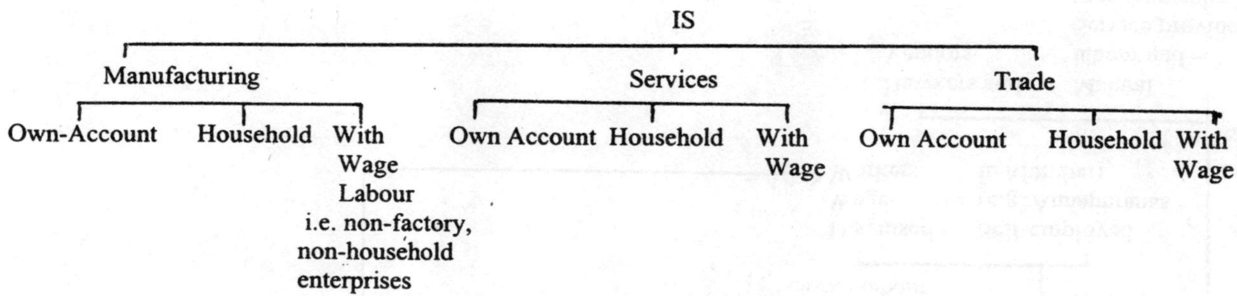

(In reality, there is not much of a difference between own-account and household activities. The latter denotes use of non-paid family labour.)

Chart 2: Classification II

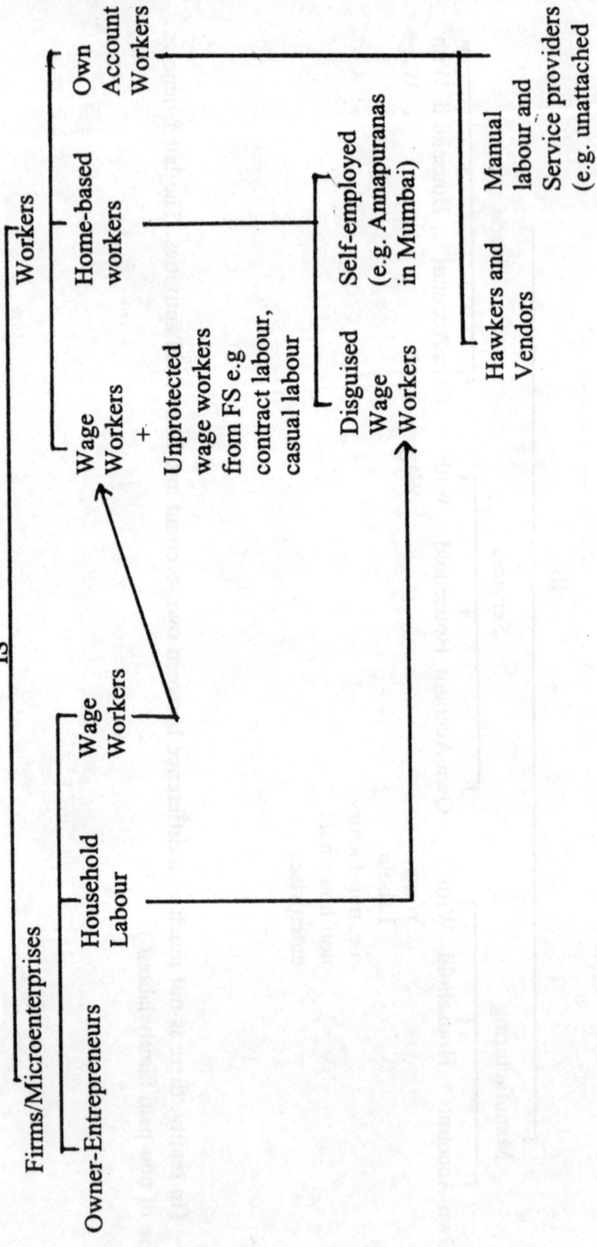

Chart 3: Classification III

IS

Hawkers and Vendors	Home-based workers (e.g., weavers Potters, garment and quilt-stichers, Embroiders, bidi and papad rollers, incense stick makers, spinners, milk-producers, basket and broom weavers, carpenters, cobblers, painters, sculptors, toy-makers). They include those carrying output-Outwork for different industries such as leather products, rubber and plastics, engineering etc. Garment-stiching and papad, bidi Rolling mentioned above are carried out as put-out activities in textiles, food and tobacco processing industries respectively.	Manual Labour and service providers (e.g., agricultural lab--ourers,hand-cart pullers, Waste-paper collectors, constr-uction workers, cleaners, domestic servants, etc.

Note: There are no firms in SEWA classification

1. Micro-enterprises and their owner-entrepreneurs,
2. Own-account workers with some skill, capital, e.g. carpenters, tailors, owners of stalls, sheds, etc.,
3. Wage-workers in micro-enterprises,
4. Unprotected wage-workers in FS (casual labour, contract labour, etc.),
5. Manual labour and service providers,
6. Home-based workers.

It is possible that some types of home-based workers earn more as compared to manual labour providers such as rag-pickers. Collectivization of workers is likely to improve income level.

It is very difficult to bring home-based workers together and so they have been placed at the bottom of the hierarchy. However, some change in the relative positions of Groups 4, 5 and 6 is always possible. Even members of Group 3, wage-workers in micro-enterprises may get higher wages provided they have some skill, have undergone some learning-on-the-job and provided that their employers are interested in retaining them. (This is explored in our survey, see below.) If these conditions are not fulfilled, Groups 3 and 4 may get the same wage. Thus the income-hierarchy in IS boils down to:

1. Micro-enterprises and their owner-entrepreneur,
2. Own-account workers, and
3. Wage-workers and service providers.

Actually a hierarchy of organization forms stands behind this hierarchy. The occupational hierarchy encompasses both FS and IS. At the top are large scale, formal industrial units with access to technology and markets. The lowest end of the hierarchy is made up of own-account units or slightly larger units that use family labour. These units work for the subsistence of the owners and they have no access to modern technology. Figure 1 depicts the links among different forms of organization in manufacturing.

The different organization forms are linked together. Large-scale endowment of specialized resources, access to technology and market enable the large firms to dominate the market. At lower levels of the hierarchy, limited availability of general purpose resources, technological dependence, subsistence rather than profit-making as the primary motive and limited markets are the characteristics of operations. Because of inter-dependence, the lower level units are able to survive and the upper level units are bale to lower their operational costs. Because both types of organizations find the interdependence beneficial, it continues. It will continue as long as resource-use in the higher and lower rungs remains different.

To the extent the higher level units follow ancillary development policies and make dynamic use of subcontracting policies, this interdependence provides the lower level units with access to advanced technology, new products and machinery, etc. A few lower level units are in apposition to move upward. Support of the state (through its promotional measures for small units) and the upper level firms is crucial for such a movement. In due course of time, a few upwardly mobile small firms may reach the position of job-shops catering to the requirement of the entire market for certain specialized components or processes. At the same time, this prospect is beyond the reach of a majority of firms.

5.2 Design of the Study and Hypotheses

Against the backdrop of this conceptual framework, it was decided to explore the earnings and economic

Figure 1

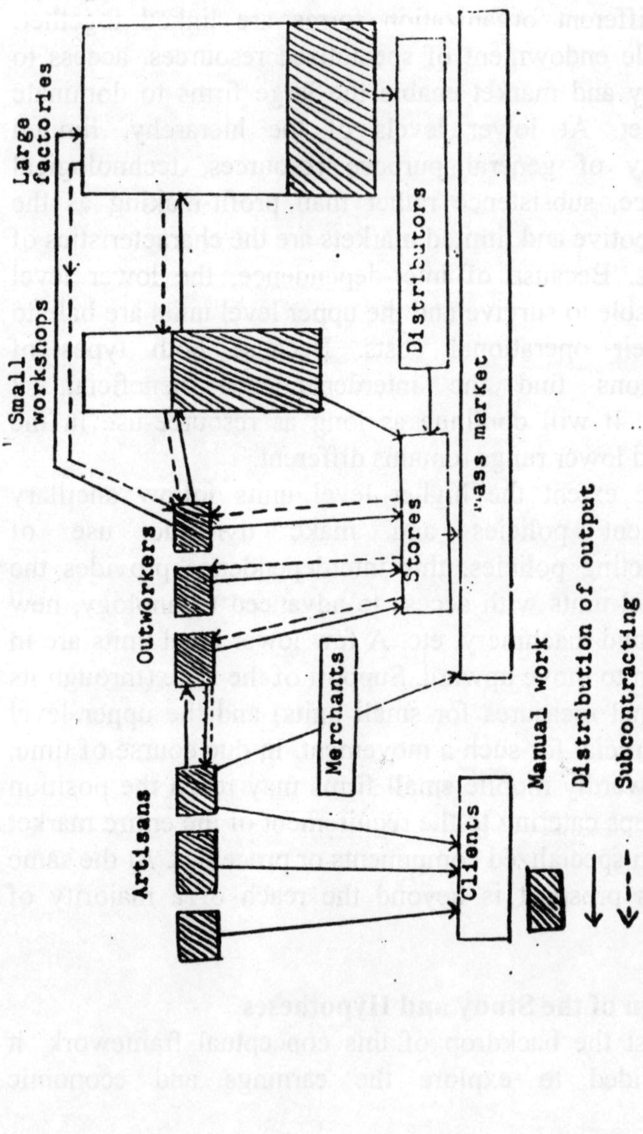

Source: Allison M. Scott, "Who Are the Self-Employed?" in R. Bromley and C. Gerry (ed.), Casual Work and Poverty in Third World Cities, 1979.

conditions of some sections of workers and enterprises in IS. A two-pronged approach was used for this purpose.

Firstly, it was decided to carry out a small survey of manufacturing enterprises in IS and their wage-workers. It was thought that these micro-enterprises would represent IS as a product-market category while their wage-workers would cover it as a labour-market category. Not much information about manufacturing enterprises was available from secondary sources. At the same time, from the point of view of understanding the growth potential of IS, they were thought to be crucially important. Secondly, on the basis of available secondary data and also the information provided by some activity in the concerned fields, a qualitative picture of different types of IS workers was pieced together. This picture is presented in Chapter 8.

Micro-enterprises were defined as unregistered firms. So registration under Indian Factories Act, 1948, was treated as the cut-off point between FS and IS. There is no other cut-off point available to distinguish between SSI and IS manufacturing units. (See our discussion on registration in Chapter 7. Shop Act registration is perhaps another cut-off point.) In other words, those manufacturing units not covered by the Factories Act were treated as unregistered micro-enterprises for the purpose of this survey. Attempts were made to look out for other features of informality – smallness, inferior resource use, etc.

Since linkages between IS and FS were important from our point of view, it was decided to concentrate on the following industry groups:

S.No.	NIC Major Group Code	Description
1.	30	Rubber and Plastic products

2.	31	Chemical and chemical products
3.	33	Basic metal and alloys
4.	34	Metal products and parts except machinery
5.	35	Machinery, machine tools and parts
6.	36	Electrical and electronic machinery, parts and appliances components

Note: NIC = National Industrial Classification.

As per the 1991 Census, there were 96,419 informal workers engaged in manufacturing other than household industry in Pune urban agglomeration. As per the 1981 Census, the number of workers engaged in the above six industry groups constituted 39.3 per cent of all main workers in manufacturing in Pune district. (Industrial classification of main workers upto major group codes – two-digit level – as per the 1991 Census is not available.) By making two bold assumption, viz. what applies to Pune district is true for Pune urban agglomeration and that what holds good for total manufacturing is good for informal manufacturing, it is deduced that 39.3 per cent of 96,419 i.e. (96,414 x 39.3% = 37,893 say,) 38,000 informal workers in manufacturing are in the above six industry groups.

It was decided to cover about 40 unregistered establishments. Each was covered through two questionnaires, viz. Enterprise questionnaire and Labour questionnaire. The former was filled in on the basis of an interview of the owner/entrepreneur and the latter by interviewing a few wage-workers in each establishment. Although larger units under the Factories Act are not intended to be systematically studied in this survey, a few such units were contacted in order to made a cursory comparison between them and surveyed units. Similarly a few officials of large companies were contacted to learn bout the subcontracting policies of these companies.

The enterprise questionnaire deals with aspects such as input use, production, market linkages, capacity utilization, employment conditions, extent of technological adaptation, etc. Opinions of these entrepreneurs about their market structures, growth prospects, ease/difficulty of entry, have also been solicited. The labour questionnaire covers aspects such as wages and working conditions, training and skill formation, standard of living, migration, change of job, aspirations and extent of upward mobility, etc.

The information collected through these questionnaires is used to build profiles of IS enterprises, their owner-entrepreneurs and workers. Then the information is used to test the following hypotheses:

Enterprises

1. Factor use in informal manufacturing enterprises has some distinctive features as compared to FS. Thus,

- Labour turnover is high indicating that labour is a general purpose input and there exists an undifferentiated mass of labour.
- Wages of workers are low and social security does not exist. Workers do not have formally acquired skills. Labour-owner relationship takes a personalized form.
- Use of cheap materials, self-assembled or self-fabricated or second-hand machinery is found in the production process.
- The enterprises mainly use non-institutional or informal sources of credit.

2. Informal enterprises use labour-intensive technology.

3. In spite of the cost advantage resulting from the special features of resource-use, micro-enterprises cannot have a net cost advantage while competing with formal enterprises, given the small scale of their operations. Price cannot hence be a tool for competition. Because of general purpose inputs, quality of work is also not very high. With limited capital at their disposal, micro-enterprises also cannot tap other souses of competitive advantage, viz. credit, publicity and advertising. Competition with formal enterprises is, hence, virtually ruled out. They, therefore, have to either become job-workers for formal firms or to find a small niche in the market. In the latter case, the boundaries of their market are determined by large formal enterprises.
4. It is easy to enter informal manufacturing. So there is intense competition among informal enterprises.
5. Due to inter-firm competition and the special resource-use pattern, growth takes the form of multiplication of enterprises of the same type. So employment grows but at the same level of support of other resources. Expansion of the same enterprise with attendant manifestations of vertical growth, e.g. quality upgradation, skill formation, technological adaptation, new product development, etc., is not a normal occurrence.

Workers in Informal Enterprises

1. Due to ease of entry, non-requirement of human capital formation and high labour turnover, informal workers are mostly young workers.
2. Workers' earnings are low and they have flat agewise earning profiles.
3. Labour productivity is low in IS owing to lower skills of workers and low level of support of other resources.

For the manufacturing component of IS, it is hypothesized that IS activities are a necessary adjunct to FS. FS used IS enterprises to cheapen its operations and IS enterprises survive by developing downstream offloading links and by resorting to general purpose resource use which minimizes cost of production. FS-IS linkages reveals an hierarchy of economic organization which is hidden behind competitive capitalism.

Chapter 6

Enterprises, Entrepreneurs and the Workforce

Information about the survey that is presented in this chapter, is grouped under the following sections:

1. Conducting the Survey,
2. Enterprises in the Survey,
3. Entrepreneurs of the Surveyed Enterprises, and
4. Hired Labour in the Surveyed Enterprises.

6.1 The Survey

The questionnaires that were prepared to elicit information from the enterprises and their workers were quite elaborate. Therefore, to facilitate better response, it was decided to approach the enterprises through some larger firms. Having regard to the major industry groups to be covered in the survey, the following companies were requested to furnish the lists of their suppliers/sub-contractors/ancillary units.

Sr. No.	Company	Industry
1.	Kirloskar Pneumatics Co. Ltd.	Engineering
2.	Thermax Ltd.	"
3.	Morris Electronics Ltd.	Electronics
4.	Amphetronics Ltd.	"
5.	Philips India Ltd.	Electrical parts and electronics
6.	Bharat Electronics Ltd.	Electronics
7.	Tata Honeywell Ltd.	Electonics and micro-processors

Out of these companies, Amphetronics Ltd. did not respond to our request. The lead of Morris Electronics Ltd. was not pursued, as it appeared to require considerable follow-up. The other five companies responded to our request readily. Kirloskar Pneumatics and Bharat Electronics gave us copies of their vendor lists. Names and addresses of suppliers had to be copied from the files of Phillips India and Thermax while the officials of Tata Honeywell telephonically communication the required information as the number of their suppliers was limited. None of these companies could give us information about the registration status of their suppliers, i.e. whether they were registered under the Indian Factories Act, 1948, or not.

So, depending upon their proximity, the listed units were contacted one by one to decide, first, their registration status and, second, their willingness to give information. Here the rate and quality of response worsened considerably. Some units refused to cooperate outright. Some entrepreneurs were polite on the telephone but abrupt in person. Some others asked us to post the questionnaires and then refused to either fill them or grant us time for an interview. The quality of information given by units that did put up with us was, on the whole, unimpressive. The reluctance of manufacturing units to supply information even for the purpose of academic research is a worrying factor. Small manufacturing units comply with different statues in a case-by-case and partial manner. This makes them extremely reluctant to give information. Individual researchers are helpless in such a situational. Both academic institutions and industries need to address themselves urgently to this problem.

The units which responded to our request were asked for an additional contact each. Some personal contacts were also used. One of them was a branch Manager at a nationalized bank and through her some of the small borrowers of the bank could be tapped. Through Mahratta Chamber of Commerce and Industries, we learnt about one Mr. Hiralal Kirad who is trying to organize tiny industrial units in Pune. Mr. Kirad agreed to help us and the information provided by units suggested by him turned out to be comprehensive and substantial. We could finally collect information from 39 manufacturing units. Their break-up on the basis of mode of contact is given below.

Mode of contact	Number of units
1. Vendors/ancillary units of large companies	16
2. Personal contacts	2
3. Contacts suggested by persons in the above categories	12
4. Organization of tiny units	4
5. Nationalized bank	5
Total	39

Two units (engineering Units) from the above refused to give any information about their capital structure and earnings, expenditure flows. They supplied the rest of the information. So some of the information presented below pertains to 37 units and some to 39 units.

The industrial units were also requested to grant us some time with their workers – one or a few workers per unit. the request alarmed some entrepreneurs and they did not entertain it. One entrepreneur answered all the questions on behalf of his workers. One entrepreneur allowed us to interview a worker but did not fill in the enterprise questionnaires. In all, 32 units returned the completed labour questionnaires. Two trade unions, viz. Sarve Shramik Sanghatana. An activist of Sarva Shramik Sanghatana contacted some workers employed in small manufacturing units in Pimpri-Bhosari area and returned four questionnaires. In the CITU office, we could interview eight workers and complete their questionnaires. Since August 1994, CITU had taken up the cause of workers in small, unorganized units and on any Thursday (industrial holiday) a large number of these workers would be present in CITU office.

Our interviews hence turned out to be group interviews. With the help of another trade unionist-cum-social worker, we visited Mangalwar Peth which is a cluster of slum industries in the heart of Pune. About 10 workers in this locality were contacted. Many of them were working as casual workers without having a fixed employer/place of work. They did not have the time to answer all our questions, many of which they did not appear to understand. The information provided by them was used as a qualitative input for drawing inferences.

In addition we spoke to three entrepreneurs who are running Factory Act units. They gave us important qualitative information. One of them in particular gave us enough time to cover both routine, procedural and policy matters. Another one gave us fruitful contacts with two micro-enterprises. Some officials of large companies who are familiar with their sub contracting operation polices the information given by them was used to develop a comparative perspective. The willingness of these participants in the higher circuit to share information and to discuss the relevant issues stood in stark contrast with the approach of the surveyed units.

Large companies were contacted in May 1994 for their vendor lists. A major part of the field-work for the survey was carried out from June to December 1994.

Reluctance of small units to give information has been mentioned above. We found that entrepreneurs were extremely touchy about the crucial aspects of their working, viz. labour and finance. They gave cryptic and approximate answers to our queries regarding them. In the case of labour questionnaires that were filled with the help of employers, it was feared that workers would give correct-sounding rather than truthful information. Information collected through trade unions is expected to provide balance to the overall information presented below as workers were found to be more open and forthright in the union officers. We sincerely feel that, on the whole, comparable information about small manufacturing units is not available easily and so, in spite of all its limitations, the survey findings are relevant.

The 39 enterprises covered in this survey employed about 400 wage-workers. Our enterprise questionnaire covered some questions about wage workers. It plus the 32 labour questionnaires returned by wage-workers in these surveyed enterprises can be wage-workers in these 400 wage-workers. Thirteen labour questionnaires canvassed through trade unions plus the qualitative information given by casual workers in Mangalwar Peth can be said to represent the case of a larger number of workers. This coverage is considered to be adequate for a qualitative survey such as this.

6.2 Enterprises in the Survey

The surveyed enterprises belong to the following industrial groups:

Industry	No. of enterprises
1. Engineering, fabrication and machining	24
2. Chemicals	4
3. Electrical and electronic parts and assemblies	6
4. Rubber and plastics	5
Total	39

The predominance of the engineering industry in Pune is fully reflected in this survey.

The enterprises were located in different areas of Pune as given below:

Area/Locality	No. of enterprises
Shivaji Nagar	1
Kasba Peth	1
Mangalwar Peth	3
Shukrawar Peth	2
Parvati, Sahakar Nagar, Satara Road	5
Katraj	1
Vitthalwadi, Manikbaug, Hingne, Vadgaon	1
Kothrud industrial estate, Karvenagar, Erandwane	3
Hadapsar Industrial Estate	6
Hadapsar	4
Kondhwa	1
Shivne	1
Bhosari	9
Chikhali	1
Total	**39**

Eight enterprises were outside municipal limits (of Pune Municipal Corporation and Pimpir-Chinchwad Municipal Corporation). This ensured exemption from certain important statutory regulations/taxes. The Maharashtra Shops and Establishments Rules, 1961. Were not applicable to these units. This aspect is discussed in detail later.) Two enterprises had set up their offices at better localities while their manufacturing operations were carried out away from municipal limits. This was a convenient arrangement because the office satisfied the representatives of bigger industrial units desirous of subcontracting while the factory managed to reduce manufacturing costs.

As shown in Table 6.1, seven units conducted their operations from residential accommodations, outhouses or residential-cum-industrial areas. They can be viewed as house hold industrial units. Eight units in Gram Panchayat area were not under the Shop Act. Table 6.2 presents classification on the basis of space per worker. Table 6.3 highlights the shift-working pattern and available space in the units. Table 6.4 portrays number of working hours per month. Literature on IS has made a reference to 'slum industries'. Goods demanded by IS may not be produced by FS; slum industries which have minimal capital investment and which pay very low wages to their workers produce low quality, cheap imitations of FS products. Low capital investment leading to low labour productivity discourages employers from forming stable relationship with their workers while low wages mean that workers also have no incentive for such a relationship with employers. Therefore labour turnover is high and slum industries fail to graduate to FS (Datta Chaudhari, T., 1989). Lack of or dearth of infrastructural facilities and non-compliance with statutory provisions are the special features of these industries. 'Gav Khate' is a local term that is used to refer to such industrial laws. Now the term is used in a derogatory sense to denote industrial activities which violate the expected norms and turn in inferior goods. Fifteen units in this survey – seven household industry units and eight non-Shop Act units – can be said to belong to the category of Gav Khate or slum industries.

A majority of units – 27 out of 38 – operate on single-shift basis with or without overtime. In Brahme-Paranjape study also it was found that most of the units operated on single-shift basis. The study reported that 15 per cent of the

Table 6.1 : Classification of Surveyed Units as per Industry and Type of Building/Structure

Industry	Type of structure				Total
	Industrial shed	Residential accommodation, outhouse	Residential-cum-industrial area	Gram Panchayat Area	
1. Engineering	14	1	3	6	24
2. Chemicals	4	-	-	-	4
3. Electrical and electronic parts and assemblies	5	1	-	-	6
4. Rubber and plastic	1	-	2	2	5
Total	24	2	5	8	39

Table 6.2 : Classification of Surveyed Units as per Industry and Size-Class of Space Per Worker

Industry	Space per worker (sq. ft.)					Total
1. Engineering	1	7	6	3	6	23
2. Chemicals	-	-	-	2	2	4
3. Electronic	-	1	-	4	1	6
4. Rubber and plastic	-	1	2	2	-	5
Total	1	9	8	11	9	38

Table 6.3 : Shift-working and Available (Covered) space in the Surveyed Units

Shifts	Space per worker (sq. ft.)					Total
1	4	9	1	3	2	19
2	2	4	-	1	-	7
3	-	3	-	-	-	3
1 with regular overtime	4	3	-	-	-	7
1 with regular overtime	-	-	1	-	-	1
2 with regular overtime	-	-	1	-	-	1
Total	10	19	3	4	2	38

Units with 1 shift working with/without overtime = 27
Units with multiple shifts = 11
38

Table 6.4 : Classification of Surveyed Units as per Industry and Number of Working Hours Per Month

Industry	Working hours per month			Month
	Standard month X standard day (26 days x 8 hours per day)	Standard month x longer day (26 days x 9 or more hours per day)	Longer month x longer day (30 days x 9 or more hours per day)	
1. Engineering	10	8	4	22
2. Chemical	1	2	-	3
3. Electrical and electronic parts and assemblies	8	1	-	9
4. Rubber and plastic	-	7	-	7
5. Miscellaneous	3	-	1	4
Total	22	18	5	45

Note : This table has been prepared on the basis of labour questionnaires rather than enterprise questionnaires, as satisfactory information about the length of the working day/month was not available in ;the latter. Therefore, the total number of enterprises in this table does not tie up with the total number of enterprises in other tables.

surveyed units operated on double shift basis and just 1 per cent – 5 units out of 374 – operated on triple-shift.

In Table 6.5, an attempt has been made to distinguish between job-shop production or job-work and production in anticipation of customer demand. Job-shop production is on the basis of known orders of customers. Job-work means carrying out or a few operations or parts in the production process as per specifications provided by customers. Pure job-work is referred to as labour charges since the unit carrying out the work operates on the basis of customer's materials and drawings and is involved only in processing. In our survey we came across only one unit which was involved in this type of work. The remaining job-work units bought their own materials. These units made one more distinction within job-work. The distinction is based on the variety of operations. Some job-work involves producing one or a few components in bulk. Variety is limited but volume is high. The other type means handling varied jobs on a limited scale. The former does not require much skill but chasing deadlines, supervising workers to get the required volume of production are the main problems. Where volume is limited and variety high, workers' skill counts and it is necessary to retain them in service. These were important operating considerations for the job-work units.

Job-work and job-shop production entail some dependence on a given number of customers. Job-work means tying up one's prospects totally with those of some larger unit. in comparison, production in anticipation of demand means producing standard goods which may not satisfy some specific requirements of customers. It denotes greater independence. This independence, of course, means greater responsibility to react to changes in demand and

Table 6.5 : Classification of Surveyed Units According to Industry and Type of Work

Industry	Type of work				Total
	Job-work, job-shop production	Independent manufacture (production in anticipation of demand)		Job work + independent manufacture	
1. Engineering	12	6	1	5	24
2. Chemical and chemical product	1	2	1	-	4
3. Electrical and electronic parts and assemblies	-	4	2	-	6
4. Rubber and plastic	1	2	2	-	5
Total	14	14	6	5	39

competitive pressure. Provided this responsibility is discharged reasonably well, the manufacturer enjoys some presence and stability in the market. A distinction can be made between manufacturers who deal with their customers directly and who deal with middlemen and distributors. Only a few of the companies that dealt with customers (3 or) employed salesmen in this survey. The presence of middlemen denotes a more structured market-place in which middlemen can reduce/usurp the importance of producers. According to one of the entrepreneurs interviewed in this survey, it is more profitable to deal directly with the consumers as it eliminates middlemen's commission and also lets the supplier establish his identity in the eyes of the customers.

All the job-work and most of the job-shop units surveyed here, on the other hand, experienced a feeling of being at the receiving end. Their clients were large companies whose policies would never permit small suppliers to become indispensable. It was said that they also actively promoted competition among the suppliers leading to a feeling of frustration and helplessness on the part of these suppliers.

Some units in this study combined job-work with independent manufacturing. Job-work is easy to start with but has little scope for growth, according to them. Pursuit of growth has led them to the exploration of the prospects for independent manufacture.

Table 6.5 reveals that in our study, the number of independent manufacturers exceeds that of job-workers. In the engineering industry, however, the situation is reversed. This is to be expected since the nature of the production process in this industry makes it easy to farm out some operations. Extent of job-work was limited in other industries.

A classification of surveyed unites according to industry and type of legal organization is made in Table 6.6.

Overall average age of the surveyed enterprises was 15.87 years. Industry-wise, the average age of these enterprises was:

1. Engineering 16.96 years
2. Chemicals 13.25 years
3. Electrical and electronic parts 12.83 years
4. Rubber and plastic 16.40 years

Age-distribution of the surveyed enterprises in Table 6.7 shows that nearly half of the enterprises belong to the age-group of 6-15 years. The proportion of young units, i.e. those within the age-group of 0 to 5 years, is low – 7.7 per cent. A majority of surveyed units is of old established units.

The surveyed units appear to have got concentrated in employment size of upto 15 workers (Table 6.8). The average number of workers per enterprise turns out to be 9.56. Employment in excess of 9 workers in an enterprise using power in the manufacturing process without the coverage of Factories Act might appear to be surprising but what actually happens is that many entrepreneurs keep forming new units along with the growth of employment. On paper, the number of workers per enterprise is kept forming new units along with the growth of employment. On paper, the number of workers per enterprises is kept pegged at 9 so as to avoid the Factories Act. In actual practice equipment is kept at one lotion; work is carried out from the same location and workers mostly work there. The entrepreneurs whom we interviewed were quite ambiguous about demarcation of capital and labour among their different units. At least five entrepreneurs explicitly indicated their policy of starting new units with constant strength of eight or nine workers per unit. Nearly half the

Table 6.6 : Classification of Surveyed Units as per Type of Organisation

Industry	Type of organisation				Total
	Sole proprietary concern	Partnership	Private limited company	Hindu undivided family	
1. Engineering	6	15	2	1	24
2. Chemical	1	1	2	-	4
3. Electrical and electronic parts and assemblies	2	-	4	-	6
4. Rubber and plastic	4	1	-	-	5
Total	13	17	8	1	39

Table 6.7 : Age Distribution of the Surveyed Enterprises

Industry	Age group (years)							Total
	0-5	6-10	11-15	16-20	21-25	26-30	31-35	
1. Engineering	1	4	8	4	3	2	2	24
2. Chemical	-	1	2	1	-	-	-	4
3. Electrical and electronic parts and assemblies	1	2	1	-	2	-	-	6
4. Rubber and plastic	1	1	-	-	3	-	-	5
Total	3	8	11	5	8	2	2	39

Table 6.8 : Classification of Surveyed Enterprises by Industry and Employment Size

Industry	Employment size					Total
	1-5 workers	6-10 workers	11-15 workers	16-20 workers	21-25 workers	
1. Engineering	1	4	8	4	3	24
2. Chemical	-	1	2	1	-	4
3. Electrical and electronic parts and assemblies	1	2	1	-	2	6
4. Rubber and plastic	1	1	-	-	3	5
Total	3	8	11	5	8	39

enterprises, 18 out of 39, had sister concerns. Twelve of them had one sister concern each, while six had two or three sister concerns. It, therefore, appeared to us that in practice it was quite easy to defy the legal provisions regarding the strength of workers.

Average sales per month per enterprise amount to Rs. 2,55,720 (Table 6.9). As many as 21 enterprises fall below the mark of monthly sales of Rs. 2 lakh. Within the size class of sales of Rs. 2,00,000, to Rs. 3,00,000 there are six units with sales values below the average. In all, there are 27 enterprises which fall below the average value of sales. The survey, thus, shows a tilt towards smaller enterprises. However, only two units have monthly sales that are less than Rs. 50,000.

Classification of enterprises on the basis of fixed capital employed similarly shows clustering around lower values of upto Rs. 3,00,000. In case of productive capital the same tendency can be observed upto an amount of Rs. 6 lakh. However, the data regarding capital is at best approximate and hence nothing further is attempted right not on the basis of Tables 6.9, 6.10 and 6.11.

6.3 Entrepreneurs of the Surveyed Enterprises

Eleven among the 39 entrepreneurs heading the surveyed enterprises were second-generation entrepreneurs, whereas 28 were self-starters. With one exception, the second-generation entrepreneurs were looking after units that were more than 10 years old. The exception was one three-year old engineering unit that had been entrusted to a younger member of the business family having similar other units. Two exceptions was one three-year-old engineering unit that had been entrusted to a younger member of the business family having similar other units. Two surveyed units were

Table 6.9 : Classification of Enterprises by Industry and size of Sales Per Month

Industry	Sales per month (Rs.)							total
	Upto Rs. 50,000	50,001 to 1,00,000	1,00,001 to 2,00,000	2,00,001 to 3,00,000	3,00,001 to 4,00,000	400,001 to 5,00,000	5,00,001 and above	
1. Engineering	1	6	6	5	1	-	4	23
2. Chemicals and chemical products	-	1	1	-	-	-	2	4
3. Electrical and electronic parts and assemblies	1	2	-	3	-	-	-	6
4. Rubber and plastic	-	3	-	1	1	-	-	5
Total	2	12	7	9	2	-	6	38

Table 6.10 : Distribution of Surveyed Enterprises by Industry and Fixed Capital Employed (on written-down value basis)

Industry	Size-class of fixed capital (Rs.)							Total
	Upto Rs. 50,000	50,001 to 1,00,000	1,00,001 to 2,00,000	2,00,001 to 3,00,000	3,00,001 to 4,00,000	400,001 to 5,00,000	5,00,001 and above	
1. Engineering	5	1	7	3	1	3	3	23
2. Chemicals and chemical products	2	-	2	-	-		-	4
3. Electrical and electronic parts and assemblies	1	-	3	1	-	-	1	6
4. Rubber and plastic	1	1	1	2	-	-	-	5
Total	9	2	13	6	1	3	4	38

Table 6.11 : Distribution of Surveyed Enterprises by Industry and Productive Capital (Fixed + Working Capital) Employed

Industry	Size-class of productive capital (Rs.)							Total
	Upto 2,00,000	2,00,001 to 4,00,000	4,00,001 to 6,00,000	6,00,001 to 8,00,000	8,00,001 to 10,00,000	10,00,001 to 12,00,000	12,00,001 and above	
1. Engineering	4	6	6	2	2	1	2	23
2. Chemicals and chemical products	2	-	1	-	-	-	1	4
3. Electrical and electronic parts and assemblies	1	1	3	1	-	-	-	6
4. Rubber and plastic	1	3	1	-	-	-	-	5
Total	8	10	11	3	2	1	3	38

more than 30 years old and they were being looked after the second-generation entrepreneurs. Enterprises of self-starters were clustered around the age-bracket of 6 to 15 years.

Tables 6.12 and 6.13 bring out some details about the educational attainment and working experience of the entrepreneurs in charge of the surveyed units.

Twenty-five out of 39 entrepreneurs have technical diplomas or degrees (technical or non-technical). Thus, the informal entrepreneurs here have got a high level of educational attainment. (Among industries, the engineering industry shows the greatest variation. The chemical industry shows a higher than average level of attainment, while rubber and plastic industry shows a tendency towards lower educational standard. The electronics industry also reveals a high educational level but the presence of two non-technical degree holders among its entrepreneurs is to be noted. The importance of technical education in the background of entrepreneurs in this survey is in contrast to Holmstrom's observation that commercial acumen rather than technical expertise is more important to a small entrepreneur.

As per Table 6.13, 25 entrepreneurs have precious working experience. It is mostly in terms of wage employment in the formal sector. We came across only one example of an entrepreneur whose previous jobs were in both the formal and informal sector. The extent of previous experience in family business (i.e. a business other than the present one owned by the family) is limited. As per the Brahme and Paranjape study, p. 120: "... Administrative and managerial positions can be seen to be a hothousing towards the formation of the section of proprietors of modern small units." It appears to us that even junior technical positions in

Table 6.12 : Classification of Entrepreneurs as per Industry and Educational Attainment

Industry	Educational Level								Total
	Matric	Higher Secondary or Inter	Tech Nical certificate	Technical diploma	Technical degree	Non-technical degree	Non-Technical Post graduation	Doctorate	
1. Engineering	3	3	-	6	6	3	2	1	24
2. Chemicals and chemical products	-	-	-	-	1	2	-	1	4
3. Electrical and electronic parts and assemblies	-	-	1	1	-	2	-	2	6
4. Rubber and plastic	1	-	-	3	1	-	-	-	5
Total	4	3	1	10	8	7	2	4	39

Table 6.13 : Classification of Entrepreneurs According to Industry and Previous Working Experience

Industry	Experience		Total
	Family business	Wage employment	
1. Engineering	2	13	15
2. Chemical and chemical products	-	1	1
3. Electrical and electronic parts and assemblies	1	4	5
4. Rubber and plastic	-	4	4
Total	3	22	25

formal firms are looked upon as a perpetration for starting a small unit later on.

Fourteen entrepreneurs do not have previous working experience. Their educational level is generally higher and they, too, reveal a clustering around the qualifications of technical diplomas, degrees and non-technical degrees.

On the basis of the revenue-expense details given in the enterprises questionnaire, we have tabulated profits of the surveyed units. Since the respondents were tight-lipped about their margins and since cursory details of expenses were given, the profits reported by them are at best indicative. We, therefore, do not feel confident in reporting the quantum of profits.

It appears to us that the income of the entrepreneurs in this survey marginally exceeded the salary income they would have got in the formal sector, given their qualifications and experience. However, the quality of working life in FS is far better. The so-called independence that allegedly drove these persons to self-employment actually means being a price-taker in the market and in the case of job work units, it is not even that. In terms of number of working hours alone, these entrepreneurs have put in far more work as compared to employees in FS. The choice thus seems to be:

FS	IS
1. Regulated income	1. Unregulated income, possibility to bolster it through sweated labour and violation, by passing of rules and laws.
2. Good quality of life	2. Primitive working conditions and poor quality of life.
3. Fair career prospects	3. Little or no career prospects.

Independent manufacturers earn the highest income, according to this study. Those who combine such manufacture with job-study come next. Job-workers' income is the lowest.

Industry-wise classification of the data regarding profits reveals that the electronics industry has come up with the highest profits. Engineering and rubber and plastics come after the chemical industry in respect of profits.

Both in chemical and engineering industries, independent manufacturers earn more as compared to job-workers. Between the two industries, they earn more in the chemical industry. Competition in the engineering industry is reflected in lower margins. There were seven independent manufacturers of engineering products in this surrey. Almost all of them were in charge of slum industry units. Their profits were high. Working long hours (stretching one shift to 10 to 12 hours), paying low wages, paying single rate for overtime, defying all labour laws, making maximum use of dirty, cramped surroundings and space shortage, using second-hand machinery, relying on reverse engineering techniques and capitalizing on the above 'lower circuit' resource use are the features of these units and through them the owners earn a high income. They reinvest their income but the result is horizontal growth. If these units were to grow vertically, they would have to observe some labour laws and get registered under the Shop Act. Production technology might also change and the special features of factor use which guarantee profits now would diminish. Investment limit announced by the government to define small-scale enterprises and Factories/Shop Act (the latter is not so much dreaded as the former; it mainly decides the location, i.e. whether outside or within municipal limits, of the units) are behind the policy decision of horizontal growth.

6.4 Hired Labour in the Survey

Information about hired workers in the surveyed enterprises was available from both the enterprise and labour questionnaires. The enterprise questionnaire gave information about skill-wise, age-wise, age-groupwise break-up of all the hired workers in an enterprise, their average wages, educational qualifications, etc. Through enterprise questionnaires, information was available from 417 hired workers and employees in the 39 surveyed enterprises. There were 400 workers and 17 employees employed in these enterprises.

Labour questionnaires, on the other hand, were filled in by 45 workers.

Forty-one male workers and four women workers were included in the present survey of hired labour in micro-enterprises. Thirty-eight workers and four women workers were married and seven were unmarried. There were seven secondary earners among the surveyed workers and only two of them were women. The average age of workers was 31.9 years with a standard deviation of 6.74. the average age of all hired workers in the surveyed enterprises was available from the enterprise questionnaires. It was 28.8 years. It can, therefore, be inferred that the labour questionnaires were filled in by older workers. This is particularly so in case of workers who were approached through their enterprises. Workers responding to the labour questionnaires had, on an average, 9.64 years of experience in their current jobs.

Twenty-nine out of the 45 workers had migrated to Pune. A majority among them had come from outside Pune district. They were also older migrants in the sense that they had migrated to Pune more than 10 years ago. Most of them had small holdings of rain-fed land at their native places. There was one worker whose family had 5 acres of irrigated land near Pune. Two workers had landholdings in excess of 10 acres but their families staying at the native place were large. Many of the migrant workers (17 out of 29) remitted money back home but it appeared as if these remittances were not gratis. In other words, they represented an exchange of cash for foodgrains produced at the native place.

Employment was the basic reason for migration. Education and father's/husband's transfer were the reasons mentioned in a few cases. One worker came to Pune from Bhuinj in Satara district for undergoing apprenticeship at a large company (Kirloskar Pneumatic Company Ltd.). He had completed one year's training at I.T.I., Satara, before he came to Pune. His apprenticeship lasted for about 9-10 months and he was not absorbed in the same company. So he took up a job in one of the surveyed enterprises that had been started by a former employee of the same company. Another worker who was employed as a casual worker came from a nomadic family and had moved among several places at regular intervals with his family. He was just 19 years old and had joined the enterprise where he was interviewed barely 1½ months ago. His parents were working as casual construction workers.

6.4.1 Workers' Skills and Employment Status

Out of the 45 workers surveyed here, eight worked as casual labour. One of them was actually a sub-contractor of an enterprise. His name did not appear on the muster-roll of the enterprise. He employed two-three workers himself. He was a skilled worker. He reported a sizable variation in his earnings every month. The sub-contracting arrangement had, thus, been worked out with an eye on labour legislation and the convenience of passing on output fluctuations outside the firm. Another casual worker was an I.T.I certificate-holder. A majority of the entrepreneurs had given us to understand that formally trained workers were scarce and were, therefore, much sought after. This skilled casual worker was then a baffling case. The Brahme-Paranjape study observes that such workers are employed on a casual basis for filling up temporary demands due to absenteeism. In this survey, however, there was no other indication of the above arrangement. For one thing, labour absenteeism was not a problem according to the entrepreneurs surveyed. Secondly, the number of casual workers was quite small and there was just the above one case of a trained casual worker. From the information given by enterprises about the number and type of workers employed by them, it was seen that out of 400 workers employed by all of them together, casual workers were just 19. Barring the above two cases, the rest of the casual workers were mostly unskilled workers.

Although most of the workers were literate, their schooling had not gone beyond and in some cases higher secondary level. There were some non-matriculate workers. The number of matriculate workers was limited. In the labour questionnaires, 33 workers described themselves as skilled, eight as semi-skilled and four as unskilled. Semi-skilled workers were employed in rubber, electronics and engineering industries. In the rubber industry, rubber moulding work was seen as semi-skilled work. Wage-wise there was virtually no difference between skilled and semi-skilled labour. (From the point of view of the formal sector, the skilled workers in this survey are best treated as semi-skilled workers given their limited exposure to technology and machinery.) So it can be said that the labour hierarchy in micro-enterprises comprised only two layers – casual or unskilled workers at the bottom and skilled/semi-skilled workers on top. Supervisory and administrative staff was strictly limited according to the information in the enterprise questionnaire. The number of trainees, too, was very limited. Thus, in all the surveyed enterprises 17 supervisory staff-members managed 400 workers among whom six trainees were included.

Though the proportion of skilled workers is sizable, the proportion of formally trained workers is expectedly limited. Five held I.T.I. certificates. One worker held a private wireman's diploma. Two workers held some certificates in their trades.

Out of the 33 skilled workers in this survey, six were formally trained and 27 workers had acquired their skills by learning on the job. One formally trained worker – and I.T.I. certificate-holder – was employed in an electronics firm as a junior engineer, while one I.T.I. trained worker was working as a casual worker (mentioned above).

6.4.2 Wages

Data on wages was available from two sources. In the enterprise questionnaire information about wages paid to all the hired workers in the enterprise was asked for. In the labour questionnaire, individual workers had mentioned their own wages. A scrutiny of these two sets of figures revealed that the overall average wage per month per worker from the labour questionnaires was higher than that from enterprise questionnaires (see Table 6.14). The interpretation of this is: the enterprise questionnaire had reported average wage of all the hired workers in the enterprise, whereas the

Table 6.14 : Average Wage of Surveyed Workers

Industry (1)	Average wage as per labour questionnaires (Rs. p.m.) (2)	Average wage as per enterprise questionnaires (Rs. p.m.) (3)	Average wage of unionised workers (Rs. p.m.) (4)
1. Engineering	1614	1436	1375
2. Chemical and chemical products	1642	1316	-
3. Electrical and electronic parts and assemblies	1422	1278 (corrected)	1588
4. Rubber and plastic	1699	1466	1150
5. Miscellaneous	1095	-	1095
Overall	1526	1406	1287

labour questionnaires were mostly answered by senior workers in enterprises. This is particularly true of the workers contracted through their enterprises.

In case of the electronics enterprises surveyed, two units have reported high wages of Rs. 2,891 per month and Rs. 3,750 per month. Both employ qualified engineers and carry out the business of manufacture and sale of power electronic equipment and software packages respectively. Their wages are, in fact, salaries of employees. If these two units are excluded, the average wage in electronic units drops down to Rs. 1,278 per month and then these units, too, conform to the above-mentioned pattern of wage in labour questionnaires being more than wage in enterprise questionnaires.

The following data is presented in terms of monthly wages. In many cases, workers have reported daily wages. Their conversion into monthly wages assumes that these workers are able to get work on all the days in a month. Our respondents concurred with this assumption.

Column (4) in Table 6.14 shows industrywise average was calculated separately from labour questionnaires filled wages in enterprise questionnaires except in the electronics units. That wages in labour questionnaires are higher – except electronics – than wages of unionized workers is taken to mean that workers on the lower rung in the hierarchy within micro-enterprises have started getting unionized but that unionization has not reached senior workers. It also shows that employers got the labour questionnaires filled from their trusted, loyal senior workers. It is well-known that the extent of unionization in the workforce in the unorganized sector is limited. However, it would appear that unionization has begun from below.

All the workers in the survey were daily-rated workers. The range of monthly wage reported in the labour questionnaires was from Rs. 500 to Rs. 3,100. The person drawing Rs. 3,100 per month was working as an Assistant Manager in an engineering units. He was promoted to this position after 12 years of service. Before this job, he had worked for seven years in another unit at Thane as an assembly operator. One entrepreneur who filled in the labour questionnaire on behalf of his workers informed us that older workers could earn upto Rs 3,000 per month in his plastic factory. This unit had a history of labour unrest and it had been closed down once due to that reason. Operations had been resumed only after revamping the entire workforce. Another worker who was a sub - contractor (see above) earned Rs. 2,375 per month on an average.

There were five workers in the survey whose monthly wage was above Rs. 2,000. A majority of the surveyed workers' wage was below this limit.

The average monthly wage of a worker was Rs. 1,526 (Table 6.14, column 2). The minimum wage in the engineering industry at the time of the survey was Rs. 64 per day. This would mean a monthly wage of Rs. (64 x 26 =) 1,664. Skill-wise bifurcation of the wage data reveals that unskilled workers earned only Rs. 767 per month on an average, while skilled and semi-skilled workers earned Rs. 1,618 per month on an average. If the above-mentioned case of the assistant manager in an engineering unit is excluded, then the average wage for skilled workers drops down to Rs. 1,581. The information is presented in Table 6.15. L.K. Deshpande, in his study of Bombay (1985), has found that skill differentials gave rise to narrower wage differentials in IS as compared to FS. The observation is supported here.

Table 6.15 : Skill-wise Variation in the Wages Reported by Workers

Industry (1)	Average wage per month reported in labour questionnaires (Rs.)	Average wage per month by skilled and semi-skilled workers (Rs.)	Average wage per month reported by casual/unskilled workers (Rs.)
1. Engineering	1614	1631	700
2. Chemical	1642	1938	1050
3. Electrical and electronic parts and assemblies	1423	1423	-
4. Rubber and plastic	1699	1699	-
5. Miscellaneous	1095	1297	697
Overall	1526	(1618) 1581 corrected	767

Apart from the skill component, the following were found to exert an influence on the variation in individual wages: (a) gender, (b) industry in which employed, (c) difference in the number of working hours.

6.4.3 Gender-wise Variation in Wages

Only four completed labour questionnaires of women workers are available with us. Among them the case of one lady supervisor in a non-Shop Act unit near Hadapsar stands out for she earned Rs. 1,875 per month. Otherwise, women workers earned much less than the male workers. Including the lady supervisor, women workers' average monthly wage came to Rs. 1,206. Women workers who were contacted in CITU office did not fill in our questionnaires but the information given by them indicated that their wages were much below those of male workers.

6.4.4 Industrywise Variation in Wages

Workers in rubber and plastic and engineering unites have reported higher wages as compared to workers in electronic and chemical units. The case of chemical units in the survey is dubious since there is a large variation in their wage in the labour and enterprise questionnaires. In case of the electronic units a wide disparity between the wages of technically qualified employees and workers was seen. These units resort to piece-work and sub-contracting on an extensive basis in order to keep their labour costs down. The entrepreneur running a medium-scale electronic unit under the factories act informed us that he farmed out work and encouraged his workers to form small workshops busy did not let their consciousness develop and by cutting down or withholding the volume of work to be farmed out work and encouraged his workers to form small workshops. This policy kept the workers busy; did not let their consciousness develop and by cutting down or withholding the volume of work to be farmed out allowed the entrepreneur to control them totally. One woman worker in an electronic unit in this survey asked us to do something to get her a wage hike because the employer had turned a deaf ear to her pleas. She had undergone a technical training certificate course of Meltron (Maharashtra Electronics Corporation Ltd.) and had eight years of service but her wage was only Rs. 875.

6.4.5 Wage Difference Due to Varying Number of Working Hours

In order to isolate the effect of varying number of working day of 8 hours and a working month of 26 days (i.e. 208 hours per month) at the reported hourly rate of wages was calculated. These calculations yielded the following results presented in Table 6.16.

It can thus be seen that the surveyed workers have been putting in more working hours compared to the norm of 208 hours per month. With standard working hours, and plastic units, chemical and engineering enterprises all extract more work from their workers in exchange for the reported wages. The electronic units, on the other hand, are more or less observing the norm regarding working hours.

It has been mentioned above that a majority (71 per cent) of the surveyed enterprises operated on a single shift basis. Many among them worked for longer than the standard day depending upon their location. In other words, units located in industrial estates were probably constrained to observe the standard length of a shift (8 hours), while slum industries worked for 10-12 hours in a shift on a routine basis. That observation explains the result in Table 6.16. (we came across one regularly extracted four hours' overtime from its

Table 6.16 : Effect of Varying Working Hours on Wages

Industry (1)	Average wage as per labour questionnaires(Table 7.14, col. 2) (Rs. p.m.) (2)	Average equivalent wage (Rs. p.m.) (3)	Difference (2-3) (4)
1. Engineering	1614	1408	206
2. Chemical and chemical products	1642	1338	304
3. Electrical and electronic parts and assemblies	1422	1403	19
4. Rubber and plastic	1699	1304	395
5. Miscellaneous	1095	1059	36
Overall	1526	1356	170

workers every day, depending upon the availability of work!)

6.4.6 Mobility

Out of 45 workers who have filled in labour questionnaires, 41 have given information about the jobs changed by them. Two-third of these workers have changed jobs and one-third have not. Of the former, a sizable number has changed two jobs or more. The extent of job-mobility is less in non-Shop Act units. This could be due to the employed women workers in these units and due to the limited availability of other jobs.

Employment histories of workers who have changed their jobs are complex. This is particularly true of unionized workers. They have experienced spells of unemployment following redundancy of closure of their units. Consequently, periods of agricultural labour and/or casual labour on daily wage (e.g. hiring themselves out as carpenters, masons, etc. depending upon availability of work) are found in-between their industrial employment.

Workers also spoke of upward mobility. Promotion from helper to a machine operator was the most common type of upward movement that was referred to by the workers. Helpers carry out all and sundry activities and over a period of time become proficient in machine operations also. It is upto the proprietor of the unit to recognize such a proficient helper as a machine operator. If he chooses not to, in order to avoid paying higher wage, he can do so. The promotion is not accompanied by a rise in wage or status, at least initially. The promotion does denote that the worker has been given greater responsibility and that he is recognized as a stable (and perhaps loyal) worker by the employer. Banerjee (1986) found labour turnover in the wage employment segment of IS I Delhi to be largely voluntary. We, on the other hand, found it to be mostly involuntary.

6.4.7 Perquisites and Facilities

Apart from their daily wage, workers in micro-enterprises are assured of only one facility, viz. Diwali bonus. Employers declare it to form a certain percentage (in some cases, 20 per cent) of profits but given the secrecy surrounding their revenue transactions, it is not possible to verify this claim. The usual practice is to hand over a round sum amounting to less than a month's wage to the workers on the day of 'Laxmi-Poojan' in Diwali.

Advances from the wage called withdrawals are also permitted by the employers. Many employers also give loans to workers and charge interest on them almost all the workers who reported having borrowed some money in this survey, mentioned their employer as the lender.

Leave was another facility mentioned by the workers. Generally one day's leave accrued for 21 days of attendance. This meant 11 days' leave for 240 working days or 14 days' leave for 300 working days. Although the workers enthusiastically gave information about their annual leave entitlement, it was not even clear whether it was leave with full/half pay or leave without pay. In all probability, it was the latter. So the leave facility actually meant that workers' absence from duty would be condoned provided it was within the leave entitlement.

Attendance bonus, increments, tips, uniform, tea, 'nasht', daily allowance, contribution to labour welfare fund, permission to attend to personal work during working hours, etc., were the benefits mentioned by some workers. The incidence of these was, however, restricted to just a handful of workers. These workers also did not receive all these perquisites together. One-odd benefit was reported by the individual workers.

There was a great resistance among employers to pay Employees' State Insurance (ESI) or Provident Fund (PF) contributions on behalf of their workers. Compliance with the statutory provisions regarding these contributions is generally coextensive with the Factories Act. The Factories Act, Employees State Insurance Act and Provident Fund Act constitute the main reason why many employers keep the workers' strength restricted to 8 or 9 per unit and choose to grow horizontally.

ESI and PF contributions are to be deducted from the employee's pay and together with contribution from the employers (matching contribution in case of PF and more than matching contribution in case of ESI) they are to be deposited with the government. This automatically confers job security on the worker. Out of the 45 workers surveyed here, six enjoyed PF benefit while 11 enjoyed the ESI facility.

Some employers tried to rationalize their opposition to these statutory facilities. "Why make a contribution to the government and ask the workers to wait in long queues to the government and ask the workers to wait in long queues for sub-standard medical facilities? We can provide better and speedier attention," said one employer. The alternate facilities rarely materialized. Only five workers ıeported that they got some health-care facilities. Four of them received a medical allowance. One worker was asked by his employer to go to a certain dispensary run by the employer's friend and it was said that the employer settled the bills subsequently.

6.5 Conclusion

Considering the above information, it can safely be said that workers in the surveyed micro-enterprises receive a monthly wage of Rs. 1,526. They do not get any other facilities except Diwali bonus. If this bonus is assumed to amount to Rs. 750 per worker per annum, then a worker's annual wage amounts to Rs. 19,062 (i.e. Rs. 1,526 p.m. x 12 + Rs. 750 bonus). This is equivalent to Rs. 1,589 per month. This wage can be used for comparison with other sectors in the economy, with the understanding that workers in micro-enterprises put in more hours of work per week/month as compared to the formal sector.

Chapter 7

Findings of the Survey

7.1 Resource Use in Surveyed Enterprises

Manufacturing activities have to be registered unless they are illegal. Registration bestows State recognition upon the concerned activity. It means an officially accepted existence usually supported by a licence, charter or certificate which eliminates the fear of eviction or harassment by the law enforcement machinery. The certificate or licence is essential for or helps in procuring infrastructure facilities also. Registration may simultaneously provide for compliance with some regulations.

Manufacturing activities can be distinguished according to their approach to registration. The higher circuit approach consists of compliance with all the statutory provisions while the lower circuit approach means weighing the benefits and cost at each step of the registration process and compliance with only those which are unavoidable. In the higher circuit approach, whether to register or not is a non-issue since registration is taken for granted. In the lower circuit approach, however, it is a very important matter as profitability depends upon lower costs made possible by non-registration. With considerable State presence as in India, total non-registration is worked out.

The idea of a differential approach to registration was suggested by Lisa Peattie (1981) and Gus Edgren (1990). In her study of shoe-making in Colombia, based on 20 interviews with owners of shoe-making firms ranging in size from one-man firms to plants employing more than 100 workers, Peattie makes the following observation:

"... Upto a certain a point it is possible to produce shoes by following either of two strategies. Either one takes the legal and open route, pays the legally required fringe benefits and tries to be competitive by capturing special markets ... and by being industrially efficient. Or one may remain inconspicuous, utilise relatively few pieces of machinery and relatively more workers and try to be competitive through flexibility and low wages." She places the cut-off point of the latter strategy at around 15 workers. The similarity between this description and our observations regarding the working on non-Shop Act and even non-Factory Act units is indeed striking.

Registration in the context of this survey, means registration with Small-Scale Industries (SSI) Directorate at the first level. This registration is voluntary but essential for receiving the benefits and concessions for small-scale units that are announced by the government from time to time. Of late, banks have started asking for this registration before considering loan application. Similarly Maharashtra State Electricity Board also insists on it before giving electricity connection. SSI registration does not seek to regulate the working of the registered units. So, apart from the initial expenses of some fee and furnishing of documents, it does not impose subsequent recurring costs on the registering unit. All the 39 units covered in our survey had this registration.

The second level of registration means compliance with the Indian Factories Act, 1948, or The Maharashtra Shops and Establishments Rules, 1961, popularly known as the Shop Act. Factories Act is applicable to larger manufacturing units – those employing 10 or more workers with the use of power in the manufacturing process or those employing 20 or more workers without power. Since our intention was to concentrate on smaller manufacturing units, Factories Act units were excluded by us. However, during the course of the survey it was learnt that the Factories Act is now applicable to all chemical units irrespective of the number of weeks employed. (The remaining surveyed units ought to have come under the Shop Act.) The Shop Act is applicable to commercial activities and smaller manufacturing activities not covered by the Factories Act, located within municipal limits. Out of the total 39 units surveyed here, 24 came under the Factories/Shop Act while as many as 15 were outside its purview. The Factories Act constituted a crucial cut-off point for the surveyed units.

The Shop Act also seeks to regulate working hours, holidays and leave rules of the covered units. It prohibits the employment of children and prescribes health and safety standards for employee's well-being. It stipulates that overtime at twice the normal rate be paid and 14 days' to 30 days' notice be given to employees before termination of their services. Non-compliance with these provisions is considered to be a sure method of reducing costs, at least by the non-Shop Act units in our survey. Hadapsar, Vitthalwadi, Manikbaug, Hingne, Vadgaon, Shivne, etc., are preferred areas under Gram Panchayat jurisdiction for this reason and each area has a sizable cluster of small-scale industrial units. (Some of these areas have recently come under municipal limits).

In these non-Shop Act units, weekly-offs are eschewed, working hours per shift stretch upto 10 hours or more, overtime is paid at single rate, multiple shift working is carried out even in residential accommodation, wages are very meagre and safety measures are conspicuous by their absence. These units employ a sizable number of women workers or put out work to them. These units also avoid the payment of octroi and thus save on their material cost. CITU has been trying since August 1994 to organize the workers in SSI units in Vitthalwai, Manikbaug areas. Office-bearers of CITU narrated stories of grave exploitation of workers that was going on in these area. For instance, we were told that in one large industrial unit there which came under the Factories Act and employed about 45 workers, almost all the workers had lost a finger or two while working and had received no compensation for this loss.

We met a number of women workers in non-Shop Act units in the CITU office. Women workers are preferred because they can be presumed to be secondary workers and can be paid low wages. One woman worker got a pricely wage of Rs. 250 per month under a piece rate system. The employer assured her that as she became quicker in her work, he wage would automatically go up. Another woman worker got a monthly wage of Rs. 450. She worked for 10 hours every day. (Luckily a weekly off was observed in her unit.) She had studied upto the 4th standard and had joined the workforce at a rather advanced age of 40 years due to family responsibilities. Her employer constantly reminded her of this and emphasized that he preferred young girls who were at least matriculates and who learnt things fast. We found that narrations of these women workers shocked the experienced union office-bearers.

Engineering non-Shop Act units in Hadapsar paid Rs. 500 to Rs. 700 per month to their casual workers. Senior, more experienced workers in one unit had started with a wage of Rs. 30 per day and were earning Rs. 40 per day when we contacted them. One employer called this the 'market wage'. He knew that the minimum wage in engineering industry was around Rs. 64 per day in that zone and he defended himself by saying that he did not want to invite the wrath of neighbouring employers by paying higher wages to his workers. In Manikaug, Vitthalwadi, Vadgaon, areas too, the average wage would be similar, though greater stratification of labour could be found there. CITU has begun to ask for the minimum wage in some units.

The third level of registration is with tax authorities. All the surveyed units had Sales Tax registration. Two or three employers proudly talked about the payment of income tax by them. Further details about income tax were, however, not forthcoming. Sales tax registration is essential for conducting any transaction of exchange of goods and services and it does not impose any concomitant regulatory costs on the registered unit. The positive response of the surveyed units to this registration is hence not unexpected.

The fourth level of compliance is with social security legislation. Out of the major 39 labour laws in the country the following provide for social security :

1. The Workmen's Compensation Act, 1923.
2. The Employee's State Insurance Act, 1948 (ESI).
3. The Employees' Provident Funds and Miscellaneous Provisions Act, 1952 (PF).
4. The Maternity Benefit Act, 1961.
5. The Payment of Gratuity Act, 1972.

These laws are broadly applicable to industrial units covered under the Factories Act. Therefore the second and fourth levels of registration coincide generally. The Workmen's Compensation Act obligates an employer to pay compensation to his workers for accidents arising in the course of employment. Both ESI and PF Acts require in the course of employers to deduct a certain amount from the wages of employees and together with some contribution from the employer, deposit it with concerned government authorities. This enables the workers to enjoy the benefit of insurance cover against illnesses and medical facilities in the case of ESI and provident fund and gratuity upon retirement in case of PF and Gratuity Acts.

Out of the 45 workers interviewed in this survey, six claimed PF benefit and 11 ESI benefit. Most of the employers showed a good deal of resistance to these Acts because of the direct cost in terms of employer's own contribution which they impose. The Maternity Benefit Act which is reportedly a stumbling block for women's employment even in FS was not implemented in any surveyed unit. Similarly gratuity for the workers was nowhere mentioned.

The Minimum Wages Act, 1948, is applicable to industrial and commercial enterprises irrespective of the number of workers employed. Minimum wage rates applicable to different industries and different geographical zones are announced by the government from time to time.

In this survey it was found that the wages paid in non-Shop Act units were lower than those in the Shop Act units. If a minimum wage of Rs. 1,560 per month (Rs. 60 per day × 26 days) is roughly assumed then the average wage reported by workers in labour questionnaires in both Shop Act and non-Shop Act units at Rs. 1,526 per month is lower. When wages reported by skilled and semi-skilled workers only are considered, the average wage goes up to Rs. 1,581 per month. However, when higher working hours per month reported by half of the surveyed workers are taken into account (see Chapter 6, Table 6.16), then the average wage drops down significantly (Rs. 1,357 per month) the minimum wage.

It was observed that registration level and resource use were tied together. Thus, the Shop Act and non-Shop Act units were found to differ in respect of the availability of space also. Average covered are per worker was 155 sq. ft. in the surveyed units. A majority of the surveyed units had upto 200 sq. ft. of covered space per worker with them (Chapter 6, Table 6.3. Non-Shop Act units had lower average covered space of 134 sq. ft. per worker. However, among them, there was one engineering unit which reported a higher space of 262 sq. ft. per worker and which influenced the average. The other non-Shop Act units were quite small. Thus the lowest space availability per worker that was reported by the non-Shop Act units was 27 sq. ft. After the largest unit (262 sq. ft. space per worker) is excluded, the average available space per worker in non-Shop Act units drops down to 95 to sq. ft. with a range of 27-157 sq. ft. Shop Act units located in residential areas in the heart of the city, e.g. in Kasha Peth, Shukrawar Peth, Mangalwar Peth, etc., were small, congested units while the non-Shop Act units located on the outskirts of Pune were relatively roomy. Thus location-availability and price of land or rent-and registration status seem to effect the availability of space in manufacturing units and the pattern appears to be:

Non-Shop Act units - more space due to lower land prices,
Shop Act units - less pace due to central location,
Factory Act units - more space.

Location, registration status of an industrial unit and its shift-working are also related. Registered units, situated in industrial areas can resort to multiple shift-working. Units located within municipal limits and registered under Shop Act cannot have multiple shift working. Non-Shop Act units located outside municipal limits, operate double or even triple shifts but they do not admit this. Among them also, a few units carry out triple shifts. Operating single shifts but stretching it to 10 or 12 hours – no extra payment for overtime is involved –is the preferred pattern.

All this has an important implication capacity utilization in small units is low as compared to big units. The former try to reduce their expenses to the minimum level but their capacity utilization remains low. Bigger units have high expenses but considering their scale of operations (which includes triple-shift working and high capacity utilization the burden of expenses per unit of output turns out to be lower in their case.

Non-Shop Act unit which illegally operate more shifts, can upset this pattern. This creates tension which could be observed by us in the withering comments made by the proprietors of units in industrial estates about the slum units.

It was observed that the Factory Act units and particularly those located in industrial estates were generally bigger than the surveyed units both because of Factory Act requirements and larger resources of these enterprises. In his study of informal activities in Calcutta, Bose (1974) has referred to an older study of manufacturing industry in Calcutta which had reported that informal units had larger space per employee as compared to factories. (Among factories also, it was reported that larger factories had less space per employee and smaller factories had more). Absence of multiple shift working in informal units was suggested as one of the possible reasons for this intriguing result. It would appear that this finding holds goods for our survey also.

Thus, it can be said that the Factory Act units start with larger space per employee. After multiple-shift working is introduced, their space availability per employee comes down. In case of the non-Factory Act units, however, space availability per employee is likely to remain constant over a period of time. (This pattern is not unlike that for total investment/total costs for these two types of units).

All the surveyed units made use of bank finance (nationalized and urban cooperative banks) for their working capital requirement. For fixed capital, the usual pattern was: initial investment was made from own savings. The entrepreneurs who had left salaried jobs for starting their units, applied their provident fund and gratuity amounts for this purpose. Loans from relatives and friends were used to supplement the initial investment. Deposits from relatives and friends were also used in a few cases. Then banks were tapped for buying machinery. Reinvestment of profit was mentioned as an important source but no further details were available. Only a few units mentioned special financial institutions, e.g. National Small Industries Corporation in this connection. The surveyed units thus had access to formal sources of finance.

Machinery used in the surveyed units was mainly of the general purpose type and the use of old, second-had and self-fabricated machinery was widespread. Machines were made by small manufacturers at Ludhiana, Rajkot, Coimbatore, etc. These manufactures are famous for their rough and ready methods and cheap, adaptive technology. It was found that 10 surveyed enterprises were using/had used second-hand machinery; 12 units were using self-fabricated and self-modified machinery, 13 units were suing Ludhiana/Rajkot/Coimbatore makes or cheap, local makes of machinery. Lower cost of machinery meant a smaller capital base and the use of old, unsophisticated machines meant that quality and precision of work were of a lower order.

Fifteen out of the 35 units which had provided information in this regard operated from rented premises.

The is one reason why these units have lower fixed capital at their disposal.

Very definitive information about the materials used by the surveyed units is not available. Thirty-one out of the total 39 surveyed units have provided some information about their material procurement. Four of the 31 units procured materials from wholesalers/manufacturers, two from parent companies, and 25 units bought materials from retailers/dealers/combinations of all sources including manufacturers and wholesalers but with retailers being invariably included. Among retailers also, reliance had to be placed on local retailers as 'Bombay dealers', in the words of one entrepreneur, demanded advance payment. Since this tended to raise the materials cost, it was necessary to use lower grade materials. Metallurgical testing of materials was skipped and ingenious methods were used to reduce materials consumption.

One entrepreneur who carried out both job work and own manufacturing explained to us how he saved on materials cost in case of the former. He bought bars of smaller size than were specified by parent companies and then heated them so that they expanded and acquired the required shape. The bars were also forged for this purpose. Profit cutting of bar components was also carried out to save on material costs. The non-Shop Act units saved on octroi and some of them were actually advised by the parent companies to go beyond municipal limits for this purpose. Other studies have made similar observations. In a study of the electrical fan industry in Calcutta, it was found that the rates offered by parent companies were so unremunerative that the small units were forced to save on inputs. They used just water instead of a weak acid solution for the sanding (rubbing a component with sand paper) operation and while painting the parts, applied less number of coats and did not apply paint of the required thickness. The same study mentions that small sandal-makers in Calcutta doing put-out work for large firms save on the glue. Handloom weavers save on the yarn given by the agents while weaving those parts of sarees which are not directly seen. A study of outwork in food processing industry – in rolling 'papads' – in Bombay observes that women add wheat flour to the papad flour that is supplied by the producer/agent so that more papads can be rolled from the given papad flour and since they are paid on the basis of the weight of rolled papads they hope to earn more.

The surveyed units also practised extensive downstream sub-contracting. Twenty-eight out of the 39 surveyed units off-loaded work. Cost of sub-contracted work formed 12.5 per cent of the cost of materials of all the surveyed units. Sub-contracting is used first to avoid making investment in fixed assets and the concomitant obligation to ensure adequate work-load for machinery and secondly to reduce costs. Cost reduction is possible because the units-mostly individuals – to whom work is off loaded have hardly any overheads and by making extensive use of family labour they save on wage costs as well. The entrepreneur of one non-Shop Act unit in Hadapsar making automobile spare parts informed us that he got 70 per cent of the work done from outside and tried to carry out only finishing work in house. They practise facilitated fast growth. He owned seven units side by side (he was an adherent of one shift, one unit policy) and complained of the tremendous work-load which left him with very little time for personal matters. Due to sub-contracting, the surveyed units could achieve a good rate of capacity, the surveyed units could achieve a good rate of capacity utilization – the range of capacity utilization percentage reported was 80 to 100. Some units even exceeded 100 per cent capacity utilization on the basis of extensive sub-contracting with the retention of only the final/finishing operations with themselves.

All in all, the surveyed units, as compared to bigger industrial units under the Factories Act, appeared to :

- use less space.
- Pay lower wages to their worker while also making them work for longer hours (except in the case of electronic units),
- use locally available and lower quality materials,
- use second-hand /self-fabricated /self-modified machinery extensively.

Inputs used by these units were thus predominantly general purpose inputs. This was particularly evident in the case of machinery and labour. In case of the latter, the reported shortage of formally trained, skilled labour, on-the-job skill formation in case of other workers and the absence of division of labour – all pointed towards the non-specialised nature of labour input. No wonder, therefore, that these units are unable to make distinctive products. Even the independent manufacturers in the survey did not make distinctive products. It is for this reason that small units are considered ideal for offloading low-technology jobs in the engineering industry.

The above pattern of resource use – the lower circuit rescource use pattern – helped the surveyed units to reduce cots. The tendency to use general purpose and lower quality inputs for reducing cots was particularly accentuated in the case of the non-Shop Act units studied. Lower costs enable these units to earn profits in the short run. At the same time, their resources commit these units to a subsidiary, dependent position in the market.

Some information about the economic performance of the surveyed units is presented below. An attempt is also made to compare it with the performance of small-scale units reported elsewhere and with the performance of larger units/factories.

Information regarding the revenue-expenditure profile of the surveyed units is presented first (Table 7.1). Surveyed units have also been classified as engineering job-work units and others- independent manufacturers – here. For 37 out of 39 units surveyed, revenue-expenditure details were available. One chemical unit carried out job-work for a Bombay-based large unit. It was excluded from the category of job-work units as the rest belonged to engineering industry. Units that were engaged in both job-work and independent manufacture were treated as job-work units.

The striking thing about the data in Table 7.1 is the very low share of overheads – establishment expenses, rent, depreciation – and other expenses – power and fuel, interest – in the cost structure of the surveyed units. Salaries and wages at 8 per cent of turnover are also very low. The figures of value added and profit per unit have therefore turned out to be usually high.

Two factors are at work behind this result. Firstly, because of their extreme uneasiness and reluctance to give information of this type to an individual researcher, the surveyed entrepreneurs gave only the briefest possible answers to the concerned queries. In some cases only material consumption percentages was indicated and another percentage figure was mentioned for all other expenses. In some other cases, percentages for material consumption and salaries and wages only were indicated. Therefore some estimation of expenses was unavoidable. It appears that such estimates have been made on the lower side.

Table 7.1: Average Monthly Revenue-Expenditure Percentages of Surveyed Units

	Particulars	All Units	Engineering Job-Work Units	Independent Manufacture Units
1.	Turnover	100.0	100.0	100.0
2.	Cost of materials	51.3	45.5	53.8
3.	Sucontarcting charges	6.4	5.3	6.9
4.	Power and Fuel	2.0	2.2	1.9
5.	Establishment expenses	2.8	2.7	2.6
6.	Depreciation	1.9	3.2	1.4
7.	Net Value Added [1-(2+3+4+5+6)]	35.6 (100.0)	41.1 (100.0)	33.4 (100.0)
8.	Salaries and Wages	7.9 (22.2)	10.1 (24.8)	6.9 (20.8)
9.	Rent	0.5 (1.4)	0.6 (1.3)	0.5 (1.5)
10.	Interest	1.2 (3.3)	1.4 (3.3)	1.1 (3.3)
11.	Profit	26.0 (73.1)	29.0 (70.6)	24.9 (74.4)

Secondly, the overheads of the surveyed units– particularly the non-Shop Act units – were actually low. The location of the units, their machinery, other equipment and the shed housing these facilities, all gave us this clear impression. This follows from their resource use pattern outlines above. For example, average monthly rent paid by a surveyed unit came to Rs. 2, 568. While four or five units had rent bills exceeding this amount, the non-Shop Act units paid much lower rent. The average monthly rent of Rs. 2,568 was thought to be reasonable. Similarly salary rates were low in the surveyed units and they employed few white-collar employees. The annual average wage per worker that has been considered in the above computations is Rs. 20,200 or Rs. 1,683 p.m. The figure was reported by the entrepreneurs in the enterprise questionnaire and it includes the value of perquisites given to workers. In Chapter 6, the annual average of perquisites given to workers, inclusive of perquisites, was calculated at Rs. 19,062 p.a. or Rs. 1, 589 p.m., on the basis of labour questionnaires. Had the latter figure been adopted, the share of wages is net value added would have declined further, though not significantly. (Table 7.2)

Although value added figures which have been computed from our survey are very high, the value added: output ratio is comparable with NSS data. Given the difference between turnover and output, this correspondence needs to be accepted cautiously. The ratio of value added to emoluments is higher in the case of the surveyed units except in electronic and electrical units. This underscores the high figures of value added derived in our survey.

Some data about capital intensity – fixed and productive capital per worker – are presented in Table 7.3.

Table 7.2: Comparison of value Added in Surveyed Units with NSS data

	Industry Group	NIC No.	Value Added / Emoluments NSS 45th Round	Value Added / Emoluments Survey	Value Added / Output NSS 45th Round	Value Added / Output Survey
1.	Rubber and Plastic	30	4.20	4.88	0.20	0.36
2.	Chemicals and Chemical products	31	3.46	5.72	0.32	0.32
3.	Engineering	33	3.38		0.25	
		34	3.13	5.05	0.36	0.37
		35	3.62		0.39	
4.	Electrical and Electronic parts and Assemblies	36	3.36	2.25	0.38	0.32

Note: 1. The two sub-columns in column 4 are not strictly comparable since the NSS ratio is value added to out put while the ratio computed on the basis of own survey pertains to turnover. The difference between turnover and output arises due to addition/deletion to finished stock during the year. No details about finished stock levels were available in our survey.

2. The NSS 45 th Round pertains to only own account enterprises and non-directory manufacturing and repair establishments (i.e. those employing less than 6 hired plus household workers). The cut off point for the number of workers in our survey was 10. Surveyed enterprises therefore are bigger than those covered by NSS.

Table 7.3: Capital Availability Per Worker

			Fixed capital per worker (Rs.)	Productive capital per worker (Rs.)
I.	1.	Overall	28,365	51,399
	2.	Engineering industry	27,277	44,791
	3.	Chemical industry	16,600	80,840
	4.	Electrical and electronic industry	25,054	43,143
	5.	Rubber and Plastic industry	21,081	41,892
II.	6.	Engineering job-work units	21,673	42,907
	7.	Others - independent manufacturers	35,643	60,989
		(From point 1 to 7 above, the figures are at current prices and are based on survey data.)		
	8.	Modern small industry (PMR - Brahme and Paranjape study, 1977. The amount pertains to capital per employee.)	14,594	26,534
	9.	Traditional small industry (PMR - Brahme and Paranjape study, 1977. Capital per employee)	5,749	12,797
	10.	ASI factory sector (All India, 1987-88)	1,29,454	1,74,903
	11.	SSI units (All India,1987-88)	25,378	-
		$\text{Rs.}\frac{1,59,625^{*}}{6.29}$ = Rs.25,378 (employment per unit)		
		* Σ fixed investment at book value = Rs.929603 lakhs / 582368 units		
	12.	Factories in Maharashtra employing less than 20 workers (1992-93)		97,600

Notes: 1. Survey figures of fixed assets indicate the book value or written down value of these assets.
2. Fixed assets + working capital = productive capital.

Source: 1. SSI units: Report of the Second All-India SSI Census, 1987-88;
2. Factories: ASI data, Handbook of Industrial Statistics, 1991.
3. For Small factories in Maharashtra: Economic Survey of Maharashtra, 1994-95.

Assuming that the figures of fixed capital per worker are all right, we have tried to compute capital productivity of the surveyed units. Our tabulations and their comparison with small scale units in the country are presented in Table 7.4

Both the above measures of capital productivity show that the surveyed units have very high productivity. Productivity cannot really be so high given our reservations about the unusually high figures of value added reported by the surveyed units. Figures of fixed capital per worker, presented in Table 8.3 seem fine when compared with SSI figure. Still, it needs to be borne in mind that :

1. Fixed capital figures for our survey computation are book values or written down values.
2. In case of older units (28 out of the 39 surveyed) units were in the age group of 11 to 35 years) the net block (fixed assets – depreciation) can become near-zero in this period, unless fresh investments are made regularly.
3. Given the widespread use of second-hand, self-fabricated and general purpose machinery in the surveyed units the gross block has lower values.

In can, therefore, be said that capital productivity of our surveyed units is high but not so high as is suggested by our computations.

We then attempted to compare the overall productivity of surveyed units with that of factories covered by Annual Survey of Industries. This comparison is presented in Table 7.5.

Even here the surveyed units are more productive as compared to the factories. Before dismissing this as an absurd conclusion, we tried to cross-check it with earlier studies (Table 7.6). These studies have reached opposing conclusions. Broadly, however, the position is this :

Table 7.4: Capital Productivity of Surveyed Units

Industry	NIC No.	Output / Fixed capital: Our survey	Output / Fixed capital: SSI Census	Net value added / Fixed capital: Our survey	Net value added / Fixed capital: SSI Census
Rubber and Plastic	30	15	4	6	1
Engineering	33) 34) 35)	9	(7 (4 (3	4	(1 (1 (1
Electrical and Electronics	36	9	6	3	1

Notes: 1. Instead of output:fixed capital, the survey results pertain to turnover:fixed capital.

2. Chemicals and Chemical Products industry (NIC No.31) units in the survey gave some absurd results which have been omitted.

Source: For SSI units: Report of the 2nd All India SSI Census, 1987-88.

Table 7.5: Comparison Between Non-factory and factory Act Enterprises

(1) Industry	Major Group Code No.	(2) Fixed capital to Net Value Added (NVA)		(3) Fixed capital to Gross Output (Turnover)		(4) NVA to Gross Output (Turnover)		(5) Wages to NVA	
		Sur-veyed units	Fact-ories	Sur-veyed units	Fact-ories	Sur-veyed units	Fact-ories	Sur-veyed units	Fact-ories
1. Engineering	33, 34, 35	0.28	2.47	0.10	0.44	0.37	0.18	0.20	
2. Chemicals and chemical products	31	0.08	2.10 1.50*	0.02	0.38 0.30*	0.32	0.18	0.17	
3. Electrical and electronic parts and assemblies	36	0.33	1.00	0.105	0.24	0.32	0.24	0.44	0.40
4. Rubber and plastic	30	0.18	1.42	0.065	0.19	0.36	0.13	0.20	

* Figures for Maharashtra as per Economic Survey of Maharashtra, 1994-95.

Source : 1) For Surveyed units - our tabulations.
2) For Factories - Handbook of Industrial Statistics, 1991.

Table 7.6: Comparative Economic Performance of Large and Small Enterprises

Sr. No.	Authors, year of study	Data base	Definitions, criteria used	Findings: Labour intensity	Findings: Labour productivity	Findings: Capital intensity	Findings: Capital productivity	Findings: Overall productivity
1.	Dhar and Lydall, 19[illegible]	CMI data (1956) for 9 industries, Perspective Planning Division data (1959) for 15 industries. Data relates to registered factories under Factories Act.	Employment size criterion for defining small scale enterprises. Capital input = Total productive capital.			Highest in modern small enterprises employing 20-49 workers.		
2.	Hajra, 1965	CMI data (1955, 1958) for 17 industries.			Low in SS enterprises.		Low in SS enterprises.	
3.	Sandesara, 1966, 1969	CMI data (1953-1958) for 28 industries.	Employment size criterion to define SS enterprises. Capital input = Fixed capital.			Not related to size of enterprise.	Rises with size.	
4.	Mehta, 1969	ASI data about registered factories (1960-63) for 32 industries.	Capital employed or investment criterion to define SS enterprises. Capital input = Fixed capital.			Rises with size.	Declines with size.	
5.	Bhavani, 1980	ASI data (1973-74) for 46 industries at 3-digit level, both Census* and sample sectors for registered factories, Census of SSI units, SIDO for SS enterprises. (*Census sector = larger factories)	Capital input = Fixed capital.		Highest in larger enterprises. Low in SS enterprises accounting for 40% of total value added.	Highest in larger enterprises.	High in large enterprises in 18 out of 46 industries. Low in SS enterprises accounting for 40% of total value added.	
6.	Goldar, 1982	RBI survey of SSI units (1977), ASI data re. Census sector (1976-77) for registered factories.	Investment criterion to define SS enterprises. Capital input = Fixed capital, both gross and net fixed capital considered.		Low in SS enterprises as compared to large units. High in large enterprises.	High in large units as compared to small units.	High in small units - 21/37 industries with gross capital basis, 15/37 industries with net capital basis.	Low in SS enterprises as compared to large enterprises.

Notes: Studies 1-5 use partial productivity approach to compute factor productivity. Goldar uses relative productivity approach in which relative labour productivity = $\frac{\text{labour productivity in SS units}}{\text{labour productivity in large units}}$; relative capital productivity = $\frac{\text{capital productivity in SS units}}{\text{capital productivity in large units}}$. He has also computed a relative efficiency index. It is nothing but a ratio of total factor productivities in small and large enterprises. Total factor productivity is computed as a weighted average of relative labour and capital productivities.

Source: Compiled from Goldar, B., "Relative Efficiency of Modern Small Scale Industries in India," in K.S. Suri (ed.), Small Scale Enterprises in Industrial Development; The Indian Experience (1988).

Labour productivity: Low in small units,
High in larger units.
Capital productivity: High is small units,
Low in large units.

Overall productivity is low in small units, high in large units, basically as a result of capital intensity.

It can be seen from the above data that profits and wages are inversely related in the surveyed units. Profit maximization requires minimization of wages. Large factories in FS in Pune pay comparatively higher wages – 3.5 times those in surveyed units, inclusive of benefits – to their workers and treat the wage bill as fixed. This points to a fundamental difference in the logic governing resource-use. Large companies use the far-sighted rationale of mature capitalism (Fordism) in which initial commitment of resources is high and short-run profits can be overlooked for enhanced long-run profits. The logic of early capitalism (perhaps, pre-Taylorism), displayed here by the surveyed units, concentrates on the short run. This basis difference gets reflected in all the operational decisions. Thus, small units believe that low wages and absence of job security are essential for securing efficiency and personal relations are sufficient to obtain workers' commitment while large companies grant job security and high wages to their workers for the same purpose.

The difference in perspective arises because of capital and not any subjective factors. Availability of capital and its continuous regeneration in the production process govern this difference. To be sure, micro-enterprises also have access to capital and they do reinvest their profits but the difference of scale in initial availability of capital and its subsequent accumulation introduce a qualitative difference between them and large businesses. As a consequence, micro-enterprises grow horizontally while large businesses have the prospect of vertical growth before them.

Dependency school in the Marxist tradition uses the terms core capitalism and peripheral capitalism respectively in place of the terms mature and early capitalism referred to above. Its insight is that growth is not linear and unidirectional facilitating automatic development of early capitalism into mature capitalism. Relationship between peripheral and core capitalism is more complex as they belong to a hierarchical order.

Looking at the information collected in this survey, it can be said that the Factories Act and the accompanying labour laws constitute the watershed between the two perspectives. They also constitute the demarcation line between the higher and lower circuit approach to resource-use mentioned earlier in this chapter. Diagrammatically:

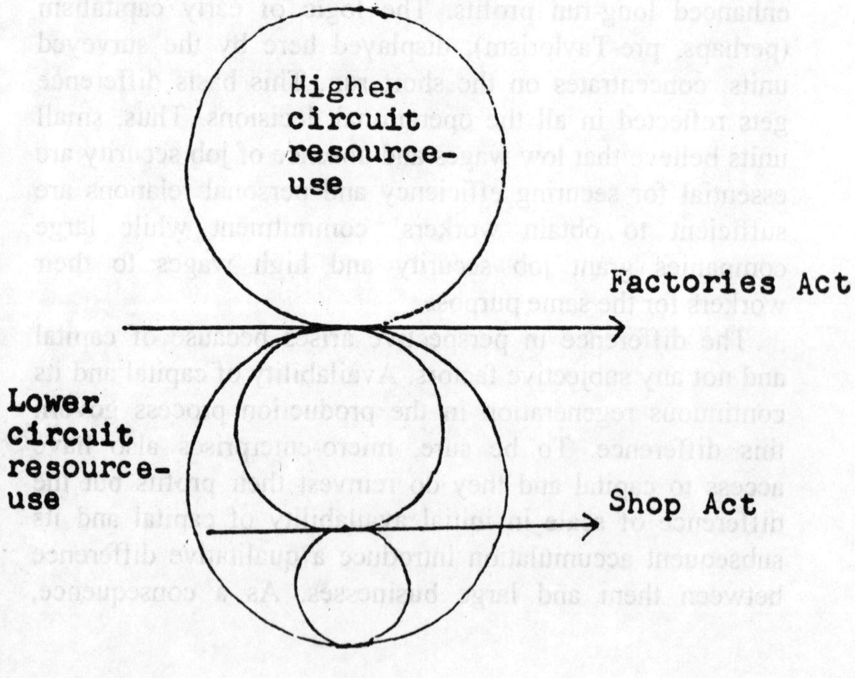

The Shop Act also constitutes an important point of departure but since it does not attract other labour laws and since its implementation is less stringent it is probably not viewed as a great barrier. (We understood that it was common practice among surveyed units, particularly non-shop Act units to come together and approach the shop inspectors unofficially 'to persuade' them not to visit the units at all.) The non-Shop Act units in this survey had consciously decided to grow horizontally so as to retain the advantages offered by non-registration. Among the Shop Act units, independent manufacturers had realized that their prospects for vertical growth were limited. As such, the eventuality of crossing the barrier did not figure much in their thinking. Some job-workers viewed the prospect with equanimity because they were simultaneously experiencing the pressure to cope up with the growing volume of work offloaded by parent companies.

7.2 Subcontracting Polices of Large Companies

Subcontracting policies of large companies become relevant here. Some do not directly deal with small units that are not covered under the Factories Act. They maintain that these units do not have the minimum stability or where withal required to undertake large-scale and continuous work. At the same time, they disregard the considerable down stream subcontracting links their own sub-contractors develop over time. Their policy therefore, amounts to an avoidance of any direct linkage with the lower circuit units. Actually, given the hierarchy of organization forms in the market and the down-stream putting out linkage from the higher to the lower form, the formal and informal sectors have been firmly integrated today.

Other companies encourage their ancillary units to take advantage of various loopholes in the existing laws. For instance, one Shop Act unit engaged in both job-work and independent manufacture of engineering products has taken the decision to grow horizontally at the behest of its major parent company. This company's officials advised the entrepreneur to locate his new units outside municipal limits so as to save octroi. There were other instances where large companies had encouraged their employees to seek self-employment on the basis of assured job-work from the employers along with a suggested course of action to take care of the initial stage. On the whole, therefore, it can be said that large companies in the formal sector are consciously using the lower circuit resource use pattern through sub-contracting.

Relations between large companies and their subcontractors are, of course, complicated. There are entrepreneurs who have been helped to cross the divide and to enter the higher circuit. The pressure and the work-load involved in the process has been 'killing' according to one entrepreneur. His unit had recently been covered under the Factories Act and, therefore, information about it could not be included in the survey. This entrepreneur complained of the very elaborate costing and documentation system that he had been required to install. The system left him with little time to attend to production and related matters. He spoke very warmly about the parent company but pointed out that it took a very long time to grant rate increases to its vendors.

Parent-ancillary business relations hinge upon three factors, viz. (1) job guarantee, (2) rate increases, and (3) timely delayed payment of bills of suppliers can be a significant source of working capital for the parent companies. The surveyed units made their supplies against a credit period of 90 to 120 day. Their experience was that larger companies were reasonably prompt about payment, while medium-size companies delayed them. One entrepreneur recalled how concerted pressure by all suppliers had been necessary to make one very large engineering company in Pune prompt and regular in its payment schedule. One job-work unit-owner saw a 'caste' pattern in the payment politics of parent companies. His contention was that Marwari businesses released payment more promptly to Marwari sub-contractors, Maharashtrians (Kirloskars) to Maharashtrian sub-contractors and so on.

Parent companies were willing to provide a reasonable assurance about work in the foreseeable future, subject to the supplier's performance regarding quality and delivery. Given the low-technology nature of most of the offloaded work, quality was not a very important factor. Some parent companies had started zero inspection policy with a stringent provision that a defaulting supplier could be blacklisted. Timely delivery was far more important to the parent companies. The relationship between the parent companies and sub-contractors was such that the latter could not insist on any 'guarantee' of job. They had to be content with the work given to them. Large companies did not want to commit themselves in this regard. At the time of carrying out this survey, the engineering job-work units were coping with the problem of excessive workload. Some entrepreneurs had memories of recessionary conditions in the past but they did not have time to dwell on them.

Parent companies also did not want to rely exclusively on one supplier. They developed a number of suppliers simultaneously and wanted to allocate their requirements among all of them depending upon their performance. The sub-contractors could do nothing about this arrangement but in private they expressed very vehement opposition to this usurpation of the role of the market by large companies. 'They foist competition on us so that we are never free from pressure' said one entrepreneur. Job guarantee by large companies thus meant assurance about future work with the following constraints :

- only in the short run. Cyclical market fluctuations were not even mentioned since subcontracting's major advantage lay in flexibility,
- not allowing monopoly to develop,
- appraisal of suppliers' performance with regard to delivery and quality.

Rate increase turned out to be Achilles' heel of subcontracting transactions. All the job-workers in the survey unanimously complained that parent companies were not willing to grant rate increases. They asked for detailed cost breakup before agreeing to any rates and were said to exercise tight control over the rates once granted. When they did increase the rates, the time gap was though to be very long with no prospects for recovering the losses sustained in the meantime. Officers of parent companies agreed that this happened. They candidly informed us that when confronted with a demand for rate increase from the subcontractors, their response was guided by the policy, "squeeze them further; they will come round". They justified this practice by pointing out that small units lacked any mechanism whereby continuous improvement in productivity could be registered by them. Pressure of parent companies was thought necessary to keep them on their toes. Without it, they would become slothful, it was felt.

A few large companies had separate vendor/ancillary development departments. They carried out the work of providing technical know-how, inspection and quality control dependable suppliers who adhered to the delivery schedules given to them. At times, specialized machinery and inspection equipment – particularly if they were written off in the parent company's books – were also provided to the subcontractors. Once the sub-contracting unit overcame teething trouble and got stabilized, the subcontracting relationship had become established. Large companies wanted to keep only critical component-making and assembly work with themselves and offload the rest progressively. This policy was necessary to release resource into new, diversified areas and to gain flexibility in case of old, established products. The principle that standardized and generic functions are more efficiently performed by the market as compared to in house production in the hierarchy was fully understood and practiced by the parent companies (Williamson, 1981). Subcontracting thus helped them to reduce their cost, use greater specialization and become more effective in the market.

Only in a few companies, detailed cost-benefit analysis of offloading had been carried out initially. Since the price of bought-out components was found to be at lest 50 per cent less than the cost of in-house manufacture, cost-benefit analysis was deemed unnecessary. Each company has developed some rules of thumb in this regard. The cost of initial development effort was not usually calculated by these companies. If it were to be amortized and if the cost of equipment were to be taken into account (unless it were zero) then the difference between outside price and in-house cost would naturally come down but the difference was still expected to be substantial, if not overwhelming. In a few cases outside price was thought to be higher but offloading was continued because the opportunity cost (and not historical cost) of parent companies resources was judged to be higher.

Officials of parent companies in the engineering industry unanimously indicated that more and more operations would be progressively subcontracted and only a few, critical operations would be retained by them. Given the low wages, low overheads and the resultant lower operational cost in the ancillary units, this would be a sensible course of action for the parent companies. According to them, it will, however, be wrong to link subcontracting policies of large companies exclusively with the lower circuit resource use of the small ancillary units.

Subcontracting offers a number of advantages to the parent companies. They are:

1. If the production process comprised some capital intensive and some labour intensive operations then putting out labour intensive operations to another unit with lower unit labour costs results in more fruitful use of plant and machinery of the parent company.
2. This putting out also reduces the burden on management wherever the produce process is very elaborate
3. When there exists a mismatch between the technically efficient scales of different processes, subcontracting is advantages.
4. Because of subcontracting it is possible to switch resources from investment in plant and machinery and other infrastructure to research and development, marketing, brand building, etc.
5. Subcontracting reduced the cost and risk of entry into a new filed.
6. It releases working capital by reducing investment in inventories.

7. To the extent, subcontractors have personal relations with their workers, risk of disruption in work due to labour unrest can be avoided.

These advantages are in addition to the usual ones, viz. lowering cost of production and gaining flexibility. (The latter is possible since subcontracting enables a company to produce without creating its own production capacity or to produce in excess of installed capacity.)

Theoretically, in the product market, operational division of labour is expected to enhance efficiency. Whenever the hierarchy and the market exist side-by-side and the same operations are carried out in both, operational cost considerations favour the market while transactions cost considerations favour the hierarchy. Innovations, technology and dynamic changes in the market affect these costs. For examples, technical progress lowers transactions costs ad so favours the market. So impersonal services are performed more and more in the market. Thus hierarchies are engaged in a continuous learning process to lower their total cost through an up-to-date make or buy decision. Then the formation of job-shop unit which specializes in a particular operation and performs it for any customer in any industry will reduce the unit cost and thus promote efficiency. Subcontracting policies of large companies also try to find out and nurture such units. Mutually beneficial partnership is possible only between these customers and suppliers.

The job-work units covered in our survey were basically different from such units which have the potential to develop into specialized job-shops serving the market. Units surveyed by us were like poor artisan units. They were dependent on a limited number of parent companies; had access to very elementary technology; had little information about market developments (save what was happening in the parent companies) and they had severely limited scope for upgrading their skills. Emergence of a modern, efficient job-shop was bound to make them unemployed. The relationship between large parent companies and their small, artisan-like ancillary units hence resulted in a one-way flow of benefits to the former.

According to Nigel Crook (1993), greater use of subcontracting and contract labour is a global strategy of capitalists, worked out in the mid-1970s to lower costs and to counter the strength of organized labour. The extent of sub-contracting and with it the integration of FS and IS is an hierarchical mode can thus be expected to be accentuated in the Indian economy in future.

To find out the extent of savings made by parent companies through subcontracting, some rough calculations were made by us. The procedure adopted is as below:

Four large companies in Pune Metropolitan Region, viz. Kirloskar Cummins Ltd., Bharat Forge Ltd., Bajaj Auto Ltd. and Miroloskar Oil Engines Ltd., were chosen. These were the major parent companies of the surveyed job-work units. TELCO was also a major parent company but it was not included because, from its published reports, it was not possible to get information about only its Pune plant.

The above four companies bought materials and components worth Rs. 1,22,207.64 lakh in the financial year 1003-94. The purchase manager of TELCO was of the opinion that material purchases from small sector units formed 5 to 10 per cent of the total purchases in the ordinary course. This was supported by an old RBI study which had found that this proportion was 9 per cent (RBI Study Committee on the problem of payment of bills by large and medium industries to small enterprises, 1971, RBI Bulletin Supplement, 1972). It was, therefore, assumed that the large companies bought materials worth Rs. 9165.57 lakh from small units. On the basis of our survey, we had developed a cost profit of the engineering job-work units. Assuming that the cost profile of small scale units in general was the same as that of the surveyed units, total cost to small units for a sales volume of Rs. 9165.57 lakh @ 70.97 per cent came to Rs. 6504.81 lakh. As per our estimate this total cost comprised the following :

Per cent to turnover		Amount in Rs. lakhs
50.70	Material cost+sub-Contracting charges	4646.95
10.19	Wages and salaries	933.97
5.47	Overheads	501.36
3.23	Depreciation	296.05
1.38	Interest	126.48
70.97		6504.81

(a) In the survey it has been established that the annual wage of a worker in a micro-enterprise was Rs. 19,062. Total expenditure of Rs. 933.97 lakh on wages and salaries at Rs. 19,062 per person per annum represented 4900 man-years of work. It was assumed that annual wage of a worker in these companies was 3.5 times that in micro-enterprises. It was, in other words, Rs. 66,717 per annum. At this wage rate, 4900 man-years mean a wage bill of Rs. 3269.13 lakh. (It is assumed that large companies will take the same number of man-years for if they were to engage in in-house manufacture.) If the large companies were to make the bought-out components in-house, their wage bill would have been Rs. 3269.13 lakh whereas it was Rs. 933.97 lakh in the micro-enterprises. This meant a saving of Rs. 2335.16 lakh.

(b) From the balance-sheets of the four large companies for the year 1993-94 it was calculated that their overheads were 2.12 times their employees emoluments. Thus, the overheads in large companies would have amounted to Rs. 6930.56 lakh (Rs. 3269.13 lakh × 2.12). Overheads in micro-enterprises have been Rs. 501.36 lakh, yielding a saving of Rs. 6429.2 lakh.

(c) The large companies bought materials on a credit period of 3 to 4 months. The small units found it difficult to get trade for their own purchases. The interest earned by large companies on this credit amounts to Rs. 366.62 lakh.

[Rs. 9165.57 lakh x 3 months x 16 rate of interest]
(Purchases from 12 months ˙100
Small units)

The combined saving : A+ B+ C =

Rs. 2335.16 lakh (wages)
Rs. 6429.20 lakh (overheads)
Rs. 366.62 lakh (interest)
Rs. 9130.98 lakh

Operating profits (profit before tax) of the four large companies amount to Rs. 33953.27 lakh in the year 1993-94. The above saving amounts to 26.9 per cent of the operating profit of these companies.

The above calculations are of a rough nature but they do show the magnitude of the cost savings that are possible through sub-contracting. Sub-contracting is, thus, a very profitable proposition for the large companies.

7.3 Entry and Growth Prospects

It has been observed above that some large companies encouraged their employees to set up small units and to start supplying components to them on a sub-contract basis. The strong advocacy of self-employment by the government also has its effect and the result is that being one's own master in a small production unit appears to be an attractive proposition. In the survey, 13 of the 24 entrepreneurs in the engineering industry had previous wage-employment experience. All of them could be said to have been influenced by these two factors. The lower circuit approach to registration means lower resource commitment. Entry into micro-enterprises must, therefore, be said to be easy and, indeed, is actively promoted.

Only later probably do the entrepreneurs realize the grim reality of an hierarchical order that lies behind the façade of competitive capitalism. Either as small independent manufacturers or as job-workers the entrepreneurs find them-selves encumbered on all sides. There is a constant struggle to overcome problems regarding stability in production, getting skilled workers, establishing a foothold in the market, etc., The units learn to survive while taking care of these problems. Four of the surveyed units had experienced major production stoppages leading to temporary closing down of the units. Two of these units had allegedly faced labour trouble, on had experienced in-fighting between partners and one lack of demand. One of the entrepreneurs who had closed down hi unit due to labour trouble said that the was disgusted after he found that the South Indian – Keralite – workers were cheating on him. He closed his unit and went to the UK. He returned after some time and made a fresh start. This time he consciously chose the lower circuit resource use pattern and has prospered since. Today he has taken other younger entrepreneurs under his wings and can be seen dispensing advice about the do's and don'ts of the formative stage.

Barring these four units, other units in the survey did not experience closure. Thus, micro-enterprises face problems continuously but these problems do not lead to closure in normal circumstances.

The independent manufactures covered in this survey had become weary because of their experience with the market mechanism. Some had even lost the will to continue although they had to keep going. A few had become disenchanted because their sons were not willing to continue. All of them agreed tacitly that vertical growth was out of their reach. Job-work units were more confident in comparison but their fortunes had got linked with those of their parent companies.

7.4 Dual Labour Force

At the time of conducting the survey, it was though that hired workers in informal enterprises would represent an undifferentiated mass of labour. Because of negligible skills possessed by these workers, employers, it was thought, would have no incentive to retain them in enterprises and so mobility among these workers would be very high.

Information collected during the survey revealed that the above conditions applied primarily to women workers. Employers attached no importance to the skills embodied in women workers by virtue of experience and seniority. They instead wanted a fast turnover so that younger and more educated workers could be recruited. This had a dual advantage from the point of view of the employers. Firstly, smarter workers would be available without any efforts of the employers, thanks to the rising educational level in urban areas. Secondly older workers could be denied benefits such as wage hike and other perquisites that normally accrue with seniority.

Since total replacement of the old workforce by new workers is not possible at a point of time, workforce would always comprise some older and some junior worker. Employers made use of this mix to their advantage. Older workers were portrayed as inefficient, quarrelsome workers and new workers were individually promised better treatment if they performed better and if they did not become demanding like the older workers. When the new workers succumbed to this or tried to obtain job security by working were beaten. These tactics also resulted in a festering suspicion at the place of work and kept individual workers apart from each other.

In the case of the male workers surveyed here, instead of an undifferentiated mass of labour, a dual labour force could be seen in its formation. The casual, unskilled workers who got very low wages comprised the second, lower tier of the workforce in micro-enterprises. Except pressing economic necessity, they had no other incentive to hold on to their jobs nor did their employers expect them to stay around for long. They were expected to quit any moment and so very impersonal relations between the lower tier workers and employers could be seen. Fast turnover and frequent absenteeism were the problems mentioned in case of casual workers.

The upper tier comprised older, skilled workers. Their skills were formed while working on the job. They could be regarded, at best, as semi-skilled workers by the standards of large formal firms. At the same time their skills were considered crucial for continuing operations. Hence employers had an incentive in retaining these workers. They drew higher wages – a little less than the minimum wage – as compared to casual workers but their commitment to the job appeared to have been based on personal relations with the employers. Because of long standing relations with the employers, these workers considered themselves to be secure in their jobs. What strengthened this belief was the shortage of trained workers observed in these micro-enterprises. Personal relations with the employers and the feeling of loyalty following from them were the factors mostly used by employers in retaining these skilled workers. At the same time, the fear of these workers setting up their own operations and becoming competitors was ever-present in the minds of the employers. Keeping the workers insulated from the commercial and financial operations was the only way to guard against this danger.

Workers in micro-enterprises, therefore, on the whole, do not constitute an undifferentiated mass. What we observed made us painfully aware of the many divisions among workers. As Nirmala banerjee (1991) has observed : "Employer's strategies are obviously designed to divide the workforce into as many fragments as possible : men-women, factory-home-based workers, regular-casual workers. Each fragment is treated differentially. Each groups is isolated from other groups and made to fell weaker. Limitations are placed on opportunities of work available labour cost is minimised. Militancy of workforce is also reduced in the face of sudden and frequent closures, irregular working hours and cuts in wages."

Most of the entrepreneurs of the surveyed units had indicated that difficulties connected with the labour market were the most substantive difficulties faced by them. "Skilled workers were simply not willing to work in small-scale industries," lamented one entrepreneur. "All ITI-trained workers have their sights firmly fixed on Telco and Bajaj," added another. One entrepreneur in charge of a non-Shop Act unit at Hadapsar complained that he was unable to get a skilled supervisor; otherwise he would have started second shift and doubled his output. Employers also felt that bigger companies had distorted the market by offering very high wages to their workers, thus reducing the supply of labour for micro-enterprises.

To overcome this problem, the entrepreneurs had to accept such unskilled workers as were available. These workers picked up trade over a period of time. The process whereby a raw worker was converted into a semi-skilled one was a long one during which the employers constantly watched the workers and finally chose a few as being eligible for their trust. The latter enjoyed higher wages and probably also job security. These were denied to the raw workers. Because of this stratification, all jobs in micro-enterprises cannot be regarded as easy-entry jobs. For this reason, it is also not possible to maintain that hired workers in micro-enterprises have flat age-wise earning profits. The statement is broadly true in the sense that seniority and job-workers' earnings. At the same time, it is not entirely true due to the presence of some experienced and loyal workers who earn a little more.

In large, formal firms there exists an elaborate division of labour which offers a promotion ladder to the workers, Upward progress along the ladder can be fairly smooth at least upto a point. In micro-enterprises there are only two categories and hence naturally a jump from the lower to the higher grade is an important even – both from the point of view of the concerned worker and the employer. It appeared to us that the dependability or reliability of the worker for the employer governed the logic o this upgradation.

7.5 Conclusion

The major conclusions that can be drawn from the survey are as follows:

1. Registration status is a major issue for informal manufacturing units. Several registrations exist for manufacturing units and informal units have a selective approach to them. Registrations which do not have recurring cost implications and which do not involve continuous monitoring are opted for. The Indian Factories Act, 1948, is the most created legislation and informal manufacturing units stay away from it. This simultaneously exempts them from a number of Acts giving social security to workers. A policy of horizontal growth by starting new units is consciously followed by nearly half of the surveyed units in order to avoid this Act.

   The Maharashtra Shops and Establishments rules, 1961, popularly known as Shop Act constitutes another level of registration. Input use in non-Shop Act units and Shop Act, non-Factory Act units is clearly different with the former constituting slum industrial units with the lowest possible cost of production.

2. Surveyed units used substantial downstream subcontracting to reduce their costs, to avoid the commitment of fixed resources and to improve their capacity utilization.

3. Although a systematic observation of Factories Act units and their comparison with surveyed units was not undertaken, casual observation suggested that surveyed units

- used less space,
- paid lower wages to their workers while simultaneously making them work for more than 8 hours a day,
- used locally available and lower quality materials, and,
- made extensive use of second-hand/self-fabricated/self-modified machinery.

4. The monthly wage of women workers covered in the survey was found to be Rs. 1206. Male workers earned Rs. 1589 per month which was less than the minimum wage for engineering industry. These wages were inclusive of Diwali bonus which was the only additional benefit that was received by a majority of workers. Except in electronic units, many of the surveyed workers were working for more than the standard 208 hours (26 days × 8 hours per day) per month.
5. Instead of an undifferentiated mass, a dual labour force could be observed in the surveyed units. Experienced, skilled workers (skill formation was mostly on-the-job) were in short-supply and employers wanted to retain them. Unskilled, casual workers were treated as temporary workers and employers expected them to quite their jobs any moment. Women workers were more likely to be treated as casual workers. Employers actively differentiated among their workers so as to divide them and keep them at each other's throats. Instead of retention, employers preferred brisk turnover among casuals and women workers so as to keep wage down.
6. The advantages of subcontracting were so many and the cost differential between in-house production and offloading was so much that large companies did not even carry out a cost-benefit analysis of the offloading decision. Time taken for payment of bills, rate increase and job guarantee were the crucial parameters of parent company-subcontractor relationship. Al least two/three sources of supply were developed by parent companies so as to avoid dependence and to keep up pressure on subcontractors. Subcontracting integrates FS and IS and goes against the idea of functional autonomy of IS.

7. Entry into a manufacturing activity is not easy. Within IS also, manufacturing activities are at the top of the hierarchy. So entry is not easy. Family background, technical experience are important factors determining entry. Yet, "Entry is not difficult in our field, survival is" said one independent manufacturer and he appeared to echo the general sentiment in this regard. The preferred point of entry was experience of wage-employment in FS. Large companies encouraged their wage-workers to become self-employed. It could also be said that FS firms encouraged competition among IS firms. Thus wage-workers in FS and owners of manufacturing units in IS were found to be functionally close together. Within IS, however, employers dreaded the prospect of their skilled workers leaving them and becoming rivals.
8. Overall productivity in surveyed units was found to be high. However, its implications were : low wages and long hours of work for labour and limited availability and low quality of capital.

Chapter 8

Earnings and Economic Conditions of Informal Sector Service Workers in Pune

In this chapter, we propose to take a closer look at some other categories of informal workers. These workers are much lower in the occupational ladder of IS as compared to workers in small workshop about whom information has already been presented. The information presented below is based on secondary sources and a few field trips with concerned activists. These activists are trying to organize informal workers in order to improve their conditions. In the last section of this chapter a temporal comparison of their earnings is attempted. Information about the following types of workers is presented below:

1. Load-bearers
2. Sweepers and scavengers
3. Domestic servants
4. Rag-pickers
5. Bidi-workers
6. Child labour
7. Vendors of second-hand tins and bottles
8. Other home-based workers
9. Construction labour.

8.1 Load-bearers for 'Hamals'

As per the 1981 Census (Occupational Classification of Workers) there were 12696 materials handling, equipment operators, loaders and unloaders in Pune district-urban (NCO, 1968, Divisions 7-8-9, group 97). There were 11702 male materials handlers and 994 women. Activists of 'Hamal Panchayat', an innovative union of these workers in

Pune, have estimate the number of load-bearers in Pune in 1996 to be around 10000-11000. This was, according to them, the figure of load-bearers registered with Pune 'Mathadi' Board. Out of them, around 4000 hamals were members of Hamal Panchayat (HP).

HP was established in 1955 and it had to struggle continuously till 1970 to make its voice heard. Today it has reached a position where merchants in foodgrain, vegetables and timber market cannot hire or fire hamals without its permission. It has managed to get rid of intermediaries between merchants and hamals. It has ensured that new entrants join the trade through its offices only. Merchants approach HP whenever they need hamals. HP and they work out how many hamals would be needed taking into account various factors such as types of work, distance to be covered work already in process, 'badli' (alternate) hamals available, etc. Rates for different types of work have been fixed and HP also negotiates periodically with merchants' association for a hike in rates. New comers – mostly migrants from rural areas – who wish to join this occupation, have to apply to HP and depending upon the availability of work, work is provided to them.

HP has struggled valiantly to reach this position. Many strikes, hardships and continuous efforts to provide social to members and to improve their quality of life have enabled it to unite members on a very low rung of IS and to regulate entry into load-bearing work.

HP runs a nutritious meals centre which provides cooked food every day to the needy through its twelve distribution centres. While sufficient work is not available to HP members the year round, this activity is able to provide regular employment to around 100 persons- mostly women ! HP also provides medical facilities to its members at affordable rates, school books to their children and a quick lump sum assistance to family members in the event of accident/death of members. It was formed a housing colony of hamals on land provided by government. A cooperative society has also been formed to accept contracts of load-bearing work from government. HP has made a lot of efforts to create political awareness among its members and to build bridges with other sections of the toiling masses. It has started organizing rag-pickers, rickshaw drivers, footpath vendors, etc.

In economic terms, however, HP's contribution has been circumscribed because it has been unable to find a solution to one basic problem of all unprotected workers, viz. lack of sufficient work opportunities.

Almost every hamal is forced to wait for work and stay idle. This period of forced idleness varies depending upon the type of goods handled. In the vegetable market, work slack was reported for 4 to 5 months every year. In timber and tiles trade, work not available for 5 to 15 days in a month. Hamals working at the railway loading, unloading shed ('maldhaka') had virtually no work available during the rainy season. Women hamals could find work for at the most 15 to 20 days in a month. Forced idleness was comparative less in handling tea, chemicals, iron and steel products, etc.

A sample survey of the working, living conditions and incomes of 220 HP members and their families was made in 1984-85. The survey calculated that the average monthly income of hamal families was Rs. 640. After cross-checking it with the records of Mathdai (head-loaders) Board it was scaled down to Rs. 515. Yet 168 out of 220 families surveyed (76 per cent) reported a monthly income of less than Rs. 500. On the basis of the information available with the Board, the study stated that 52 per cent of the hamals earned less than Rs. 500 p.m. Thus 50 per cent of HP members – 1500 hamals – earned less than Rs. 500 p.m. Hamals who were not members of HP must have earned less. Out of 220 hamales, 82 (37 per cent) reported that there were two or more earning members in their families. This is in conformity with the observed inverse relationship between per capita income and labour force participation rate in a family. Lack of adequate work was hamals' main problem and HP could not do anything about it.

According to a very rough estimates, a porter who was a member of HP earned Rs. 1,700 in a month in 1996. This figure has been worked out assuming that the works for 20 days in a month at Rs. 85 per day.

8.1.1 Hamal Women in Pune

Unlike male hamals who carry sacks and gunny bags on their backs, hamal women are head-loaders and they work in different localities in Pune, e.g. Bhavani Peth (foodgrain market), Mandai/Gultekdi (vegetable and fruit markets), Timber Market, Maldhakka (railway goods yard), Shivajinagar (government foodgrain godown), etc. Some of them carry out the work of stitching gunny bags at Somwar Peth. Lack of sufficient work and very low earnings when it is available are their main economic problems. In 1976, their average daily earnings were Rs. 2 or less. There was some fluctuation in earnings depending upon location and type of work. For example, in the foodgrain market, they earned around Rs. 3 during the busy season. (This work was handled by Maratha women who had formed a close-knit group which effectively restricted entry. Also this type of work-handling grains- was not available to Scheduled Caste women.) In the vegetable market, hamal women were either attached as regular workers to particular merchants or were casual workers. The former earned Rs. 2 per day and the latter Rs. 1.80 per day. Stiff resistance of organized merchants in the vegetable market meant that these workers could not be organized. Women hamals in the timber market represented the absolute border line between the lowest rung of unskilled work in cities and destitution. Availability of work and rate or earnings were both so poor here that it was not necessary to restrict entry.

At Maldhakka, all women hamals were members of HP and since 1970, HP has secured exclusive rights to unload coal. So there is some stability but the problem m of under-employment and seasonal fluctuations persists. At the government godown in Shivajinagar, a cooperative society has been formed to secure and distribute the work of unloading and arranging sacks of foodgrains. Sweeping and mending torn bags was another job that these women did. These women constituted a privileged group, each earning Rs. 250 p.m. along with the facilities of interest-free loans and maternity leave. In gunny bag stitching work at Somwar Peth, women could earn upto Rs. 4 in a day at the availability of work was very poor.

8.2 Sweepers and Scavengers

Table 8.2 that follows shows that only this group of workers has been able to register an improvement in earnings from 1958 to 1996. The sweepers employed by Pune Municipal Corporation (PMC) belong to Poona Municipal Workers' Union established in December 1943. The union today has around 8,000 members, 5,000 of whom hold permanent jobs with the rest being employed on a casual basis.

As per 1981 Census there were 4,773 male building contractors, sweepers, cleaners and related workers and 3,

527 female workers in Pune district-urban (NCO, 1968 – division 5, groups 54). This is the total number, whereas the figure given by the union relates only to municipal sweepers but for the year 1997.

In 1958 the average monthly earnings of sweepers were Rs. 61. They started working in the salary scale of Rs. 30-1/2-35 in PMC and were made permanent after 3 years of service. Today the starting salary of sweepers is Rs. 793 p.m. or Rs. 8C5 (basic), including scavenging allowance. Those who work in casual capacity average Rs. 52 per day. The casual sweepers work on a casual basis. The latter are able to work for no more than 5 or 6 days a month. There are many casual who are working for years as casuals. Legally, a casual ought to be made permanent after 240 days of work but the union has to struggle on a case-to-case basis for securing permanence. Break in service proves to be a contentious issue.

On an average a permanent sweeper earns Rs. 2,750 p.m. approximately (Table 8.2). There is some variation in earnings depending on years of service and type of work. Permanent sweepers are entitled to paid leave and provident fund facility. They also get an annual bonus along with the other municipal workers plus 'bakshis' for which the union negotiates separately with PMC once in three years.

8.3 Domestic Servants or 'Molkareeni'

As per the 1981 Census, there were 10,220 domestic maids in Pune district-urban, comprising 1,011 males and 9,209 females. Activists who are trying to organize these workers place the current number at around 30,000. According to them, there were cases of young women who worked in factories nearby but now preferred this work because of the high costs of commuting from the city to the outlying industrial areas. This amounts to a considerable lowering of status because of the domestic context of work and personalized relations which surround domestic work. Unlike in Mumbai, there are few male domestic servants in Pune.

'Molkareen Sanghatana', attached to the Poona Municipal Workers' Union is trying to organize domestic servants in Pune 'Molkareen Sanghatana' was established in 1980. Today it has approximately 5,000 member. Every time the union gives a strike-call an agitation, there is a temporary surge in its membership. Thus it claims that about 8,000 domestic servants supported the strike that was declared in 1995. The union is strong in certain localities such as Deccan Gymkhana, Karve Road, Narayan, Shaniwar and Sadashiv Peths, etc. Else-where it does not have much influence. In posh localities of Koregaon Park, Camp, Aundh, Pashan, etc., domestic servants command a higher fee but there is little unionization. In the expanding suburban areas, charges are much lower.

Full-time domestic servants attached to particular households have now become an extinct breed. Part-time domestic help has become the norm. In Maharashtrian families, employment of a maid-servant is one indicator of upward mobility or of a family's graduation from working into middle class. Should a Maharashtrian middle class family fall onto bad times, the first means of exercising economy is to fire the maid and the lady of the house then takes over the menial work of washing utensils, clothes, sweeping and mopping the floor, etc. In non-Maharashtrian families, requirement of domestic help is much greater. Muslim middle class families and Bohra Muslims rely on domestic servants to a much greater extent. Same is the case with Sindhi, Punjabi families.

Personal factors such as the employer and the maid having the same religious background, knowing each other and getting along, knowing each other for a long time, etc., are important matters in this line and therefore entry is not free, nor is the option of more work, more earnings easily available. (In case of a tiff between an employer and the servant, the servant does not allow anyone else to take up that work). In the early 1980s, Molkareen Sanghatana had raised an important issue, viz. whether this work would die out in the course of economic development in developed countries or whether it would continue to exist thanks to the labour surplus in IS. It is not possible to give a clear-cut answer to this question but in all probability, domestic servants, like the rest of IS would remain forever!

Domestic servants normally begin their work at 8 a.m., finish it by 2 p.m. and return home to attend to their own household duties. Working for 6 to 8 hours every day is the norm and for these hours, they earn on an average Rs. 700 per month. Sanghatana activities maintained that by working longer and by staying attached to particular families, some workers earn upto Rs. 2,000 per month also. Along with a wage in cash, in-kind earnings, e.g. tea, sometimes breakfast, taking cooked left-over and old clothes home, over-drawing the wage, occasionally borrowing money, also exist but individual practices vary and there is little uniformity.

Molkareen Sanghatana has worked out the following schedule of rates for different types of work performed by maids:

Type of Work	Amount per head in Employing family (Rs. p.m.)
1. Cleaning Utensils	30
2. Washing clothes	30
3. Sweeping, dusting and	30 (per room)

4. Making chapatis 200 (per kg.)
5. Cooking 112.50

Apart from a hike in wages on the above lines, Sanghatana has demanded bonus, gratuity and paid leave for its members. The demand for one month's wage as bonus was made in 1980 and some resistance apart, it was met rather easily. The demand for paid leave and gratuity has proved to be much more difficult.

Because of fluctuations in wages of these workers in different localities and because of the limited influence of the union, we have assumed that all domestic servants in Pune earn Rs. 500 p.m., in spite of the figure of Rs. 700 p.m. quoted by union workers.

8.4 Rag-pickers

Rag-picking is regarded as the last resort activity in modern urban economics. Early economic surveys (1936 and 1954) do not make any mention of this activity. It is a new activity, an offshoot of the prevalent industrialization and urbanization pattern.

In occupational classifications of workers in 1981 Census also there was no separate mention of rag-pickers. They must have been put in Division 7-8-9, groups 99-labourers not elsewhere classified. There were as many as 24,229 such workers, 19,661 males and 4,568 females. Hamal Panchayat is trying to organize these workers. Its activists estimate that between 8,000 and 10,000 persons are currently in Pune in rag-picking and garbage recycling.

Two independent activists, late Group Captain Oak and Manisha Paranjape have studies the problem of garbage collection in Pune in detail. According to them, each day 1,000 tonnes of garbage are generated in Pune city: 80 per cent of it according to HP activists and 60 per cent according to Oak, i.e. between 800 and 600 tonnes of its are collected by local authorities and the rest, 200 to 400 tonnes, are handled by the rag-pickers. HP activists place this figure at 250 tonnes, which is mind-boggling.

They maintain that a rag-picker processes about 30 kgs of garbage every day and daily covers the distance of 5 to 10 kms while searching for it. Collection of garbage varies from locality to locality. Garbage bins in commercial and industrial areas yield a richer haul as compared to residential areas but entry to these 'beats' is not open. These rag-pickers can earn upto Rs. 100 every day but elsewhere earnings can drop to Rs. 5 a day also. At this lower end, entry is free. Collected waste is classified first as dry and wet waste and dry waste is further sorted into 13 different items ranging from rags, glass, plastic tin to paper. Sorted garbage is sold to merchants. Every slum has shops which buy sorted waste. The maximum number of these shops can be found at Dandekar bridge slum area in Pune.

Because of modern lifestyles and consumerism in urban areas, plenty of waste is generated and garbage recycling is one activity where there is no shortage of work. It is also an open-entry activity, as mentioned above. However, there are several cultural constraints because of which poor people resist the pressure of becoming rag-pickers. Men consider it below their status. It is also considered unsafe for young girls of marriageable age. Their chances of getting married are reduced if they engage in this work. Rag-picking women narrate that the moment the work becomes more organized and takes the form of removing garbage from housing societies or offices, their husbands become willing to carry it out.

Rag-pickers' main complaints are : lack of recognition of their contribution in waste management, harassment from local authorities or their contractors' workers. Severe health hazards, cheating by merchants, etc. Merchants who buy waste from them cheat them in recording the weight and they do not issue any receipts under the pretext of avoiding sales tax.

HP has started a separate union for organizing these waste-collectors. It has managed to reach out to nearly 4,500 or half of these workers in Pune. The union is yet to formulate economic demands. It is struggling to get recognition for the work done by its members. "Garbage belongs to us and not to anybody else" is a slogan made by it. Recently, it succeeded in getting identity cards for its members from the Pune Municipal Corporation (PMC). These cards are important because they serve two purposes: less harassment from PMC staff at garbage bins and access to free medical facilities provided by the municipality.

Because shopkeepers cheat rag-pickers, the union has started its own shop on a cooperative basis. Rag-pickers themselves are joint owners of this shop. It keeps proper records and issues receipts for all its purchases. It earned a profit of Rs. 25,000 right in the first year of working. Now each month, the earned profit is distributed among members. However, earning profit is not the union's objective. It wants to bring pressure on other shopkeepers through this endeavour. It sees the shop as its first step in a long journey to bring some regulation in the totally unregulated waste recycling industry. It has also started a saving group among its members.

Activists drew our attention to some adverse developments in their field. There is a move in posh housing colonies to appoint private contractors for collecting garbage and disposing of it either directly at the big municipal dumping ground located far away or by burning it. Supply of waste to nearby garbage bins would then be reduced. City beautification plans often envisage the elimination of garbage dumps without sparing a thought for the survival of those who eke out a living from these dumps. Pune's rag-pickers have even resorted to a 'chipko' agitation to ensure that garbage bins are not removed from particular points. The union has also demanded that the government should impose some restrictions on import of plastic and other waste in order to curb wide fluctuations in their prices as seen today.

8.5 'Bidi' Workers

As per the 1981 Census, there were 2,251 tobacco and tobacco product preparers in Pune district-urban (306 male workers and 1,945 female). These were perhaps only the factory workers in the tobacco industry. The number of out-workers (to whom the work of rolling bidis is put out) in this industry is much larger as compared to factory workers and most of these out-workers are women. Activists estimate that the present strength of all tobacco workers ranges anywhere between 12,000 and 25,000.

Factory workers in the bidi industry earn a minimum wage of Rs. 35. Out-workers earn much less-around Rs. 20 per day because there is no regulation that compels the employer to pay a minimum wage.

Bidi industry in the country is estimated to provide employment, after agriculture, to the largest number of women workers. In Pune, however, it has been stagnating and the number of workers has been steadily decline. Over the years, two major trends in this industry in Pune have been observed: closing-down of small factories and substitution of regular factory work by put-out work. Rising land prices (most of the big factories had large sheds where women workers sat down to roll bidis) and the desire to break unionization were the chief factors behind the latter trend. Elsewhere too, this pattern has been observed – it is reported that in Ahmedabad, bidi manufacturers have now resorted to a novel sale-purchase system so that workers become traders (factory workers – out-worker – traders) and are hence ineligible to demand a rise in wages.

In Pune, factory workers in the bidi industry, did not resist the move towards put-out work, hoping that they would then be able to earn more because of unrestricted working hours and help of other family members, including children. As it actually turns out, employers constantly check this desire to earn more by refusing to issue material ('tendu' leaves and prepared tobacco) for more than 1000 bidis at a time. Trade unions (unions of bidi workers have existed in Pune since 1940-42) have, right from the beginning demanded that leaves weighting 1 kilo should be issued for 1,000 bidis but the demand has never been met: 700 grams of leaves for 1,000 bidis is now the accepted proportion. Rejections of rolled bidis (known as 'chhat' bidis) are heavy and are a major tool for controlling workers. Workers are often required to buy tendu leaves on their own to reach the target of 1,000 bidis. No payment is made for chhat bidis and workers must themselves dispose of them. For these reasons, the out-workers earn less than the factory workers. The desire to get more material, to earn more and to have less rejections on hand often lands the out-workers into situations where they are sexually exploited.

8.6 Child Labour

Occupational distribution of workers in the 1981 Census gives sexwise and agewise break-up of these workers. From the agewise break-up it can be seen that there were 5,092 child labourers – 3,540 boys and 1552 girls – in Pune district- urban in 1981. (These are workers in the age group of 0 to 14 years of age.). They appear to be evenly distributed among all occupations at the first glance. This is depicted in Chart 1.

Closer scrutiny of divisionwise figures shows that these children worked mostly in the occupations listed in Chart 2.

Incidence of child labour must be associated primarily with informal sector, i.e. own account work in household industries or small production and service units. The above data shows that the highest number of both boys and girls is found on construction sites. Food processing industry also is a great user of child labour – 555 boys working as cooks, waiters, bartenders. Working as maids and housekeepers has claimed the maximum number of girls.

Apart from the above record, no authoritative figure of child workers in Pune is available. A recent study of municipal authorities puts the number of child workers in Pune Metropolitan Region at a mere 687 while according to activists, the number could be around 20,000 or even more.

Apart from construction sites, hotels and restaurants, brick kilns, garages, bakeries, laundries and shops use child labour regularly. In industries where substantial putting-out takes place and where putting-out activity is finally linked with home-based work, use of child labour is certain. Home-based work carried out by women invariably means the use of child labour. Therefore in food processing, bidi rolling, garment making and electronic industries also, there is sizable use of child labour. In all household industries and artisan units child labour is used. Children also constitute a chunk – 2,000 out of 10,000 workers – of rag-pickers.

In 1996 the Mahratta Chamber of Commerce and Industries commissioned a study on children employed in

Chart 1

NCO division	Description	Child workers Male	Female	Total
7, 8, 9	Production and related workers, transport equipment operators and labourers	1,916	838	2,754
5	Service workers	817	574	1,391
4	Sales workers	514	69	583
X	Workers not classified by occupation	114	33	147
		3,361	1,514	4,875
	Rest	179	38	217
	Total	3,540	1,552	5,092

Chart 2

Occupation group	Description	Child workers		
		Male	Female	Total
52	Cooks, waiters, bartenders and related workers	555	43	598
53	Maids and other house-keeping service workers	93	510	603
43	Salesmen and shop assistants	361	58	419
84	Machinery fitters and assemblers	334	-	334
95	Bricklayers and other construction workers	332	277	609
99	Labourers not elsewhere classified	331	253	584
79	Tailors, dress-makers, etc.	119	27	146
81	Carpenters, cabinet and related wood workers	114	-	114
89	Glass formers, potters and related workers	114	149	263
	Total	2,353	1,317	3,670

the hotel industry in Pune. The study is confined to Pune city and the township of Pimpri-Chinchwad. The study covers 97 child labourers, 100 employers, 100 hotels and about 50 parents of child labourers. Views of two trade unions active in this industry in Pune-Hind Mazdoor Sabha (HMS) and Centre of Indian Trade Unions (CITU) – were also considered as a part of the study.

The study found that the youngest child was only 7 years old and the youngest age of starting work was 6 years. Fifty-one children were between 12 and 14 years of age. Forty-five children had started work between 12 and 14 years, while 24 had started work between the ages of 9 to 11 years. Fifty-six children had been working for at least one year prior to this survey. Twenty-six children were illiterate and 35 had dropped out of secondary school. Forty-five belonged to SC/ST/OBC/NT categories and the proportion of illiteracy and dropping out of primary school was higher in their case. The proportion out of primary school was higher in their case. The proportion of illiterate children from urban areas was higher than the proportion of illiterate children from rural areas. Twenty-nine of the children were migrants and 16 of them had come from Karnataka.

The parents of most of the children were small farmers, farm labourers or unskilled casual labourers with a majority of fathers earning less than Rs. 60 per day and mothers earning less than Rs. 40 per day. Seventeen children had siblings who were also employed in hotels in Pune. Only Fifty children contributed to family income from their earnings.

Fifty-seven children were residing at the place of work. Thirty-two worked for more than 11 hours a day, while 54 worked between 8 and 10 hours every day. Seventy-nine children were paid monthly wages ranging between Rs, 400 and Rs. 700, while 16 were daily wage labourers. According to the employers, children's monthly wages were in the range of Rs. 550-850. Some children did not know their wages.

The employers were mostly young – less than 45 years old and 40 per cent had attended college. A grade hotels were found to employ more children as compared to C grade hotels such as tea stalls, pav-bhaji stalls, etc. The employers corroborated the information given by the child workers regarding working conditions. Accommodation, food, toilet, free medical aid and bonus were the facilities reported by employers but medical aid and bonus were hardly given, according to the children. Similarly, 71 employers said weekly holidays were given while only 36 children reported them. Fourteen employers stated that no weekly holidays were given but 28 children said that they had no weekly offs. According to the employers, adult workers in hotels were engaged in cooking, foods service plus any other work, whereas children were employed mostly for cleaning, washing and sweeping and to a much lesser extent in food service. While all employers agreed that education was necessary for children more than half held the parents and their economic conditions responsible for the practice of child labour.

On the basis of the above information it can be surmised that children in hotels earn around Rs. 600 for 250 hours of work – 25 days, assuming 5 weekly offs, at 10 hours per day – put in during a month. Availability of work is not a problem for them. Rather, the problem is continuous, very tiring work, low wages and horrible working conditions.

The study of action taken by the Labour Commissioner's (LC) office, Pune to eliminate child labour concentrated on cases filed by this office under the Bombay Shops and

Establishments Act, 1948 and the Child Labour Prohibition and Regulation Act, 1986. Under the former Act, the action initiated by L C was :

Year	No. of Visits	No. of Child Labourers	Cases Filed	Convictions
1992	48	25	3	3
1993	503	462	24	86
1994	1091	344	4	5
June 1995	352	126	43	3

Hotels, shops, auto garages and bakeries were main types of establishments that were prosecuted. The 16 cases that have been filed by LC's office till June 1995 under the Child Labour (Prohibition and Regulation) Act, 1956 are against builders and contractors in the construction industry.

Starting in 1992, LIC's office zealously filed cases against employers of child workers. Since 1994 the office tried to rehabilitate the children. Towards the third end, it tried to either resettle the children in their families/ communities or to enrol them in special institutions. This change of orientation perhaps explains the drop in the number of cases filed in 1994.

8.7 Vendors of Second-hand Tins and Bottles

A survey of 100 families in which women were major earners and were engaged in vending second-hand household goods was carried out in 1974-75 (Gadgil, M., 1976). It found that these women earned on an average Rs.

60 p.m. but per head monthly earning in their families was only Rs. 42. (The gap was due to the number of dependents in families). This was insufficient to procure even adequate food for at least a few days every month. Even when they had some money with them, these families could afford to eat only once a day.

These women's earnings constituted the mainstay for their families because the earnings of male members – husbands, children (boys above the age of 10 had to seek some work – were even more precarious. Their husbands were hamals or casual labourers. They had no certain income prospects. Boys who worked were engaged in running errands for nearby grocers, stitching of gunny-bags, cleaning in hotels, rag-picking, etc.

A similar survey was carried out (by the same activist-researcher) in 1979. This survey concentrates on Muslim women. Again 100 families were included in the survey. Almost every member of these families, barring very young children, was forced to be economically active. Women carried out activities like rolling incense sticks, bidis and papads, embroidery, stitching of clothes, making buffings (stuffed balls of rags used to clear machinery) and selling bakery items, groceries, vegetables, etc. All of them took their children's help in their work. The husbands of these women were petty vendors themselves or they hired themselves out as causal labourers. They had no guarantee of work. Only 14 men in these 100 families held jobs which were semi-permanent. The per head average monthly expenditure in the surveyed families was Rs. 125 or less. (Only six out of 100 families reported higher expenditure). A bulk of the surveyed families had monthly (family) incomes upto Rs. 400 but the survey has also computed per had consumption expenditure as a better indicator of the economic status of the respondent families. The average consumption expenditure represented an absolute level of poverty with many of the persons not having enough food to eat. Yet they were better off than the vendors of second-hand tins and bottles.

The activity of selling second-hand bottles possibly belongs to the lowest stratum in the informal sector, after rag-picking. Below it, begging, prostitution and destitution were the only alternatives.

8.8 Other Home-based Workers

An enormous amount of work is carried out by women and children in food processing, garment-making activities, in electronics, plastic, leather and engineering industries. An estimate of the number of these workers is difficult. The 1981 Census records that there were 10,005 males and 1,306 females working as cooks, waiters, bar-tenders and related workers (domestic and institutional). A majority of these 1,306 women were possibly rolling chapattis, papads and making other eatables for some contractors/shops. Similarly the number of labourers not elsewhere classified is 24,229-19,661 males and 4,568 females. They must also have been involved in some type of put- out work that defied Census occupational classification. It is also possible that some workers, particularly women, are still treated as non-workers.

These workers work as piece-rate workers with very low earnings as compared to time rate workers in workshop doing similar work. They also carry the burden of several work-related activities which the employers carry out in their workshops. Auxiliary material and tools such as cooking oil for making eatables, rolling pins for rolling chapattis, papads, thread and glue in stitching garments, leather purses, etc. must be bought by these workers themselves. So that net receipts in the hands are lower than would be indicated by gross piece-rates and output.

Very stringent checking of work and high rejection rates are found whenever work is put out. For exercising control, employers often resort to spreading the available work thinly among many workers. Therefore home-based workers live in constant dread of not getting enough work. They have little information about outside conditions and considered themselves to be different from other workers. Employers take full advantage of this feeling and their ignorance and pay them very low rates.

The current piece rate for rolling chapattis is 10 paise per chapatti. Women who were employed in Indira Community Kitchen, Pune – an activity which began as social work of providing low-cost meals to manual labourers but which was made sick through systematic diversion of funds for the private gain of management – used to roll 500 to 600 chapattis a day. This was a popular activity initially; there was plenty of work and these women should have been able to earn Rs. 1,375 per month. (550 chapatis a day × Rs. 0.10 = Rs. 55 per day × 25 days = Rs. 1,375 p.m.). Instead they were offered a monthly time-rate wage of Rs. 300 per month and they happily agreed because they would not have to starve any longer. Thus time rate or piece-rate whichever works out to be cheaper is used by employers in case of informal workers.

Many women carry home prepared dough, roll out papads and return them the next day. This activity is done continuously and it is hard, tiring work. From Shri Mahila Udyog, Pune, famous for 'Lijjat' papads, rolling of papads is routinely put out to many small papad makers. Its economics works out as shown in Table 8.1.

Table 8.1: Rollin Papads: Gross and Net Revenue Per Day

	Expense (Rs.)	Income (Rs.)
1) Rolling 15 kgs of papads @ Rs.5 per kg.		75.00
Expense:		
i) Oil, 150 gms.	3.75	
ii) Plastic, baskets for keeping papads to dry	4.00	
iii) Travelling	2.00	
iv) Miscellaneous	1.00	
	10.75	
2) Net income		64.25
Three women roll 15 kgs. of papads in a day		
3) Net income per worker		21.42

Source: Nandita Gandhi and Nandita Shah, 'Gharbaslya Kam: Striya ani Gharguti Utpadan' (Marathi), 1993.

Plenty of work is put out in the leather industry. In a simple activity of making pouches or spectacle cases of leather or rexine, there exist as many as twelve different steps and each of them or bunches of them are put out. The subcontractor who accepts this work has income-expenditure particulars shown in Table 8.2:

The profit margin is thus high but the sub-contractor earns, if work is available continuously, not more than Rs. 4,000.

Worse is the conditions of artisans such as sandal makers who work as account workers at home and use family labour.

The break-up of production cost of one pair of sandals in 1977 was as shown in Table 8.3.

It was found that the supply of materials to home- based sandal-makers was controlled by a few retailers. Purchase

Of sandals from artisans was also controlled by big retailers or wholesalers. (There was at least one retailer who supplied materials and also bought sandals.) Through a stringent rejection policy these traders forced the artisans to sell their sandals at less than the cost price. Artisans realized only Rs. 12 per pair while the wholesalers sold it for at least Rs. 22.

8.9 Construction Workers

As per 1981 census, there were 24,212 bricklayers and other construction workers (19,016) males and 5,196 females) in Pune district-urban. As per our calculations in Table 4.10, in 1981 there were 15,834 unorganised construction workers in Pune urban agglomeration and their number rose to 71,650 in 1991. This is a reflection of the

Table 8.2: Making Rexine Spectacle Cases

Description	Expenditure (Rs.)	Income (Rs.)
1) 32 cases @ Rs. 3 each		96.00
Expenditure:		
i) Rexine, 1 metre	42.00	
ii) Metal strips	4.80	
iii) Worker's wages	6.60	
Total	53.40	
Therefore, Net Income		42.60

Table 8.3 Sandal Making: Expense Incurred

	Rs.	Rs.
<u>Material Cost</u>:		
a) $\frac{3}{4}$ sq.ft. upper leather @ Rs.3/sq.ft.	2.25	
b) $\frac{1}{2}$ sq,ft. lining leather @ Rs.1.60/sq.ft.	0.80	
c) 115 gms insole @ Rs.22/kg	2.53	
d) Micro-sheet (sole)	3.67	
e) Adhesives, solutions, polishing materials	1.50	10.75
<u>Labour Cost</u>:		
a) Labour charges @ Re.0.75 for upper leather, Re.0.50 for sole and Re.0.25 for fitting	1.50	
b) Grinding, spraying and stamping charges	0.65	2.15
<u>Overheads</u>:		
Rent, electricity and other expenses		0.18
Total		13.08

<u>Source</u>: Basu, T., "Calcutta's Sandal Makers," Economic and Political Weekly, 6-8-1977, p. 1262.

construction boom that has been seen in Pune in recent times. Contract labour, often migrant labour are chief features of the lower-end construction workforce. Because of these features, it is difficult to organise them. The per day wage rate on construction sites in Pune in 1996 was Rs. 64 for male workers and Rs. 45 for female workers.

8.10 Temporal Comparison of Earnings

Some comparative data on nominal and real wages over a period of 60 years – 1936 to 1996 – is presented in Tables 8.4 and 8.5.

The information in Table 8.5 is highly tentative. To cross-check it we looked at Working Class Family Income and Expenditure Surveyed for 1981-82 for Pune. This is an authoritative (albeit, old) source as the survey was carried out by the Labour Bureau, Ministry of Labour, Government of India, with the help of National Sample Survey Organization. This survey was carried out in 76 important industrial centres in the country, of which Pune was one. The survey covered 7 sectors of employment, viz. registered factories, mines, plantations, ports and docks, electricity generating and distributing establishments, public motor transport undertakings and railways. The study pertains to organized employment but it is useful to use because it gives information about both number of workers and their per capita income and expenditure. There exist unprotected workers in each of the above sectors and even if information about them is not presented separately, information that is available is useful as it pertains to the lower end of the formal sector workforce.

The survey defined a working class family as one with at least one member working as a manual worker. Apart from workers as defined under various Acts relating to factories,

Table 8.4: Estimated Monthly earnings of Women Workers in IS, 1936 and 1956

(Amount in Rs.)

Category	1936	1956	
1. Sweepers and scavengers	12.9	55	(13.8)
2. Bidi workers	9.9	38	(9.5)
3. Servants/workers working in small factories/workshops	9.4	49	(12.2)
4. Domestic servants	8.7	23	(5.8)
5. Construction workers	10.2	28	(7.0)
6. Casual labourers/hamal women	9.2	26	(6.5)
7. Petty vendors of household goods, fruits, second-hand goods	13.5	31	(7.8)

Note : Figures in brackets indicate real wages. Prices went up by 4 times during these 20 years (Poona : A Resurvey, p. 162). So real wages in 1956 are 25 per cent of nominal wages.

Sources: 1. 1936 - Gadgil, D.R., Poona: A Socio-Economic Survey, Part I : Economic.

2. 1956 - Sovani, N.V. et al., 'Poona: A Resurvey, The Changing Pattern of Employment and Earnings'.

Table 8.5: Estimated Monthly earnings of Women Workers in IS, 1958 and 1996

(Amount in Rs.)

Category	1958	1976	1996
1. Sweepers and scavengers	61	-	2750 (206)
2. Bidi workers	57.5 (outworkers)	75 (25)	600 (45) (Outworkers: Rs. 20 per day x 30 days)
	45 (factory workers)		900 (68) (factory workers: Rs. 30 per day x 30 days)
3. Servants/workers in small factories/workshops	55	-	1526 (114)
4. Domestic servants	-	45 (15)	500 (37.5)
5. Construction workers	22	100 (34)	1280 (96) (Rs. 64 per day x 20 days)
6. Casual labourers/hamal women	-	60 (20)	450 (34) (Rs. 30 per day x 15 days)
7. Petty vendors of household goods, vegetables, second-hand goods such as old tins and bottles etc.	-	42 (14)	300 (23) (Rs. 15 per day x 20 days)
8. Rag-pickers	-	70 (24)	450 (34) (Rs. 15 per day x 30 days)

Note: Figures in brackets indicate real wages. To calculate them, the following information has been used.

Year	Annual average purchasing power of rupee (in paise)
1960	100
1976	33.8, so deflator w.r.t. 1960 = 2.96
May 1994	7.5, so " 1960 = 13.33

(Statistical Outline of India, 1992-93, 1994-95, Tata Services Ltd.)

Sources:
1. 1958: Dabholkar, V.A., 'Life and Labour of Employed Women in Poona', 1960, Unpublished Ph.D. Thesis.
2. 1976, except rag-pickers: Brahme, S., Sonalkar, V., 'Economic Plight of Hamaal Women in Poona'.
3. 1976, rag-pickers: Bapat, M. and Crook, N., "Duality of Female Employment: Evidence from a Survey in Pune," 1988, Economic and Political Weekly, 23, 31.
4. 1996: From our survey. Most of these figures are given in respective sections of this chapter. Wages of workers in small workshops are from Chap.6, Table 6.14.

mines, etc., contract labour, peons, watchmen, other manual workers, etc., were also covered in the survey.

The survey estimated that there were 90,000 working class families and 1,22,635 workers as defined above in Pune in 1981. The organized workforce in Pune district in 1981 was 3,29,100. Thus workers formed a sizable 37 per cent of it. A bulk of these workers were engaged in the manufacture of transport equipment and parts, machinery, machine tools and parts, chemicals and chemical products, etc. A sizable number worked as machinery fitters, assemblers, precision instrument makers, blacksmiths and tool makers, etc.

The average per capita monthly income was Rs. 652.88. Roughly these figures of earnings are on the higher side as compared to figures for 1976 reported in Table 8.5. This can be interpreted to mean that the same type of work attracts higher rewards in formal sector as compared to informal sector.

Table 8.5 shows that over these 40-odd years, earnings of sweepers, workers in small workshops, construction workers have improved. In other categories of workers, improvement is restricted because of insufficiency of work. The exception is of rag-pickers but because of the stigma attached to this work, only desperation drives people to it. Earnings of sweepers are high because they have unionized and because they are after all, municipal employees. Therefore actually they should be a part of the formal sector. In small workshop, some learning and skill accumulation takes place and workers benefit from it. Also availability of work has not been a problem so far, thanks to industrialization.

To some extent therefore trickling in of development can be found in the informal sector as well. Otherwise, due to both supply and demand side factors, quantitative expansion at subsistence level appears to be the general norm.

Chapter 9

Conclusions

9.1 Macro Environment

It is time to bring the scattered links of this enquiry together. The enquiry emphasizes the essential but non-dynamic and unrecognized part that IS plays in an economy. As our planners' initial faith in state-led growth with expanding manufacturing employment under a large and dynamic public sector is now buried, the topic of IS has become particularly relevant. The prospects for working class and IS appear to be invariably tied together.

Coexistence of several modes of production such as own account work, family business, putting out arrangements, subcontracting of work, etc. along with factory production was reloaded by this study and it is an important insight into the working of an economy. Because of this coexistence primitive accumulation of surplus takes place along with secondary accumulation. To understand this accumulation process and the mutual relations among these different modes, a bottom-top, subaltern, approach is necessary. This is the approach for studying IS. Its importance cannot be over-emphasized for a complete understanding of the working of an economy.

Apart from a subaltern approach, study of IS is important because the crucial task of making productive use of abundant, surplus labour in the economy remains neglected. A two-pronged employment strategy has been followed in the country. Its one prong consists of special employment generation programmes and also of measures to transfer more resources to workers with low productivity. Programmes for transferring resources, e.g. IRDP have sought to upgrade the resource-base of IS and employment generation programmes have created a safety net.

The second prong of the strategy relies on the process of economic growth and development to create more employment opportunities. Its benign belief is that progressively more employment will be created and the need for special employment generation programmes will be progressively reduced.

While it is true that economic growth is the final creator of employment, what has been seen on the other hand, is that there are severe limits to labour absorption in the organized sector. The public sector did give a boost to the organized sector. The public sector did give a boost to organized employment in the past but it is not going to do so in future. Already its rate of growth in employment has turned negative. (Economic Survey, 2001-2002 reports that this rate was -0.03 per cent during 1994 to 2000.) What is more, the public sector as a whole is not likely to play an important, dynamic role in the economy. In large enterprises in the private sector, a wage-employment trade-off is seen clearly. Also, a hard core of permanent employees is getting surrounded by more secondary, casual, non-permanent workers.

Thus, our present dilemma is that employment generation and resource transfer programmes continue but the organized sector continues to be very inferior to that envisaged by the planners. The basic point to note here is that capital has and continues to generate more surplus to take the economy forward but at the same time, it has failed to provide productive employment to all labourers.

More employment is being generated in construction, trade and service sectors. Often, however, this is employment of temporary, casual and unprotected nature. It is seen that large enterprises in the organized sector have Fordist relations with their permanent workers. Their wages are indexed to cost of living. So permanent employees are expensive and there is pressure to economise on them.

Therefore, large enterprises have every incentive to make use of cheap, unprotected labour in small firms and IS. This is reflected in widespread use of contract labour in the organized sector. It is used in large enterprises invariably for housekeeping, material handling, transport and maintenance activities. It is used also for managing temporary peaks in regular production work. Subcontracting of some parts of the production process itself has been increasingly resorted to since the mid-1970s. It offers two substantial benefits, viz. lowering costs because of cheap labour and flexibility. Containing the strength of organized labour has also been a motive behind subcontracting. It can be maintained that the segmentation of labour market (its divisions between FS and IS) has induced complementarity between large firms and small firms.

Large enterprises particularly in the private sector have used a variety of means to pressure protected labour and to use unprotected labour in its place. Cost-reduction and restructuring in these enterprises has basically meant only this. Thus industrial units have been closed down where this labour substitution has been resisted. Blue-collar workers have been shifted to non-unionised, lower managerial positions only in terms of designations, i.e. without any change in job content or wage. Permanent workers' names have been struck off the muster in some cases and these workers are then shown as sub-contractors of the firm. Many firms have encouraged their white-collar employees to start small workshops and to become suppliers to their employers. So promotion of self-employment is also a part of this strategy. And, of course, all large enterprises have completed voluntary retirement schemes. The lump sum amounts of separation packages have been enormous and in spite of deferring their write-off, some public sector banks went into the red because of them. Still, nobody doubts the future benefits that will result from a lean workforce.

It has been mentioned above that in terms of all economic indicators except employment, the organized sector continues to surge ahead. In the 1980s and 1990s small-scale industries have grown in terms of both value added and employment. Small-scale industrial units belong to both formal and informal and to sub-contract work, there is a shift of activity from large to small firms. This shift is clearly seen in engineering, food processing, electronics, textiles and garment industries. In the textile industry, powerlooms have gained an upper hand over mills. Actually there is little competition between powerlooms and mills and powerlooms are being promoted, because of their flexibility and sweated labour, by mill-owners themselves with the connivance of the state. In other industries also, small firms which previously had a competitive relationship with large firms, have become the latter's ancillaries. The vibrancy of thesis units is thus largely due to the policies of large enterprises. Not competition but complementarily explains the relationships between large enterprises and small firms.

Atomistic competition assumes that equality exists among competing units on at least some points. This equality is hard to come by. Mostly an hierarchical order links different economic units. When the focus is on different modes of production, the economy must be conceptualized as an hierarchy. Gradiation of economic units is inherent in this arrangement. Duality is a stark representative of and simultaneously an abstraction from this reality. Hierarchical existence means dependence and limited growth products at the lower end and the ability to use lower forms at the higher end. This is the reality behind market mechanism.

IS comprises lower ends of this hierarchy and it too has been conceptualized by us as an hierarchy with small manufacturing firms at the top. Our analysis shows that these firms have been hemmed in by large firms. The small firms in turn make use of own-account and home-based workers. This hierarchical order allows the lower forms to barely exist after a lot of hard work and it simultaneously allows higher forms to seize any opportunities for profit making that come to the lower forms.

IS can be defined as all of the following:

(a) A buffer before open unemployment or a self-evolving safety net of the working poor. It is a cluster of survival strategies and thus plenty of family labour, i.e. women's labour and child labour is found in it.

(b) A sector of inferior modes or technique of production; an abode or primitive accumulation.

(c) A storehouse of backwash effect of industrialization and technological change.

(d) A sector 'beyond the pale', i.e. where state regulation does not reach.

(e) A reserve army of labour. Its ability (which is nothing but a supply-driven desperate response) to absorb more people and to grow in quantitative terms help it perform this role. As is inherent in an hierarchy, there is one-way dependence between FS and IS. In other words, FS dropouts reach IS but IS members find it very difficult to reach FS. Also IS expands when FS contracts but it does not contract when FS expands because of the limited labour absorption in FS.

A view of IS as a staging post or a temporary abode or rural migrants was not considered in our analysis

Keeping the above analysis in mind, it is very difficult to visualize any improvement, beyond bare subsistence, in the working and living conditions of people in IS. It has been suggested that the post-World War II era with Bretton Woods institutions creating the basic framework and with Foredims defining capital-labour relations is taking place in all the countries in the world. Indian capitalists too are moving from ad hoc attempts to limit labour's demands to a systematic strategy of Neo-Talorism for getting more out of works. The entire working class is hence expected to be pressurized by capital. Policies for IS must be thought of against this background.

9.2 Improving the Conditions of Informal Workers

Conventional wisdom treats economic growth as an autonomous process. While the choice of goods and services is now beyond state intervention, choice of techniques of production can still be influenced through incentives and taxes. In every industry there exists a number of techniques of production ranging from the most capital-intensive one to the most labour-intensive one. A tilt in favour of favour-intensive techniques will result in more subcontracting of work which will help IS. This is already happening in engineering and construction industries. However, the state must simultaneously impose an ancillary development tax on predicting units putting out their work. This tax revenue must be used for providing income and social security to IS workers.

The state is on the retreat in the present times. A number of protests would be made about the above proposal and many of these protests would centre round the reduced ability of the state to impose and collect new taxes. We, however, firmly believe that the state must continue to intervene and to regulate the process of economic growth in an imaginative fashion.

Because IS is a neglected sector, neither state, nor trade unions but non-government organizations (NGOs) have been active in it. Their experience shows that government measures to improve the conditions of IS workers have been marked by rigidity and a strait-jacket approach and a greater role for NGOs will be preferred.

What informal workers basically need is income security and social security. For providing the former, an employment guarantee programme for urban areas can be added to the existing battery of special employment programmes. However, it will be better to build on existing strengths. For example, government programmes have a broad reach and have access to finance-both from government budget as well as from special cesses but administratively they are rigid, often insensitive to the needs of beneficiaries, are not cost-efficient and do not deliver in a timely fashion. NGOs, on the other hand, are responsive, timely and often cost-efficient but do not have access to large finance and they find it difficult to expand beyond a certain scale. So a contributory or tax-based welfare fund should be started for informal workers and its administration should be left in the hands of NGOs.

Trade unions have not been active in this field because they require at least a few permanent workers at a fixed location to become operational. In small, informal firms few workers are permanent, personal relations exist between workers and their employer and workers may keep moving in and out of firms and indeed out of the workforce because an attempt to do so means loss of job even in FS. Casual workers and contract labour keep moving from place to place in their jobs. For home-based workers, workplace is home; they rarely met other workers and they do not regard themselves as workers. The first step in organizing them is to make them aware of their status as workers. Trade unions have found this to be an uphill task.

Protest, opposition and confrontation are building a block of trade union activity. What is seen in small firms is threats of employers to close down firms the moment workers try to organize themselves. An attempt to unionize means job-loss for everybody. Under these circumstances, trade unions have to be prepared to take over the closed units or to start some other activity for generating income. Trade unions have been opposed to either of these as they logically maintain that this is not their work.

Thus trade unionism works when class identities are clear-cut and when battle-lines are clearly drawn between capital and labour. In such situations, industrialists have a firm understanding of either role as capitalists and they have a commitment to the activity of production. They understand that containing labour is one of the fundamental issues to tackle while carrying out production. This they are prepared to do without closing down their firms. This does not happen in IS. Therefore the negligible trade union presence in IS is partially due to the very character of the petty bourgeoisie.

Of late, trade unions have started paying more attention to the plight of informal workers. In our own survey, we observed the efforts of the Centre of Indian Trade Unions (CIPU) to organize workers in small firms located in a particular area of Pune. These efforts were basically for making workers bold enough to vocalize their experiences (rather than demands), to create a sense of class-solidarity among them and to force employers and the state bureaucracy to implement existing laws such as the Minimum Wages Act. The union activates were fully alive to the risks attached to a confrontationist stand for going beyond these steps and for resorting to direct action.

NGOs which have attempted to help informal workers have proceeded along the following lines:

(a) organizing workers,
(b) undertaking income-generation activities by forming cooperative societies and implementing various government schemes and accepting contracts for work through them,
(c) supplying credit to home-based and own-account workers, by forming self-help groups or credit cooperatives to help them to become viable,
(d) imparting new skills to workers,
(e) pressurizing government to enact laws, particularly for home-based workers and to implement the existing minimum wage laws.
(f) networking with other NGOs to build up strength.

Income generation activities of NGOs used to be dismissed by leftists and trade unions as reformist measures for they involve the acceptance of status quo with perhaps some change at grass-root level. Now it is realized that they are indispensable in IS. At the same time, these activities are very time-consuming, they require full-time committed cadre and they mostly require protected markets to sustain them. Barring some exceptions, their scope remains confined to some pockets. While some NGos e.g., SEWA, Amul, Anapurna, Lijjat, etc. have become successful, several others have failed. In fact, failure rate and stagnation are very high among these NGOs.

SEWA or Self-Employed Women's Association started its activities in 1972 as a trade union with Gandhian values.

It realized the limits to conventional trade unionism while working among own account women workers in Ahmedabad. Paucity of work, lack of access and resources were these workers' major problems and they desperately needed income security. So SEWA undertook appropriate income generation activities and organized them as cooperatives. Thus it started cooperatives of artisans, vendors, service providers, milk collectors, etc. It has freely made use of the existing welfare and promotional schemes of government and it implements some of them on behalf of government.

SEWA has gown in the process responding to different needs of its members and it has also provided a number of support services to the cooperatives in the form of banking (by starting its own bank!), child and health care, housing, legal aid, insurance and training, etc. Its experience is that social security is of utmost importance to these unprotected workers and its membership took a high jump when it introduced a social insurance scheme for members. It has found that provision of social security becomes an income generating activity by itself. Apart from its innovates and flexible approach, unceasing lobbying with government and international bodies, foreign funds, skilful public relations have made SEWA highly successful. This SEWA model of provision of training, income, credit and social services to members in the interest of self-sustenance is likely to succeed in IS. The crucial difference between Pune's own Hamal Panchayat and SEWA is that the former functions like a traditional trade union and does not undertake income generation activities. It has a more militant approach to labour problems.

Trade union activities are also necessary in IS in order to force the implementation of existing laws and to bring more activities under their coverage. Organizations of home-based workers, coolies and porters, domestic servants, rag-pickers, etc., have helped, first of all, to give visibility to their work and the problems surrounding them. This work takes the trade unions much beyond the conventional scope of their activities. The union of rag-pickers in Pune has, after a lot of efforts, won identity badge for its members from the municipal corporation and is now demanding regular, free medical check-ups since there are several health hazards in this activity. Because of a large number of women and child workers in IS, a number of familial and domestic problems, e.g. alcoholism, domestic violence, child-care, lack of drinking water, etc. also have to be solved by unions.

It appears that after organizing workers engaged in a particular activity, the union should negotiate with the employers (they might mean local authorities also) and strive to provide work to its members in an equitable manner. Formation of local tripartite boards with representatives of workers, employers and the State will be beneficial. Hamal Panchayat has followed this pattern. It has succeeded because it has secured monopoly rights over the supply of load bearing services.

As regards employment programmes of government, SEWA has made an important suggestion, viz. these programmes should have built-in social security arrangements in the form of insurance schemes, welfare funds, savings and credit schemes, etc. It further suggests that administration of these social security arrangements should be handed over to workers' bodies or tripartite boards as above and finances for them should be made available from workers' contributions, contributions from industry, cess on products and government budget.

9.3 Conclusion

The issue of IS always raises uncomfortable questions which however, lead us straight to the basis of capitalism, viz. the supremacy of capital over labour, the continuing adjustments that the working class must adapt itself to capital's requirements and the elaborate machinery that is also being fashioned continuously to sustain this supremacy.

The recommendations made above stem from our belief that it is the responsibility of the state to ensure that the accumulation process takes place within a framework which guarantees some basic minimum rights of labour. In order to maximize profit, capital looks out for every opportunity to externalize its costs. It wants the state to create infrastructure out of public money and it wants free access to it. The State must be strong enough to resist this pressure and to force some internalization of costs on capital. Cost of maintenance and reproduction of labour force must be borne by capital. Hence the suggestion for tax on ancillarization and subcontracting.

Appendix

Case Studies

I. Entrepreneurs of Micro-Enterprises

1. GSG (A non-Shop Act slum industrial unit located at Hadapsar)

I am 53 years old today. After obtaining a diploma in mechanical engineering at Hubli, I worked in HMT, Bangalore first as a trainee and then as a supervisor. Then I came to Pune and joined Bharat Forge. I got all-round exposure in both the companies. In 1976, I opened this machine shop along with a partner. I was still serving then.

We started with three workers. My wife used to help in general supervision. Our initial capital consisted of only Rs, 6,000, contributed by the two partners equally. We started producing auto-turned components on job-work basis. We made rapid progress but my partner quit in one year. I took three additional partners and started a small forge shop nearby. There my partners started cheating me. When I found out, the forge shop had become a sick unit. It is still sick but I have separated from my partners. Now, my son and I look after the two units. The forge shop has created financial difficulties otherwise my progress would have been much more.

I employ 12 persons today including two lady inspectors. My units work on two-shift basis. In each shift, workers work overtime for 2 hours. If skilled supervisors are available are available, I can introduce third shift and my turnover will really increase then. However, skilled persons are just not available. So I have had to adopt the policy of taking only unskilled workers and training them. I pay daily wages to workers. A new unskilled worker gets Rs. 30 per day. After three months, I raise his wage. After one year, it is raised still further. But each year 50/60 casual workers come and depart quickly. I do not want to run a mine not accepted by big companies. Yet the turnover is high. Once automatic machines are set up by me, the problem will become worse because then work will be routinized further. I know, my wages are below the minimum wage prescribed by government. In slum industries nobody pays the minimum wage. What I am paying is the market wage. If I try to pay anything more, other producers will be displeased.

Today's workers do not know the meaning of discipline. They leave the moment you try to tighten control just a little. Other small producers must be facing the same type of labour problems. Our education system is faulty and so these problems arise. There should be greater vocationalization.

I have quite a few lathes and grinding machines. The recent acquisitions are of second-hand machines. I will soon buy a CNC machine for Rs. 10 lakhs. I am supplying parts to really big companies. I have recently received an export enquiry also but there is no capacity to fulfil new customers' demands. My turnover has increased continuously over the last three years but gross profit has declined. So I will, in future, select only high value items.

I have carried out plenty of modifications in our machines for improving their performance. I use the warm forging method for treating material and my skill lies in using forged components in the place of turned components. Officers in the big companies often refer their problems to me and I solve them.

Getting payment in time from customers is a problem but not a major one. I have supplied components to many big companies and I know about their subcontracting policies.

Only a few of them operate professionally and do not favour their own communities while selecting suppliers. Some companies pay suppliers' dues in time, others are notorious for delayed payments. A supplier needs three things from the customer company – job guarantee, timely rate revisions and in-time payment. A company that gives all three is extremely rare.

On the basis of my experience of the last 29 years, I have realized that quality plus delivery requirements of the customer and price of the supplier is a long-lasting equation. I concentrate on only quality and delivery schedules and find that customers seek me out.

2. BDJ (A Shop Act Unit in Shivjinagar)

Ours is an 18 year-old engineering workshop run in partnership. We manufacture marine duty pumps which are supplied to different marine engine manufacturers as original equipment (OE). We, the partners, are both engineering diploma-holders and have worked in big companies. My partner, was, in fact, in charge of the Tool Engineering section of Kirloskar Oil Engines Ltd.

This unit was started with a capital investment of Rs. 18 lakh and six hired workers. Today we have five workers. Three of them have been with us for the last 13 years. The wages that we pay to workers are above the minimum wage. We work on one-shift basis. We have good, well-maintained machines of both local and standard (Shimoga, HMT, Mysore Kirloskhar) makes including one CNC machine.

Getting credit was a problem till we established ourselves. The need for technological change and adaptation never arose because our customers have not changed their specifications. The problem of technological change does not really bother job-shop units. Getting skilled workers is the biggest problem as skilled, ITI trained workers are not willing to work in small-scale units. New workers have no work work-ethic. Workers do not welcome change and new equipment. They are not included to acquire new skills. I think there are no easy solutions to the problems faced by small units.

Starting a new unit in our line is not a problem, survival is. It is difficult to earn enough to cover all the expenses. So few persons are attracted to this activity. If a person did enter the line, he would, of course, find it difficult to compete with us. Our investment, engineering know-how and contacts have given us an adequate lead.

Quality and delivery together give you a sustainable competitive advantage. Price is not a competitive tool but it can be used as such where value addition is high.

Because of the constraints on growth in this line, we have started two new units with a new product.

3. DD (A Shop Act Unit in Mangalwar Peth)

I established this unit nine years ago. For the first six years, I had one partner. Since the last three years, this has been a sole proprietary business.

After doing B.E. (Mech.), I worked in Buckau Wolf for five years as a project engineer. While I was there, I started this unit. One year was very hectic when I carried out both, my job as well as all the running around that is required for a young business.

We started by undertaking job-work for Buckau Wolf. Initially we got all the work done from outside. Slowly machinery was acquired. One milling machine was second-hand. I sold it last year. Our initial capital investment was Rs. 500 only. The area of our present workshop was acquired only for Rs. 30,000, out of which Rs, 22,000 was spent on renovating this place. The written down value of our fixed assets is zero. Since 1988 I have not invested any money in this unit. I have acquired a bigger plot at Manik Baug and we will soon shift there.

I make spare-parts for textile machinery. The textile industry is a continuous process industry in which production stoppage is very costly and so supply of spare-parts is considered to be very essential. My market is therefore secure.

I carry out reverse engineering. I do not engage in design. Modifications are also made as per customer's requirements. Original equipment manufacturers are my competitors. The real competitor is only one. It is a German firm-Barmag. They know we are copying their parts. Their spare-parts are costly. They use high quality materials, carry out metallurgical testing and also incur heavy engineering costs. They safeguard their market by selling additional sets of spare-parts with the original machine. People come to us after these sets are over. We use alternative materials, have no metallurgical testing and we do no incur engineering costs. So obviously our spare-parts are cheaper. If continuous process plants are buying them then it means that their quality is goods.

I have also started making rotary automisers required in the chemical industry. I make 10/12 such units each year. I still give out plenty of work. My capacity utilization is above 100 per cent, thanks to subcontracting. High precision work is contracted out. So I am saved the headache of buying special purpose machines and ensuring adequate work-load for them.

Material consumption roughly amounts to 35 per cent of my turnover and subcontracting 30 per cent. Gross profit is around 30 per cent of turnover.

I employ six workers today. Four of them have been with us right from the beginning. There are two apprentices as well. Workers' daily wages vary from Rs. 25 to Rs. 70 depending upon their seniority. It is not necessary to differentiate wages according to skill differentials among workers. Workers work over-time for three hours every day. They are not paid anything extra for it. I pay them annual profit-linked (8.33 per cent of profit) bonus.

Initially I was forced to sell on credit but buy for cash. Today getting credit is not a problem. The biggest problem is getting skilled workers. Here I do not face this problem but for our expansion at the new location, we are not getting any skilled workers. Big companies have vitiated the market. The fad of daily lotteries has diverted workers and reduced their supply.

In sugar, chemical and food processing industries, a lot of scope exists for machinery updating and modification. I will turn my attention to that. So my business will grow vertically. New-comers can, any time have the kind of start we had. Some technical knowledge will however be essential. Goodwill that has been earned so far and the variety of parts we produce for catering to our customers have given us a head-start.

4. KGA (A Shop Act unit in Shukrawar Peth)

This unit undertakes plastic moulding work as per customer's orders. It was established 22 year ago. I am a die-maker. I started working here and today I am the manager. I have been here since inception of the business. After the death of the proprietor, his son took over but he lost his life in a road accident. Since then his mother – she is 68 years old now – is the owner on paper. I look after everything. For the first 10 years, that is, till this accident took place, however, the only objective is to hold the fort. It is our policy not to buy any new machinery.

Initially two workers were employed in this unit. Now there are five workers. Their wages vary from Rs. 50 to Rs. 67 per day. Additional employment is not possible. We work on one-shift basis. Multiple shift working is not possible. On one-shift basis, our capacity utilization is full on an average. One of our customers holds a monopoly in making blood pressure checking apparatus. He even exports it. I do not remember any modifications in the production process or in the machinery used.

Our materials used to be imported in the beginning. Its availability was a problem then. Now that problem does not exist. Our type of business is easy to start but sustenance is very difficult here. Hard work is required. Getting dies is the biggest problem. So you have to be an expert die-maker. If you get some skilled workers, you have to hold on to them. then you can survive. Large businesses in our line are more efficient because of the productivity of their labour and production process. Quality, delivery and personal relations help a business to push ahead, according to me.

5. RSZ (A Shop Act unit in Sahakarnagar)

I carry out machining and fabrication of pressed components and manufacturing of cabinet locks, mild steel boxes, etc., in my two workshops. The first workshop was established 12 years ago. The second one became operational since January 1994 though land and machinery were acquired for it in 1992.

I have studied upto matric. While still in school, I started helping my father in his die-making businesses. Father's drunkenness led to a split following which I started a small machining shop in Somwar Peth with the help of a friend.

We used to carry out job-work for Volcan (now Alfa) Laval Ltd.

I had to shut down that unit after a prolonged strike in the parent company. Then I started the first of my present workshops with a capital investment of Rs. 68,000. I started with a few old machines, some of them were 20 years old. I carried out only labour operations in the beginning. Its proportion has now come down to about half of my total work, the other half being own production.

In the beginning we did not hire any workers. Today I employ 18 workers. They have been split up in the two units so Factories Act is not applicable. Our new unit is located outside municipal limits. This location was suggested to us by our parent company. The objective was to save on octroi. All the workers – including three women-workers – are unskilled and get daily wages which are below the prescribed minimum wage. We have only one shift of work at our first unit. Workers work overtime for ¾ hours a day for about 4 days in a week. Overtime does not attract extra payment. I give them tea and breakfast. I do not look out for skilled workers. I do not look out for skilled workers. I take raw, unskilled workers and train them myself. I consider myself very competent technically in spite of the lack of formal training. I have modified machines. We work very fast – a job which others will complete in 16/18 hours is completed by us in just 10 hours. Technical competence, personal touch and skill in handling people (I beat my workers sometimes, while training them, but help them to solve their personal difficulties) have made me successful.

Our market is competitive so the strategy that I have used for establishing myself is to be versatile and to accept every order, however, small it is. Smaller number of orders and greater variety per order is my motto.

Big companies have helped me a lot. They have given me orders plus machinery on rental basis plus valuable advice. Personal relations do matter for getting business. I do not believe in offering commission or under-the-table payment. Doing small personal jobs for the concerned officers, e.g. paying their bills, getting documents for them is a more effective method of winning favour.

Easy credit is available in the market today. So one finds a very large number of workshops. There is unhealthy competition. Corruption gas vitiated the scene even further. Small units therefore find it difficult to come up. Our own growth prospects are positive. Philips will soon give us machines worth Rs. 10/12 lakhs. So rapid expansion will take place. I will soon start the operation of metal plating on any surface.

6. RPB (A Shop Act unit Located in Electronic Industrial Estate)

This unit was established nine years ago. My father established it and have been working here since may college days. I have done B.Sc. Electronics and I hold a diploma in Radio Fingering. I manufacture temperature control soldering stations, soldering irons and solder baths. We have also started making transformers basically for in-house consumption. Initial capital invested in the unit was Rs. 6 lakh. My father's technical help was invaluable in the beginning. I started by looking after the sales side but now I combine it with production. Soldering station was, in fact, developed by me.

Initially, we employed five hired workers. Four were women workers. Now also there are five workers with two women workers. There is one trainee also. Their wages vary from Rs. 700 per month onwards. Workers do not normally work overtime.

Present capacity utilization is around 60 per cent. In 1982 we undertook a new project but it failed due to technical as well as managerial problems. So this unit was closed from 1983 to 1985. In 1987 capital worth Rs. 6 lakh was injected.

We sell our products to both dealers and consumers (60:40). It is more profitable to sell directly to consumers. With the growing popularity of ISO 9000 certification, there has been a heavy rush for soldering irons. Our solder stations represent an important effort for import substitution. Without capital, others cannot reach our position. A newcomer, too, has to be very skilled. Getting payment in time from customers is our biggest difficulty. Bigger companies in our line are better managed and are strong in marketing. Quality is the primary tool for competitive advantage. Price is secondary.

7. VKB (A Factory Act unit that upgraded itself by shifting to its own premises in Hadapsar Industrial Estate)

The unit was established in 1976. I obtained my engineering degree from Ahmedabad in 1975. Then I worked in the small workshop of a relative in Pune for about six months and then started my workshop on Pune-Satara Road.

My unit is an ancillary unit of TELCO. We make precision machined components and fabricated assemblies. We buy our own materials. – mostly steel bars, sheets and plates. Telco provides specifications of operations and helps in calibrating our gauges. Though a bulk of our work (90 per cent) is for TELCO, some is for other ancillaries of TELCO

(5 per cent), other parties (Thermax and ZF Steering Gears, 3 per cent) and even exports (2 per cent).

I started with five workers and initial investment of Rs, 2,85,000. I have reinvested profits, taken loans from banks and individuals – directors of the company and have expanded operations. We have also have our share capital. Our biggest investment was in the present factory plot – Rs. 5,50,000 in 1990. I have acquired this land for a lease of 99 years. We constructed this land for a lease of 99 years. We constructed the factory building for Rs. 10 lakhs in 1992.

At present 20 workers – 17 permanent and 3 temporary, casual workers- are employed in the company. Most of them have studied upto secondary school level. Their wage ranges from Rs. 72 per day (skilled workers). They are all daily rated workers. We work on two-shift basis. Workers ordinarily put in overtime of 2½ hours for which they are paid at 1.5 times normal wage. (By stretching the shift overtime, the factory probably remains open for 24 hours).

On two-shift basis our capacity utilization at present is around 60 per cent. Eight more workers can be accommodated in the second shift provided there is assurance of demand in the market. However, I do not want any permanent liability on account of labour and so I will not recruit any more permanent workers.

Total fixed investment in the company (original value) stands at Rs. 30 lakh (land and building Rs. 16.1 lakh, plant and machinery Rs. 10. 61 lakh). For working capital we have a limit of up to Rs. 8.75 lakh with our bank. Our monthly turnover was Rs. 9.4 lakh in 1994-95 and Rs 8 lakh in 1993-94. The break-up of cost is: material cost 47 per cent and conversion cost 53 per cent. Conversion cost included sub-contracting cost 53 per cent. Conversion costs include subcontracting charges paid to outside parties.

Technicians' time is hired and if professional charges paid for that purpose are added to wages and salaries then subcontracting charges are thrice as high as the salary bill.

My biggest worry is about the time lag between price rise for materials and expenses and rate increase allowed by Telco. They want a detailed costing system to be installed by me in this company. Unless I submit a detailed cost break-up they do not even entertain any proposal. Installing and operating the documentation system takes up so much of my time that I have to neglect production matters. I have totally neglected my family for so many years. But new pressures are such that I have no time even now. Telco wants us ancillary units to modernize ourselves by trying hard continuously. Every time I attend their vendors development conference, I become acutely aware of what distance I still have to cover. Given the manpower constraints, I do not think that upward mobility will be possible for us.

Getting payment in time is not a problem. Some time back there was a recession in the automobile industry (the industry has a trade cycle of 8-10 years) when there was stringency of cash with Telco. The pressure has eased now. Getting right quality steel is a big problem for us. The government must establish some norms for in-process inspection of steel and it must also check the spurious suppliers of steel so that small units will able to maintain consistent quality of output.

I try to sustain my position with Telco by emphasizing quality and delivery. Large companies have better management and organization techniques. If small units have to survive in the market then their individual worker's efficiency has to be high and capacity utilization percentage has to be very high.

II. Workers in Micro-Enterprises

1. AAK (A woman worker contracted in trade union office)

I am 28 years old. I have been working in (Karel Industries) for the last 13 years. I was born in Pune. I am married but I stay with my parents and two unmarried brothers. My father used to work. He is retired now.

When I started working here, I used to be paid a daily wage of Rs. 6. After 7/8 months of probation I was promoted to piece-work. My work means stamping the switch assemblies that are prepared. For 7,000 stampings, the employer has fixed a rate of Rs. 29 per day. For stampings above this limit, the rate is 1.5 times more. I work fast and manage to make Rs. 60-65 per day. I have not a minute to spare in the factory. I start work at 8 a.m. and finish by 6-30 p.m. there are other women-workers with me and we put in overtime of one hour every day.

My name does not appear on the muster. I do not sign any voucher while accepting my wage-packet. Our supervisor who is sympathetic about our lot and who came to the union office with us has advised us to make Xerox copies of the slips that are attached to the wage-envelopes. We do not get any benefits. Our fingers often start bleeding because of this work but the employer expects us to buy our own thimbles too. He does not want to provide any facilities. He just wants to minimize the costs.

I am good at my job and so I am not troubled by the employer. However, he is very harsh with the new women. There are at least 20 women workers at the location where I work. Work might be getting carried out at other locations also. He pays them around Rs. 500 per month. My friend is 40 years old. She has started working for the same number of hours every day she gets only Rs. 400 every month. The employer keeps shouting at her and he calls her slow. He frequently asks her to give up the job if she cannot cope and tells her that he would like to employ only young, matriculate girls. Really, it seems to me that our employer does not care at all for older workers like us. He wants to have a fast turnover

2. AMS

I am 24 years, old. Koregaon, district Satara, is my native place. I am a matriculate. I am not married. I came to Pune seven years ago. I am staying with my older brothers who are earning members. I am a secondary earner right now. One of my brothers is a labour contractor. I worked under him for four years. Because of his contract, I have got the present job.

I get a monthly wage of Rs. 1,050 here. I get medical allowance of Rs. 50 every month. We are given milk every day in the factory. Professional tax (Rs. 15) is cut from my wage every month. I also put aside 10 per cent of the gross wage in a voluntary provident fund account. I have a bank account and save about Rs. 100 a month. Our factory runs on two-shift basis. I work in shifts and put in extra work of about four hours. Overtime varies but I work for almost 10/11 hours every day. I am entitled to 15 paid leaves in a year.

I joined this factory as a helper. Now I have been promoted to regulating the batches. My wage was hiked by Rs. 100 p.m. after the promotion. I am looking out for a place of my own. I borrowed Rs, 2,000 from the employer a year ago for paying room deposit. I do not know about any trade union. I am not a member of any union. I have never thought of striking out on my own.

3. FMK

I am 34 years old and I migrated to Pune from Uttar Pradesh in 1980. My family owns two acres of rainfed land in U.P. I have studied upto 9th standard. I got my first job in Pune because of some contacts. I was trained in gas-cutting in that factory. I worked there for seven years and have been here since 1987. Mine is skilled work.

My name does not appear on the muster roll of this factory because I am shown as a subcontractor. The factory offloads work to me on a piece-rate basis. The rate is specified per square foot of profile cutting. I employ two workers to help me. The factory naturally does not recognize these workers. There is wide fluctuation in the volume of work offloaded. So my monthly earnings vary between Rs, 1,000 and Rs, 5,000.

I am not entitled to any leave or other facilities. We adjust our work to the pressure exerted by the factory. We take an off day whenever it is convenient.

My family consists of five persons including myself. Our monthly expenditure is around Rs. 1,175. Last year we bought a TV set for Rs. 3,500. Whenever I am in need, I approach the employer for an advance. I have not heard of any trade union. There has never been any time to bother about that kind of a thing. Our working arrangement will continue in future. I do not expect myself to be without work any time in future.

4. MMM

I am 45 years old. I migrated to Pune from Pali, Raigad district, in 1965. My mother is still there, We have no land there. I send about Rs, 500-600 each year for her maintenance. I have studied upto the 2nd standard. Economic pressure forced me out of my native place.,

It was understood that once I came to Pune, I might be able to find some work by using the contacts of people from my village. I accordingly found work in Gujarat Metal Factory in Rasta Peth. In 1968 I shifted to this factory on the basis of my uncle's recommendation. Thus I have been working here for the last 26 years.

While working I have picked up a few things and I have become versatile in work. I am engaged in packing and finishing now. As a trustworthy and experienced worker, the employer gives me additional work. I work in the general shift normally from 9 a.m. to 5-30 p.m., but the working hours are liable to be changed and stretched in a span of 12 hours depending upon pressure of work. My monthly wage is about Rs. 2,000. I get house rent allowance of Rs. 150 p.m. ESI contribution and professional tax are deducted from my wage. Dearness allowance of approximately Rs. 105 is a part of the above wage. I get increments (not always annual) of around Rs. 120 p.m. I am entitled to 15 leaves in a year. I feel secure in this job. Last year I borrowed Rs, 3,000 from the employer. He charges interest at 17 per cent p.a. on it and each month makes a deduction from my wage.

I have heard of some trade unions but did not take much interest in them. I would have liked to be self-employed but lack of education was the major hurdle.

5. BSK

I am 32 year old. I left school after failing in the 9th standard. My native place is Kololi, Taluma Barmati, district Pune. I came to Pune in 1982 in search of employment. My cousin's son had some contacts and so I made the decision. My first job was in Perfect Oil Seal. I worked as helper there. I spent five years there but I remained a temporary worker. The wage was also very low. So I left that job in

1988. I did odd jobs on a temporary basis for the next four years. There were periods of unemployment too. Then I got this job and I have been here for the last one and a half years. I now work as a moulder. My work consists of taking a rubber pipe out of the extruding machine, putting it in the die and heating it. This is a skilled job. I have acquired the skill myself by making observations and by learning on the job.

My family in Pune consists of just myself and my wife. We stay in our own house. A part of it has been converted into a shop which is run by my wife. My parents and four brothers stay at Kololi. We have a landholding of five acres there and half of it is under well-irrigation. I would like to send some money back home but somehow it is never possible.

I work from 8 a.m. to 4-30 p.m. Overtime of about two hours in a day for half the month is routine for me. My wage including dearness allowance is Rs. 1,300. Sixteen paid leaves in a year and tea are the only perquisites I get. There are seven old and two new workers in our factory. The employer has pegged the strength at tine and so we do not get ESI benefits.

I bought my house five years ago for Rs. 55,000. I borrowed money from a society that time. I have a bank account but I cannot save any amount regularly.

Because of shortage of capital, I never felt like exploring the avenues for self-employment. I have been a member of Sarva Shramik Sanghatana since 1982. Wage hike and leaves are the benefits received because of the union. It is because of the union that I am continuing in my job; otherwise the employer would have thrown me out long ago.

6. KBS (A woman worker in a non-Shop Act Unit in Hadapasar)

I am 27 years old. I have been working in this factory for the last 14 years. This is the only job I have held so far. My family consists of my mother, sister and a younger brother who is almost an invalid. My sister, also has a job but I am the primary earner. I was born and brought up in Pune. I have studied upto the matric.

I stayed at home for two years after matriculation. Then through a mutual friend of my family and the employer of the unit where I am working, I got this job. My work consists of checking the auto components machined by operators. Whenever the need arises, I perform machine operations also. I am also given supervisory duties. I am permanent here and I feel secure about my job.

I work from 8 a.m. to 6 p.m. There is overtime of two hours every day. Overtime attracts only single rate. My basic wage is Rs. 49 per day plus there is an incentive of Rs. 20 per day. My gross wage comes to around Rs. 1,800. Thursday is our weekly off day.

Our employer implements a provident fund scheme of his own. I contribute Rs. 100 p.m. to it. He makes a matching contribution. I get an annual increment of Rs. 100. I am not entitled to any leave but I can take upto seven holiday for festivals, etc. The employer provides tea and pays our medical expenses. I have not got any promotion in this work. Whoever I ask of its, the employer retorts that I do not want to take any additional responsibility and so I do not deserve one.

Our monthly family expenditure is around Rs. 2,400. Last year I had to spend Rs. 30,000 for house repairs. I had to borrow Rs. 13,000 for that purpose. A family friend lent met this amount without charging any interest.

I have not taken any steps to start on my own. Lack of capital, lack of contacts and family support have prevented me from making any efforts in this regard. The employer feels that I have no initiative and I do not want to take up additional responsibility and so I am stuck in this groove. I have access to the head of trade unions but the question of becoming a trade union member never quite arose.

7. JKG

I am 32 years old. I have passed 9th standard. I was born and brought up in Pune. The factory where I am working employs 20 workers but since it comes under Gram Panchayat jurisdiction, Factories Act is not applicable to it. Executive chairs are the principal item produced in the factory.

I have been working here for the last 12 years. A friend of mine used to work in this factory before me. He left the job as he wanted to be a self-employed painting contractor. I stepped into his place – and started working here. I worked as a helper for six years. Then I was promoted to the welder's grade. Welding is a skilled job and I acquired this skill myself by learning on the job. My name appears on the muster of our factory

My daily wage is Rs. 55. It is less than that given in the Minimum Wages Act. We have approached the Centre for Indian Trade Unions CITU) to help us in forming a trade union in the factory. This was just four months ago. No benefits have accrued to us so far. In fact, the employer has become very angry with us and he has stopped all overtime. Supervision has become very tight. We really worry that we might have to lose our jobs. But we will pull through this stage and then we expect wage increase, inform, those of

ESI benefit, etc., through the union office. Right now, we are not entailed to any leave but that too will change.

My family consists of eight persons including myself. My grandmother and my parents also stay with me. My father retired from the Ammunition Factory. I am the principal earning member of my family. Our monthly expenditure is around Rs. 1,500. I am the member of a chit fund scheme and so have to save Rs. 200 every month.

I would like to start my own unit in spite of the obvious difficulties of lack of capital and family support. There is also no place available but I will find a way out. I will be leaving this job after two more years.

8. DSR

I am 34 years old. I was born and brought up in Pune. I have studied upto the 6th standard. I had to leave school and look out for a job because of my father's sudden death. I started by working as a casual worker in a small workshop in Mangalwar Peth. I used to get a daily rate of Rs. 3 that time. I worked there for about six months. Then I got an opportunity to work in (Bharat Forge) for six months. I had temporary work. After that I could get work in Tabs India, a small factory in Gultekdi industrial area. The unit has now been closed down, but I was there for three years. After losing that job I started working as a casual worker for a labour contractor. This work fetched me a daily wage of Rs. 25. In 1989 I got married. Since then I have been working in the present factory. I joined as a helper but I now work as a skilled welder. The employer accepted my welding but did not give me the corresponding higher grade. After forming a union in January 1994, we are getting the minimum wage. So now I make Rs. 64 per day. Prior to January 1994, my rate was Rs. 41.50.

There are seven person, including myself, in my family. I am the only earning member. I used to have a bank account but I closed it because it is not possible to save anything.

The employer gives us tea and two uniforms in a year. He operates an insurance scheme for workers for which he deducts Rs. 10 from my monthly wage. After unionization, Thursdays have become a regular weekly off. Previously overtime was compulsory. Now it is optional. Some workers think that overtime is a facility but I disagree. I get 15 paid leaves in a year. Encashment of leave is not possible. Through the union, we are trying to get ESI and PF cover. Unionization has definitely helped us but it has also reduced job security. I have started taking an active interest in the union's working. I talk to other workers in our area and encourage them to unite and unionize. I used to think of self-employment but now I have abandoned the idea.

9. KMR (Works in a Shop Act Unit at Hadapasar)

I am 40 years old. I was born and brought up in Pune. My parental family is in Pune. I live separately in Hadapsar with my wife and two daughters.

I have passed the 11th standard. After that I got my first job almost immediately. That job was in Jayprabha Engineering Works. I worked there for two years as a casual worker. It was difficult to get payment of wages in time there. So I joined another factory nearby- Mane Industries. Here also I was a casual worker but I used to carry out production operations. After five years of work, I left that job following a dispute regarding the rejection of my work. I held my third job for two years. That too was in a Hadapsar-based unit. We used to get ESI facility there. But the employer did not give me the wage rise that I asked for. So I left that job. Then I came to this unit and have been here foı the last seven years. The important thing about this job is that now my name appears on the muster. So I have some status as a regular worker. In the previous jobs, my name was never entered on the muster.

Now I am a skilled turner and assembly fitter. I am also responsible for assignment of work among other workers. This is supervisory work. I was given an allowance of Rs. 150 p.m. after I was promoted to it from the earlier work of turning. I have ESI facility here but the real benefit is 21 days of leave a year. Unutilized leave can be carried forward to the next year. There are no other facilities here.

I work for 10 hours a day, sometimes more. As much overtime as one wants is available here. Overtime means single rate only. My monthly income is Rs. 1,475. I can earn more – upto Rs. 1,600 because of overtime. My family's monthly expenditure is around Rs. 1,350 and monthly savings vary from Rs. 125 to Rs. 250. I have a bank account.

I have heard trade union leaders like Rajan Nair and Datta Samant. There are no trade unions that work for workers in small industrial units. Since there is no union, the question of membership did not arise.

10. SBP (Worker in a Factories Act Unit)

I am 54 years old. I am married and I earn for a family of six, including myself. After higher secondary school, I left my native place in Pune district and came to Pune (1987). My mother used to work in this electronic factory. Because of her I got this job immediately after coming to Pune. I am working here for the last seven years. We have no land at the native place.

My work here consists of transformer testing. I am also responsible for finishing the rest of the operations from other workers and for arranging the delivery of transformers. This is skilled work. I learnt about it through observation and through the help of friends. Later I was trained in the job by the company.

I work in the factory for eight hours. My regular wage is Rs. 1,625 p.m. In addition, I take work home. For this assembly work, I earn Rs, 1,500 p.m. on an average, additionally. All other workers in the factory do the same thing.

[Mr. X, partner of this firm has made a conscious decision to subcontract work to the workers and to encourage them to form small units of work in order to avoid any unrest from workers. This work keeps the workers busy and by cutting down or withholding the volume of work to be put out he can discipline them effectively. He does not want workers' consciousness to be developed. He has decided that worker's strength would be kept below 20 so that no trade union could be formed by them. He plans to resort to automation for this purpose. 'Workers have to be under your control', he averred.]

I get a conveyance allowance of Rs. 205 p.m. I am entitled to 15 paid leaves during a year. I have not been promoted in this job any time. ESI Rs, 40, PF Rs. 135 and professional tax Rs. 20 are the deductions from my wage. If I need any advance, etc., I can approach the employer.

My family's monthly expenditure is around Rs. 2,600. I have a bank account and I save Rs. 350 p.m. I have not thought of becoming a trade union member. In fact, I do not know about any union. I have not thought of self-employment either. I sued to be uncertain about this job cut now I feel secure.

Bibliography

Bibliography

BOOKS

Amjad, Rashid (ed.). *Human Resource Planning : The Asian Experience*. New Delhi : Asian Employment Programme, ILO-ARTEP, 1987.

Aziz, Abdul. *Urban Poor and Urban Informal Sector*. New Delhi : Ashish Publishing House, 1984.

Balassa, Bela. *Policy Reform in Development Countries*. Oxford : Pergamon Press, 1977.

Balassa, Bela. *Development Strategies in Semi-Industrial Economics*. Baltimore : Johns Hopkins University Press, 1982.

Banerjee, Biswajti. *Rural to Urban Migration and the Urban Labour Market : A Case Study of Delhi*. Bombay : Himalaya Publishing House, 1986.

Banerjee, Nirmala. *Women in the Unorganised Sector*. Delhi : Sangam Books, 1985.

-------- (ed.) *Indian Women in a Changing Industrial Scenario*. New Delhi : Sage Publications, 1991.

Basu, S.K., Ghosh, A. and Ray, S. *Problems and Possibilities of Ancillary Industries in a Development Economy*. Calcutta : The World Press Pvt. Ltd., 1965.

Berger, Suzanne and Piore, M.J. *Dualism and Discontinuity in Industrial Societies*. Cambridge : Cambridge University Press, 1980.

Bose, A.N. *Calcutta and Rural Bengal : Small Sector Symbiosis*. Calcutta: Minerva Publications, 1978.

Brahme, S., and Paranjape, S. *Modern Small Industry : A Wheel Within a Wheel*. Pune : Shankar Brahme Samaj Vidnyana Granthalaya, 1979.

Bromley, R., and Gerry. C. (ed.). *Casual Work and Poverty in Third World Cities*. Chichester : John Wiley and Sons, 1979.

Bromley, R. (ed.). *Planning for Small Enterprises in Third World Cities*. Oxford : Pergamon Press, 1985.

Cairncross, A., and Puri, M. (ed.). *Employment, Income Distribution and Development Strategy : Problems of the Development Countries*. London : MacMillan, 1976.

Crook, N. *India's Industrial Cities : Essays in Economy and Demography*. Delhi : Oxford University Press, 1993.

Deshpande, V. *Hamal Panchayat* (Marathi). Bombay. Mauj Prakashan, July 1989.

Dhar, P.N., and Lydall, H.F. *The Role of Small Enterprises in Indian Economic Development*. Bombay : Asia Publishing House, 1961.

Doeringer, P, B., and Piore, M.J. *Internal Labour Markets and Manpower Analysis*. Lexington, Mass. : D.C., 1971.

Durand, J. *The Labour Force in Economic Development*. Princeton : Princeton University Press, 1975.

Fallon, P.R., and Verry, D. *The Economics of Labour Markets*. Oxford : Philip Allan, 1988.

Gadgil, D.R. Poona : *A Socio-Economic Survey, Part I : Economic*. Poona : Gokhale Institute of Politics and Economics, 1945.

Gadgil, Malati. *Daba-Batliwali* (Marathi). Pune : Pragatik Pustak Prakashan, June 1976.

-------- *Muslim Shramika* (Marathi). Pune : Pragatik Pustak Prakashan, August 1982.

Galenson, W. (Selector and Introducer). *Essays on Employment*. Geneva : International Labour Officer, 1971.

Gandhi, Nandita and Shah, Nandita. *Gharbaslya Kam-Striya ani Ghargusgi Utpadan* (Marathi translations by Meena Deval and Jaya Velankar). Mumbai : Akshara Prakashan, 1993.

Geertz, C. *Pedlars and Princes*. Chicago : University of Chicago Press, 1963.

Godbole, Madhav. *Rural Employment Strategy : A Quest in the Wilderness*. Bombay : Himalaya Publishing House, 1990.

Gregory, Peter. *The Myth of Market Failure, Employment and the Labour Market in Mexico*. World Bank Research Publications, 1986

Hariharan, S.V., and Benjamin, R.E. *Informal Sector*. Jaipur : Printwell, 1991.

Harris, Johan, Kanna, K.P., and Rodgers, G. *Urban Labour Market Structure and Job Access in India : A Study of Coimbatore*. Geneva : International Institute of Labour Studies, Research Series 92, 1991.

Holstrom, Mark. *Industry and Inequality : The Social Anthropology of Indian Labour*, New York : Cambridge University Press, 1984.

International Labour Organization (ILO). *Towards Full Employment : A Programme for Colombia*. Geneva : ILO, 1970.

-------- *Employment Incomes and Equality : A Strategy for Increasing Productive Employment in Kenya*. Geneva : ILO, 1972.

-------- *Growth, Employment and Equity: A Comprehensive Strategy for Sudan*. Geneva : ILO, 1976.

Islam, R., and Muqtada, M. (ed.). *Urban Unemployment and Underemployment*. New Delhi : ILO-ARTEP, 1986.

Islam, R. (ed.). *Employment Challenges for the 1990s*. World Employment Programme, ILO-ARTEP, March 1990.

Jagannathan, N.,V. *Informal Markets in Development Countries*. New York: Oxford University Press, Inc., 1987.

Jhabvala, Renana, Subrahmanya, R.K.A. (eds.). *The Unorganized Sector, Work Security and Social Protection*. New Delhi : Sage Publications India Pvt. Ltd., 2000.

Jolly, Richard, De Kadt, E., Singer, H., and Wilson, F. (ed.). *Third World Unemployment Problems and Strategy*, Selected Readings. Penguin Education, 1973.

Joshi, Heather and Joshi, Vijay. *Surplus Labour and the City : A Study of Bombay*. Delhi : Oxford University Press, 1976.

Kannappan, Subbiah. *Employment Problems and the Urban Labour Market in Developing Nations*. Ann Arbor : University of Michigan Press, 1983.

King. J.E. (ed.). *Readings in Labour Economics*. New York : Oxford University Press, 1980.

Kulkarni, A.P. *Employment Multiplier in Pune, Industrial and Employment Growth of an Indian City Since 1950*. Pune : Centre of Studies in Social Sciences, 1991.

Lakdawala, D.T., and Sandesara, J.C. *Small Industry in a Big City, A Study of Bombay*. University of Bombay Series in Economics, No. 10, 1960.

Lall, Vinay D. *Informal Sector in the National Capital Region*. Delhi : B.R. Publishing Corporation, 1989.

Lambert, Richard D. Workers, *Factories and Social Change in India*. Poona : Gokhale Institute of Politics and Economics, 1963.

Lambert, Richard D., Ginsberg, R.B., and Moore, S.J. *The Transformation of an Indian Labour Market : The Case of Pune*. Pune : Gokhale Institute of Politics and Economics, 1987.

Lebergott, Stanley (ed.). *Men Without Work, The Economics of Unemployment*. New Jersey : Prentice-Hall Inc., 1964.

Lindbeck, Assar, and Snower, D.J. *The Insider-Outsider Theory of Employment and Unemployment*. Massachusetts Institute of Technology Press, 1988.

Little, Ian, Mazumdar, Dipak, and Page, John. *Small Manufacturing Enterprises : A Comparative Analysis of India and Other Economies*. Oxford University Press (for the World Bank), 1987.

Majumdar, A. *In-Migration and Informal Sector: A Case Study of Urban Delhi*. New Delhi : Vision Books Pvt. Ltd., 1980.

Mazumdar, D. *The Urban Labour Market and Income Distributions: A Study of Malaysia*. New York: Oxford University Press, 1981.

Mitter, Vishwa. *Growth of Urban Informal Sector in a Developing Economy*. New Delhi : Deep and Deep Publications, 1988.

Papola, T.S., and Subramanian, K.K. *Wage Structure and Labour Mobility in a Local Market*. Bombay : Popular Prakashan, 1975.

Papola, T.S. *Urban Informal Sector in a Developing Economy* (Ahmedabad). Delhi : Vikas, 1981.

Pillai, S.D., and Baks, G. (ed.). *Winners and Losers : Styles of Development in an Indian Region*. Bombay : Popular Prakashan, 1979.

Rodgers, Gerry (ed.). *Urban Poverty and the Labour Market : Access to Jobs and Incomes in Asian and Latin American Cities* . Geneva : WEP/International Institute for labour Studies, ILO, 1989.

Rose, Kalima. *Where Women Are Leaders, The SEWA Movement in India*. New Delhi : Vistaar Publications, 1992.

Safa, Helen, L. (ed.). *Towards a Political Economy of Urban Third World Countries*. New Delhi : Oxford University Press, 1982.

Salome, Bernard (ed.). *Fighting Urban Unemployment in Development Countries*. Development Centre Seminars, OECD, 1989.

Scheafer, Kalmann. Sao Paulo : *Urban Development and Employment*. Geneva : ILO, 1976.

Sen, Amartya K. *Employment, Technology and Development.* Oxford Press, 1975.

Sethuraman, S.V. *The Urban, Informal Sector In Developing Countries : Employment, Poverty and Environment*. Geneva : ILO, 1981.

Sinclair, Stuart W. *Urbanisation and Labour Market in Development Countries*. London : Croon Helm Ltd., 1978.

Singh, A.M., and Kelles-Viitanen (ed.). *Invisible Hands : Women in Home-based Production*. New Delhi : Sage Publications, 1987.

Singh, Manjit. *The Political Economy of Unorganized Industry, A Study of Issues and Evidence*. New York: Oxford University Press, 1981.

Squire, Lyn. *Employment Policy in Developing Countries : A Survey of Issues and Evidence*. New York : Oxford University Press, 1981.

Sovani, N.V. et al. *Poona : A Re-Survey, The Changing Pattern of Employment and Earnings*. Poona : Gokhale Institute of Politics and Economics, 1956.

Sreeramamurty, Kundamala. *Urban Labour in Informal Sector (A Case Study of Visakhapatam City)*. Delhi : B.R. Publishing Corporation, 1986.

Standing, Guy, and Tokman, V.E. (ed.). *Towards Social Adjustment, Labour Market Issues in Structural Adjustment*. Geneva : ILO, 1991.

Stewart, Frances. *Technology and Underdevelopment*. London : Macmillan and Co, 1978.

Suri, K.B. (ed.). *Small Scale Enterprises in Industrial Development, The Indian Experience*. New Delhi : Sage Publication, 1988.

Swanson, Gordon I., and Michaelson, Joh (ed.). *Manpower Research and Labour Economics*. California : Sage Publications, Inc., 1979.

Todaro, Michael P. *Economic Development in the Third World* (3rd ed.). New York: Longman, 1985.

Turnham, David. *The Employment Problem in Less Developed Countries, A Review of Evidence*. Paris : Development Centre Studies, OECD, Employment Series No.1, 1971.

Turnham, David, Salome, Bernard, and Schwarz, Antoine (ed.). *The Informal Sector Revisited*. Paris. : Development Centre, OCED, 1990.

Van der Veen Jan H. *A Study of Small Industries in Gujarat State*, India. Cornell University, 1973.

Vepa, Ram K. *Modern Small Industry in India, Problems and Prospects*. New Delhi : Sage Publications, 1988.

Watanable, Susumu (ed.). *Technology, Marketing and Industrialisation : Linkages between Large and Small Enterprises*. Delhi : Macmillan India Ltd., 1983.

ARTICLES

Amin, A.T.M. Nurul, "Marginalisation versus Dynamism: A Study of the Informal Sector in Dhaka City," *The Bangladesh Development Studies*, Vol. IX, No. 4, Autumn 1981.

-------- "The Role of the Informal Sector in Economic Development : Some Evidence from Dhaka, Bangladesh, : "*International Labour Review*, Vol. 126, No 5, Sept-Oct, 1987.

Anand, Vinod, "Informal Sector in Developing Countries : Certain Crucial Hypotheses," *The Indian Economic Journal*, Vol. 42, No. 2, Oct.-Dec. 1994, pp. 75-86/

Aziz, Abdul, Review of "Employment Problems and the Urban Labour Market in Developing National" by Kannappan, S., *Indian Journal of Industrial Relations*, Vol. 22, No. 1, July 1986.

Banerjee, Biswajit, "The Role of the Informal Sector in the Migration Process : A Test of Probabilistic Migration Models and Labour Market Segmentation for India," *Oxford Economic Papers*, Vol. 35, No. 3, November, 1983. pp. 399-422.

Banerjee, Nirmala, "The Weakest Link," *Institute of Development Studies Bulletin*, Vol. 12, No. 3, July 1981.

-------- "Women's Work and Discrimination," in N. Banerjee and D. Jain (ed.). Tyranny of the Household. New Delhi : *Shakti Books*, 1985.

-------- "Small and Large Industrial Units : Symbiosis or Matsya-nyaya?" I K.B. Suri (ed.). Small Scale Enterprises in Industrial Development : The Indian Experience. New Delhi : *Sage Publications*, 1988.

Bapat, Meera, and Crook, Nigel, "The Quality of Female Employment : Evidence from a Study in Pune, "*Economic and Political Weekly*, Vol. 23, No. 31, June 30, 1988.

Bardhan, Kalpana, "Rural Employment, Wages and Labour Markets in India – A Survey of Research,: *Economic and Political Weekly*, Vol. XII, No. 26, June 25, 1977; Vol. XII, No,. 27-28, July 28, 1977.

-------- "Women's Work, Welfare and Status," *Economic and Political Weekly*, Vol.,. 20, No. 50-52, December 14-28, 1985, pp. 2207-2220, 2261-2269.

Basant, Rakesh and Kumar, B.L., "Data Base for Study of Household Manufacturing Sector, Problems and Comparability,"*Economic and Political Weekly*, Vol. XXIV, No. 20, May, 19, 1990.

Basu, T., "Calcutta's Sandal Makers," *Economic and Political Weekly*, August 6, 1977, pp. 1262.

Berry, Albert, R., and Sabot, R.H., "Labour Market Performance in Developing Countries: A Survey," *World Development*, November-December, 1978.

-------- "Unemployment and Economic Development," *Economic Development and Cultural Change*, Vol. 33, No. 1, 1984.

Bhattacharya, S.S., "The Shoe-Shiners of Patna," *Sociological Bulletin (Journal of the Indian Sociological Society)*, Vol. XVIII, 1969, pp. 167-174.

Bienefeld, M., and Godfrey, M., "Measuring Unemployment and the Informal Sector: Some Conceptual and Statistical Problems," *Institute of Development Studies Bulletin*, Vol. 7, No. 3, October, 1975, pp. 4-10.

Breman, Jan, "A Dualistic Labour System : A Critique of the 'Informal Sector' Concept," *Economic and Political Weekly*, Vol., XI, No. 48, 49 and 50, November 27, December 4, 11, 1976.

Bromely, R., "The Urban Informal Sector, : Why Is It Worth Discussing?" *World Development*, Vol. 6, No, 9/10, 1978, pp. 1033-1039.

Cole, W.E., and Sanders, R.D., "Internal Migration and Urban Employment in the Third World," *American Economic Review*, June 1985, pp. 481-494.

-------- "Internal Migration and Urban Employment : Reply, " *American Economic Review* , June, 1986.

Cole, W.E., and Fayissa, B., "The Urban Subsistence Labour Force : Toward a Policy-Oriented and Empirically Accessible Taxonomy," *World Development*, Vol. 19, No. 7, 1991.

Collier, P., "Labour Mobility and Labour Utilisation in Development Countries," *Oxford bulletin of Economics and Statistics*, Vol. 37, No., 3, August 1975.

Dantwala, M.L., "Garibi Hatao : Strategy Options", *Economic and Political Weekly*, Vol. XX, No. 11, March, 16, 1985.

Das, D.K. La, "Sex Discrimination Against Female Workers in Unorganised Sector," *Indian Journal of Industrial Relations*, Vol. 21, No. 2, October, 1985.

Datta Chaudhary, T., "A Theoretical Analysis of the Informal Sector," *World Development*, Vol. 17, No. 3, 1989, pp. 351-355.

Dighe, A., "Women's Employment in the Urban Informal Sector: Some Critical Issues," *Social Change*, Vol. 15, No. 2, June 1985, pp. 3-6.

Eapen, M., "Structure of Manufacturing Workforce: A Preliminary Analysis of Emerging Tendencies", *Economic and Political Weekly*, Vol. XIX, No. 31, 32, 33, August 1984, pp. 1454/1456.

Elkan, W., "Is a Proletariat Emerging in Nairobi?" *Economic Development and Cultural Change*, Vol. 24, No. 4, July 1976, pp. 695-706.

Fallon, P.R., and Lucas, R.E.B., "The Impact of Changes in Job Security Regulations in India and Zimbabwe," *The World Bank Economic Review*, Vol. 5, No. 3, 1991, pp. 395-413.

Fields, G., "Rural-Urban Migration, Urban Unemployment and Underemployment and Job Search, Activity in LDCs," *Journal of Development Economics*, Vol. 2, 1975, pp. 165-187.

-------- "Labour Market Modelling and the UIS : Theory and Evidence," In Turnham, Salome, and Schwarz (ed.). The Informal Sector Revisited. Paris : *Development Centre, OECD*, 1990.

Friedman, J., and Sullivan, F. "The Absorption of Labour in the Urban Economy : The Case of Developing Countries," *Economic Development and Cultural Change*, Vol. 22, No. 3, April 1974.

Gerry, Chris, "Developing Economics and the Informal Sector in Historical Perspective," *The Annals of the American Academy of Political and Social Science*, Vol. 493, September 1987.

Gibson, Bill, and Kelly, Bruce, ""A Classical Theory of the Informal Sector," *The Manchester School of Economic and Social Studies*, Vol. LXII, No. 1, March 1994, pp. 81-96.

Gindling, T.H., "Labour Market Segmentation and the Determination of Wages in the Public, Private-Formal and

Informal Sectors in San Jose, Costs, Rica," *Economic Development and Cultural Change*, Vol. 39, No. 3, April 1991.

Goldar, B., "Relative Efficiency of Modern Small Scale Industries in India," in K.B. Suri (ed.). Small Scale Enterprises in Industrial Development, The Indian Experience. New Delhi : *Sage Publications*, 1988.

Gregory, Peter, "An Assessment of Changes in Employment Conditions in Less Developed Countries," *Economic Development and Cultural Change*, Vol. 28, No. 4, July 1979, pp. 673-700.

Guisinger, S., and Irfan, M., "Pakistan's Informal Sector," *The Journal of Development Studies*, vol. 16, No. 4, 1980, pp. 412-426.

Harberger, A.C. "On Measuring the Social Opportunity Cost of Labour," *International Labour Review*, Vol. 103, 1971, pp. 559-579.

Harriss, John, "Character of an Urban Economy : Small Scale Production and Labour Markets in Coimbatore," *Economic and Political Weekly*, Vol. XVII, No, 23, 24, June 5, 12, 1982, pp. 945-954, 993-1002.

-------- "Vulnerable Workers in the Indian Urban Labour Market," in Rodgers, G. (ed.). Urban Poverty and the Labour Market : Access to Jobs and Incomes in Asian and Latin American Cities. Geneva : *ILO*, 1989.

Harris, J.R., and Todaro, M.P., "Migration, Unemployment and Development : A Two Sector Analysis," *American Economic Review*, Vol. 60, No. 1, March, 1970, pp. 126-142.

Hart, Keith, "Informal Income Opportunities and Urban Employment in Ghana," *Journal of Modern African Studies*, London, March, 1971, pp. 61-89.

Higgins, Benjamin, "The dualistic Theory of Underdevelopment Areas," Economic Development and Cultural Change, January 1956, reprinted in Gerald Meier (ed.). Leading Issues in Economics Development. New York : *Oxford University Press*, 1976 (3rd edition).

House, William J., "Nairobi's Informal Sectors : Dynamic Entrepreneurs or Surplus Labour?" *Economic Development and Cultural Change*, Vol. 32, No. 2, January 1984. pp. 277-302.

-------- "Labour Market Differentiation in a Development Economy : An Example from Urban Juba, Southern Sudan," *World Development*, Vol. 15, No. 7, 1987, pp. 877-897.

Jackson, Dudley, and Turner, H.A., "How to Provide More Employment in a Labour Surplus Economy," *International Labour Review*, Vol. 107, No. 4, April 1973, pp. 315-338.

Joshi, Heather, "The Informal Urban Economy and the Boundaries," *Economic and Political Weekly*, Vol. 29, March, 1980.

Kalpagam, U., "Labour in Small Industry- Case of Export Garments Industry in Madras," *Economic and Political Weekly*, Vol. XVI, No. 48, November 28, 1981, p. 1959.

Kannappan, Subbiah, "Urban Employment and the Labour Market in Developing Nations," *Economic Development and Cultural Change*, Vol. 33, no. 4, July 1985, pp. 699-730.

-------- "Rural – Urban Migration in Deepening Nations," (Review of Rural to Urban Migration and the Urban Labour Market: A Case Study of Delhi, by B. Banerjee, Op. cit.), *Economic and Political Weekly*, Vol. 22, No. 15, April 11, 1987.

Khundker, N., "The Fuzziness of Informal Sector : Can We Afford to Throw Out the Baby with the Bath Water?" *World Development*, Vol. 10, October 1988, pp. 1263-1265.

Krishnamurthy, J., "Some Aspects of Unemployment in Urban India," *Journal of Development Studies*, Vol. 11, No. 2, January 1975.

Kritz, E., and Ramos, J., "The Measurement of Urban Underemployment," *International Labour Review*, Vol., 113, No. 1, January-February 1976, pp. 115-127.

Lakdawala, D.T., and Mehta, B.V., "Small and Medium Scale Engineering Factories in Bombay City," *Journal of the University of Bombay*, Vol. XXVI, Part 4, January 1958.

Lewin, A.C., "The Dialectic of Dominance : Petty Production and Peripheral Capitalism," in Bromely, R. (ed.). *Planning for Small Enterprises in Third World Cities*, op. cit.

Lewis, W.A., "Economic Development with Unlimited Supplies of Labour," *Manchester School of Economic and Social Studies*, May 1954.

Leys, C., "Interpreting African Underdevelopment: Reflections on the ILO Report on Employment, Incomes and Equality" in Kenya," in Gerald Meier (ed.). *Leading Issues in Economic Development*, op. cit.

Lubell, Harold, "Under Development and Employment in Calcutta," *International Labour Review*, Vol. 109, No. 1, July 1973.

Lubell, Harold, and Charbel, Zarour, "Resilience Amidst Crisis : The Informal Sector of Dakar," *International Labour Review*, Vol. 129, No. 3, June 1990.

Mazumdar, D., "Segmented Labour Markets in LDCs," *American Economic Review*, Vol. 73, No. 2, May, 1983, pp. 254-259.

-------- "The Rural-Urban Wage Gap, Migration and the Working of Urban Labour Markets : An Interpretation Based on a Study of the Workers of Bombay City," *Indian Economic Review*, Vol. 18, No. 2, 1984, pp. 1969-1998.

McGee, T.G., "Labour Mobility in Fragmented Labour Markets, The Role of Circulatory Migration in Rural-Urban Relations in Asia," in Safa, H.L. (ed.). Towards a Political Economy of Urbanisation in Third Word Countries. Delhi : *Oxford University Press*, 1982.

Merrick, T.W., "Employment and Earnings in the Informal Sector in Brazil : The Case Belo Horizonte," *Journal of Developing Areas*, Vol. 10, No. 3, April 1976, pp. 337-354.

Mohan, Rakesh, "Industry and Urban Employment, 1961-81 : A Preliminary Exploration," Economic and Political Weekly, Vol. XXIV, Nos. 44, 45, November 4-11, 1989, pp. 2481-2504.

Morawetz, David, "Employment Implications of Industrialization in Developing Countries," *Economic Journal*, September 1974.

Moser, C.O.N., "Informal Sector or Petty Commodity Production : Dualism of Dependence in urban Development?" *World Development*, Vol. 6, Nos. 9/10 1978.

-------- "The Informal Sector Reworked : Viability and Vulnerability in Urban Development," *Regional Development Dialogue*, Vol. 5, No. 2, 1984, pp. 135-178.

Moselyu, P., "Implicit Models and Policy Recommendations : Reflections on the Employment Problem in Kenya," *Institute of Development Studies (IDS) Bulletin*, Vol. 9, No. 3, February 1978, pp. 3010.

Nagaraj, R., "Sub-contracting in Indian Manufacturing Industries : Analysis, Evidence and Issues," *Economic and Political Weekly*, Annual Number, August, 1984, pp. 1435-1453.

Nattrass, Nicoli Jean, "Street Trading in Transkei – A struggle Against Poverty, Persecution and Prosecution," *World Development*, Vol. 15, No. 7, 1987. pp. 861-875.

Nihan, G., and Jourdain, R., "The Modern Informal Sector in Nouakchott," *International Labour Review*, vol. 117, No. 6, 1978, pp. 709-179.

Pack, H., "The Employment-Output Trade-off in LDCs-Micro-economic Approach", *Oxford Economic Papers*, Vol. 26, 1974, pp. 388-404. Papanek, Gustav F., "The Poor of Jakarta," *Economic Development and Cultural Change*, Vol. 24, No. 1, October, 1975.

Papola, T.S., "Informal Sector : Concept and Policy," *Economic and Political Weekly*, Vol. XV, No. 18, May 3, 1980.

-------- "Dissecting the Informal Sector," review of The Informal Sector In Research : Theory and Practice by Jan Breman, *Economic and Political Weekly*, Vol., XVI, No. 31, August 1, 1981, pp., 1272-1274.

Parthasarthy, G., "Unorganised Sector and Structural Adjustment," *Economic and Political Weekly*, Vol. XXXI, No. 28, July 13, 1996.

Peattie, L., "Anthropological Perspectives on the Concepts of Dualism, the Informal Sector and Marginality in Development Urban Economics," *International Regional Science Review*, Vol. 5, No. 1, 1980, pp. 1-31.

-------- "What Is To Be Done With the Informal Sector? A Case Study of Shoe Manufacturing in Colombia," in H.LK. Safa (ed.). Towards a Political Economy of Urbanisation. New Delhi : *Oxford University Press*, 1981.

-------- "An Idea in Goods Currency and How it Grew : The Informal Sector," *World Development*, Vol., 15, No. 7, 1987, pp. 851-860.

Portes, Alejandro, "The Informal Sector and the World Economy : Notes on the Structure of Subsidised Labour," *Institute of Development Studies Bulletin*, Vol. 9, No. 3, February 1978.

Portes, Alejandro, and Sassen-Koob, S., "Making It Underground : Comparative Material on the Informal Sector in Western Market Economics," *American Journal of Sociology*, July 1987.

Rajaraman, Indira, "The Urban Labour Market," *Economic and Political Weekly*, Vol. 21, No. 40, October, 4, 1986.

Raj, Krishna, "Unemployment in India," *Economic and Political Weekly*, Vol. I, No. 9, March, 1973.

Ramana, K.V., "Structure and Working of Unorganised Sector in Visakhapatnam City," *Research Abstracts Quarterly*, July-December, 1988.

Ramaswamy, K.V., "Small-Scale Manufacturing Industries, Some Aspects of Size, Growth and Structure," Economic and Political Weekly, *Review of Industry and Management*, Vol. XXIX, No. 9, February 26, 1994, pp. M13-M23.

Rao, J. Mohan, "Capital, Labour and the Indian State," in Juliet Schor, and Jong-Il you (ed.). Capital, the State and Labour, A Global Perspective. *United Nations University Press*, Japan and *Edward Elgar Publishing Ltd.*, U.K. 1995.

Romatet, E., "Calcutta's Information Sector: Theory and Reality," *Economic and Political Weekly*, Vol. XVIII, No. 50, 1983.

Sabot, Richard H., "The Meaning and Measurement of Urban Surplus Labour," *Oxford Economic Papers*, 1977, pp. 389-411.

Samal, Kishore, "Urban Informal Manufacturing Sector : Its Structure and Operation (A Case Study)," *Urban India*, Vol. X, No. 2, July-December, 1990.

Sandesara, J.C., "Small Scale Industrialisation : The Indian Experience," *Economic and Political Weekly*, Vol. XXIII, No. 13, March, 26, 18\988, pp. 640-654.

Sanyal, Bishwapriya, "Organizing the Self-employed : The Politics of the Urban Informal Sector." *International Labour Review*, Vol. 130, No. 1, 1991.

Scott, Alison M., "Who Are the Self-Employed," in Bromley, R., and Gerry, C. (ed.). *Casual Work and Poverty in Third World Cities*, op. cit.

Sethuraman, S.V., "Urbanisation and Employment, A Case Study of Djakarta," *International Labour Review*, Vol. 112, Nos. 2-3, August-September, 1974.

-------- "The Urban Informal Sector: Concepts, Measurement and Policy," *International Labour Review*, Vol. 114, No. 1, July-August 1976.

Sethuraman, S.V., "The Informal Sector in Developing Countries: Some Policy Implications," *Social Action*, July-September 1977, pp. 196-205.

-------- "The Urban Informal Sector in Africa," *International Labour Review*, Vol. 116, No. 3, 1977.

Shaw, Annapurna, "Linkages of Large-Scale, Small-Scale and Informal Sector Industries : A Study of Thana-Belapur," *Economic and Political Weekly*, February 17-24, 1990.

-------- "The Informal Sector in Indian Manufacturing activities: A Regional Study," *Indian Journal of Labour Economics*, Vol. 37, no. 3, 1994.

Souza, P.R., and Tokman, V.E., "The Informal Urban Sector in Latin America," *International Labour Review*, Vol. 114, No. 3, November-December 1976.

Speare, Alden Jr., and Harris, J., "Education Earning and Migration in Indonesia," *Economic Development and Cultural Change*, Vol. 34, No. 2, January 1986.

Special Issue on Informal Sector, *Manpower Journal*, Vol. XXIX, No. 3, October-December 1993.

Stark, Oded, "On Modelling the Informal Sector," *World Development*, Vol. 10, no. 5, 1982, pp. 413-416.

Sundaram, K., and Pandit, V.N., "Informal Credit Markets, Black Money and Monetary Policy : Some Analytical and Empirical Issues," *Economic and Political Weekly*, April, 21, 1984.

Tanne, Michael, B., "Labour Markets in Northeast Brazil : does the Dual Market Model Apply?: *Economic Development and Cultural Change*, Vol. 39, No. 3, April, 1991.

Thorbecke, Erik, "The Employment Problem : A Critical Evaluation of Four ILO Comprehensive Country Reports," International Labour Review, Vol. 107, No. 5, May 1973.

Todaro, M.P., "A Model of Labour Migration and Urban Unemployment in Less Development Countries," *American Economic Review*, March, 1969, p. 138.

Tokman, V.E., "An Exploration into the Nature of Informal-Formal Sector Relationships," *World Development*, Vol. 6, No. 9/10 1978, pp. 1065-1075.

-------- "The Informal Sector in Latin America : From Underground to Legality," in G. Standing and V.E. Tokman (ed.). *Towards Social Adjustment, Labour Market Issues in Structural Adjustment*, Geneva : ILO, 1991.

Visaria, P., and Visaria, L., "Employment Planing for the Weaker Sections in Rural India," *Economic and Political Weekly*, Annual Number, vol. 8, 1973.

Weeks, John, "Does Employment matter?" in R. Jolly, E. de Kadt, H. Singer, and F. Wilson, (ed.). *Third World Employment* op. cit.

-------- "Policies for Expanding Employment in the Informal Urban Sector of Developing Economies," *International Labour Review*, Vol. III, 1975, pp. 1-3.

Williamson, O.E., "The Modern Corporation : Origins, Evolution, Attributes," *Journal of Economic Literature*, Vol. 19, No. 4, December, 1981, pp. 1539-1568.

REPORTS, DIRECTORIES

Action for the Right of the Child (ARC) and Unicef, Maharashtra. *Towards the Elimination of Child Labour in Pune* Documentation of Action Taken by the Labour Commissioner's Officer, Pune. (n.d.)

Annual Survey of Industries, 1985-86, Summary Report and Employment and Labour Cost in the Census and Sample Sectors, (Report).

Committee on Unemployment (Bhagwati Committee) Report, 1972. Government of India, New Delhi, November, 1972.

Census of India, 1951, 1961, 1971, 1981, 1991, Maharashtra, General Economic Tables.

Department of Economics, S.N.D.T. : Women's University, Bombay. *Inventory of Studies on Informal Sector in Maharashtra*, January 1995.

District Census Handbook- Poona, 1981.

District Socio-Economic Review – Pune, Directorate of Economics and Statistics, 1993-94.

Economic Census, 1980, All India Report. Central Statistical Organisation (C.S.O.).

Economic Census, 1980, Districtwise Aggregates of Principal Characteristics of Enterprises. C.S.O.

Economics Census, 1990, Summary Results, C.S.O.

Economics Census, 1990, Report (in brief) and Statistical Tables, Maharashtra State. Directorate of Economics and Statistics Government of Maharashtra.

Economic Census, 1998, All India Report, C.S.O.

Economic Survey, 1988-98. Ministry of Finance, Government of India.

Economic Survey of Maharashtra, 1991-92. Directorate of Economics and Statistics, Government of Maharashtra.

Economic Survey of Maharashtra, 1994-95. Directorate of Economics and Statistics, Government of Maharashtra.

Everett, J., and Savara, M. *Women in Informal Sector in Bombay*. Report of Household Survey, Report presented at Expert Group Meeting on Women in the Informal Sector. National Institute of Urban Affairs, New Delhi, November, 1-2, 1988.

Handbook of Industrial statistics. 1991.

Indian Labour Statistics (Annual). Labour Bureau, Shimla/Chandigarh, Ministry of Labour, Government of India.

Maharashtra Chamber of Commerce and Industries. *Industrial and Commercial Directory of Poona/Pune*, 1978, 1985, 1990, 1995.

National Accounts Statistics, Source and Methods, 1989, Central Statistical Organisation.

National Accounts Statistics of India – 1950-51 to 1994-95. EPW Research Foundation Mumbai.

National Sample Survey Organisation (NSSO). *Tables With Notes on Survey of Unorganized manufacture : Non-Directory Establishments and Own Account Enterprises* (40 Round).

-------- *Report on Own Account Enterprise – Manufacturing* (40 Round).

-------- *Tables With Notes on Own Account Trading Enterprises and Non-Directory Trading Establishments – All India* (41st Round). Report Nos. 366/1 and 2, June-September, 1989.

-------- *Unorganised Manufacture : Non-Directory Establishments and Own-Account Enterprises*, Part I – All India (45th Round).

Report of National Commission on Labour. Ministry of Labour, Employment and Rehabilitation, Government of India, 1969.

Report of the Second All-India Census of SSI Units. DCSSI, Ministry of Industry, 1987-88. August 1992.

Report of the Special Group on Targetting Ten Million Employment Opportunities, Planning Commission, May 2002.

S.N.D.T. Women's University Department of Adult and Continuing Education, Pune Centre. *Child Labour in Hotel Industry, Pune : A Situational Analysis*. Report of Major Findings, January 1997.

The Maharashtra State Employment Review (Annual), from 1968 onwards. Directorate of Employment, Government of Maharashtra.

Working Class Family Income and Expenditure Survey, 1981-82, Pune. Government of India, Ministry of Labour, Labour Bureau, Chandigarh.

World Development Report (Annual), 1979-90. The World Bank, 1979, 1990

MONOGRAPHS, WORKING PAPERS COUNTRY STUDIES

Abdel-Fadil, M. *On the Dynamics of Interface between Formal and Informal Economies in LDCs*. Institute of Development Studies, Discussion Paper No. 301, June 1992.

Agrawal K.G. *Casual Labour of Kanpur, Their Living and Working Conditions*. National Labour Institute, New Delhi, August 1988.

Alonzo, R.P., and Mangahas, A.A. *The Informal Sector in Metro Manila : Findings from a Recent Survey*. (Mimeo.) ILO-ARTEP, International Labour Office- Asian Regional Team for Employment Promotion, New Delhi, 1989.

Bairoch, P. Urban. *Unemployment in Development Countries: The Nature of the Problem and Proposals for its solution*, ILO, Geneva, 1973.

Bardhan, Kalpana. *Women Workers in South Asia : Employment Problems and Policies in the Context of the Poverty Target Groups Approach*,. Asian Employment Programme Working Papers, ILO-ARTEP, New Delhi, 1987.

Brahme, S., and Sonalkar, W. *Economic Plight of Hamaal Women in Poona*. Poona, 1979.

Deshpande, L.K. *Segmentation of Labour Market : A Case Study of Bombay*. Kunda Datar Lectures, Gokhale Institute of Politics and Economics, Pune, 1985.

Gerry, Chris. *Petty Producers and the Urban Economy : A Case Study of Dakar*. World Employment Programme Research Working Papers, ILO, Geneva, 1974.

Gregory, Peter. *The Impact of Institutional Factors on Labour markets*. The World Bank, Studies in Employment and Rural Development, No. 27, Washington, D.C., 1975.

Kanhert, Friedrich. *Improving Urban Employment and Labour Productivity*. World Bank Discussion Paper, No. 10, May 1987.

Mazumdar, D. *The Urban Informal Sector*, World Bank Staff Working Paper No. 211, July 1975.

Nanavaty, Reema. *We Can We Will- Women's Employment and DWCRA Programme*. SEWA Paper Series, Working Paper No. 3, Ahmedabad, 1994.

Papla, T.S., and Mathur, R.S. *Inter-Sectoral Linkages in Manufacturing : A Study of Mela Engineering Industry in Kanpur*, India. Giri Institute of Development Studies, (Mimel.). 1979.

Romijn Henry B. *Dynamism in the Informal Sector in a Fast Growing Economy : The Case of Bangkok*. ILO-ARTEP, New Delhi, December, 1993.

Roy, T., and Basant, R. *Urban Informal Sector : A Critical Review*, Working Paper No. 27, The Gujarat Institute of Area Planning, Ahmedabad March, 1990.

Steel, W.F., and Yasuoki, T. *The Intermediate Sector, Unemployment and the Employment*, Output Conflicts, World Bank Staff Working Papers, No. 301, October, 1978.

Town and Country Planning Organisation, Ministry of works and Housing, Government of India. *Informal Sector in a Metropolis, Case Study of Delhi*, Informal Industrial Cluster : Anand Parbat. December 1983.

World Bank. *Gender and Poverty in India*. A World Bank Country Study, Washington, D.C., 1991.

Index

Index